Injia on Investigatory Practice in Papua New Guinea and the Pacific

Salamo Injia

University of Papua New Guinea Press and Bookshop, 2013

Injia on Investigatory Practice in Papua New Guinea and the Pacific

ISBN: 978-9980-945-99-0

PUBLISHED BY:
The University of Papua New Guinea Press and Bookshop
PO Box 413
University PO, NCD
Papua New Guinea
Email: upngpress@gmail.com

FOREWORD

This textbook is one of six (6) textbooks written under my hand and supervision:

'Injia on Criminal Offences in Papua New Guinea and the Pacific'

'Injia on Criminal Practice and Procedure in Papua New Guinea and the Pacific'

'Injia on Sentencing in Papua New Guinea and the Pacific'

'Injia on Statutory Interpretation in Papua New Guinea and the Pacific'

'Injia on Coronial Proceedings in Papua New Guinea and the Pacific'

'Injia on Investigatory Practice in Papua New Guinea and the Pacific'

Each of those textbooks is an effort to offer to Judicial officers, legal practitioners and students of law a comprehensive set of principles and practical guidelines on criminal law and practice in Papua New Guinea and the Pacific. The work undertaken under the auspices of AusAID through the PNG-Australia Law and Justice Partnership Project is an extension of a similar project undertaken previously in writing the textbook *Criminal Law and Practice in Papua New Guinea* co-authored by myself, Professor Don Chalmers, Dr Weisbrot and Justice Andrew.

The textbooks will be of great benefit to the criminal justice system in Papua New Guinea and the Pacific and specifically will assist judges, magistrates, lawyers, law students and police officers in the performance of their duties.

The assistance of AusAID and its development practitioner Mr Errol Gibson who provided research and spent countless hours in the production of these textbooks is acknowledged.

Sir Salamo Injia, Kt

Chief Justice of Papua New Guinea

7th June 2013

TABLE OF CONTENTS

TABLE OF CONTENTS

TABLE OF CONTENTS

TABLE OF CONTENTS

TABLE OF CONTENTS

TABLE OF CONTENTS

TABLE OF CONTENTS

TABLE OF CONTENTS

TABLE OF CONTENTS

TABLE OF CONTENTS

TABLE OF CONTENTS

TABLE OF CONTENTS

TABLE OF CONTENTS

TABLE OF CONTENTS

TABLE OF CONTENTS

TABLE OF CONTENTS

CLIENT SERVICE

[1.0] INTRODUCTION

The role of police is often focused upon:

- the protection of life and property;
- crime prevention;
- the detection of offenders;

  and
- the preservation of peace and order.

These roles involve three main functions:

- 'law enforcement' (the use of power to control others);
- 'peace keeping' (maintaining public safety);

  and
- 'service provision' (assisting people requiring help).

A lot of emphasis is often placed on the functions of law enforcement and peace keeping with less importance placed on 'service provision'.

Success in other functions is largely dependent on the co-operation and assistance of the public.

The development of an effective police and community partnership depends on the quality of each interaction between the police and community members.

The majority of daily interactions between police and the community involve service provision.

Service provision focuses on the 'clients' of the Bougainville Police Service and the Royal Papua New Guinea Constabulary.

Addressing 'client needs' requires police to first have a clear understanding as to who are their clients.

Police then need to identify what these clients expect or need from them in terms of service or support.

Once police have established who their clients are and identified what their expectations and needs are, they can then work towards addressing these expectations and needs.

CLIENT SERVICE

Police must also develop and practice appropriate communication skills to effectively establish and address client needs in a way that respects the rights of all clients, including their rights to privacy and confidentiality.

The role of policing often requires officers to interact with members of the community and suspects in situations where conflict is more likely.

This sometimes causes police to react, rather than respond to clients.

Police must ensure they develop and practice appropriate verbal, non-verbal and written communication skills to enable them to respond to clients in a friendly, calm and courteous manner.

Police need to develop close bonds with the community and displaying courteous behaviour when dealing with the public is one of the most powerful ways of developing a positive relationship.

The display of courteous behaviour should become part of everyday interactions between police and the public.

If police can develop and maintain this behaviour they might find that community members are more likely to also respond better.

Less conflict then becomes a possible positive outcome.

However, such courteous behaviour and development of bonding relations should avoid personal relationships that would compromise the independence and integrity of the police.

[2.0] IDENTIFYING CLIENTS

A policing organisation has 'internal' and 'external' clients, and these may include:

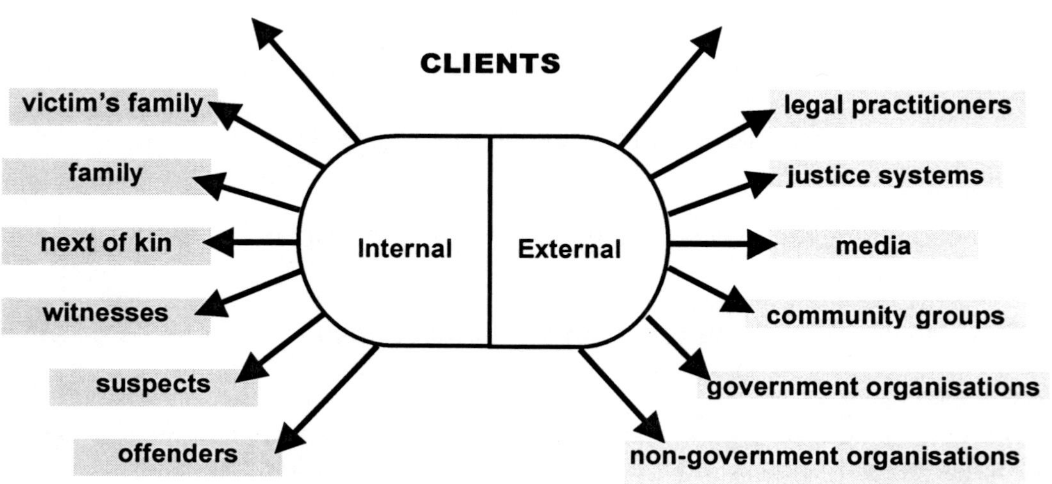

Police Clients

CLIENT SERVICE

All of these client groups will have different needs.

They will also have differing levels of need for services and support.

Police have a responsibility to:

- care for their clients;

  and

- treat all persons with courtesy and compassion and with due respect for their personal rights, dignity, and physical and mental well-being.

In the performance of their duty, police officers should respect and protect human dignity and maintain and uphold the human rights of all persons.[1]

All citizens have the same rights, privileges, obligations and duties, irrespective of race, tribe, place of origin, political opinion, colour, creed, religion[2] or sex.[3]

There should be no discrimination shown to a victim on grounds of race, colour, sex, language, religion, political or other opinion, national or social origin, property, birth or other status. Their religious beliefs and moral precepts should be respected.[4]

There will also be clients who may need special care, protection or support.

These may include:

- victims of crime[5];
- elderly persons;
- people with disabilities;

---

[1] See section 148(2)(a) and Part 14 of the *Constitution of the Autonomous Region of Bougainville*.

See also: International Human Rights Instrument titled 'Code of Conduct for Law Enforcement Officials', Article 2.

[2] See section 45 of the *Constitution of the Independent State of Papua New Guinea*.

[3] See section 55(1) of the *Constitution of the Independent State of Papua New Guinea*.

[4] See International Human Rights Instruments titled 'Convention on the Elimination of All Forms of Discrimination against Women'; 'United Nations Declaration on the Elimination of All Forms of Racial Discrimination'; 'International Convention on the Elimination of Racial Discrimination'; 'Declaration on the Elimination of All Forms of Intolerance and of Discrimination based on Religion or Belief'; 'Declaration on Race and Racial Prejudice' and 'Declaration on the Rights of Persons Belonging to National or Ethnic, Religious and Linguistic Minorities'.

[5] Refer also to the chapter titled 'Victims Of Crime'.

- abused children and/or children who have been sexually assaulted;
- adults who have been sexually assaulted;
- people in crisis;
- people suffering from critical incident stress and other psychological/psychiatric illnesses;
- alcohol affected persons;
- drug affected people;
- victims of family violence;

  and

- persons affected by transmittable diseases.

[3.0] SERVICE DELIVERY

All clients expect efficient and effective service delivery. The following are the major identified characteristics of service delivery:

Visual	• Appearance of police buildings, facilities, equipment and personnel
Reliability	• Ability to perform the promised/expected/advertised service consistently and dependably
Responsiveness	• Willingness to help customers (clients) and provide timely assistance and prompt services
Competence	• Possession of the required knowledge to perform the service
Courtesy	• Politeness, respect and consideration
Credibility	• Trustworthiness, believability and honesty of staff
Access	• Approachability of and ease in making contact
Communication	• Keeping the people informed in language they can understand and listening to them
Understanding the client	• Making the effort to know the clients and their individual and collective needs.

Major Characteristics Of Service Delivery[6]

Police need to develop close bonds with the community and displaying courteous behaviour when dealing with the public is one of the most powerful ways of developing a positive relationship.

6 See Queensland Police Service, 2001, 'Client Service Standards'.

CLIENT SERVICE

Specific behaviours that demonstrate courtesy within the station are as follows.

Behaviour	Behaviour Description	Characteristics of Behaviour
Promptness	• Attending to clients promptly	➢ When a client enters a station they should be acknowledged verbally ('Good morning/afternoon/evening') or non-verbally (smile, nod of the head) very quickly.
Voice Tone	• Friendly tone of voice	➢ Use acceptable voice tone: o normal, calm and unraised. ➢ Do not use unacceptable voice tone: o impatient, rude, indifferent, angry, hostile or abrupt.
Undivided Attention	• Attending to one client at a time	➢ Pay attention to the individual client throughout the entire interaction. ➢ Do not undertake other duties at the same time (except in emergency). ➢ Do not continue a conversation with any fellow staff members in front of client. ➢ Acknowledge the arrival of any other clients with a non-verbal response (smile, nod of head) to indicate that though you are busy you are aware of their presence.
Attentiveness	• Giving the client full attention by use of non-verbal responses (eye contact, nods) and verbal comments to indicate the client is being listened to	➢ Use appropriate verbal and non-verbal responses and behaviour to indicate that you are listening to and paying attention to the client. ➢ Do not look away or at others whilst the client is talking. ➢ Do not make or answer phone calls, unless it is in relation to the client (or in unavoidable or emergency situations).
Smiling	• Smiling or a friendly expression	➢ Smile when greeting a client and/or in parting when they are leaving.

Behaviour	Behaviour Description	Characteristics of Behaviour
Greeting/Offering to assist	• Providing an appropriate greeting	➢ Greet the client promptly in a friendly manner and offer to assist. You might ask: o 'May I help you? 'Have you been attended to?' or 'Is anyone waiting?'
Parting/Referral phrase	• Ending the interaction appropriately	➢ Use a courteous parting phrase such as: o 'Have a nice day' or 'Thank you'. ➢ If you need to refer the client to someone else, advise them who will assist them and when. If that person is busy or out, ask the client if they would like to wait or come back later or leave a message. ➢ Offer extra help if the client is unsure.
Respect	• Use of formal polite terms and attitude	➢ Address the client politely. ➢ Advise if you need to make a phone call. ➢ Assess if the client needs privacy.

Courteous Behaviour

[4.0] ESTABLISHING AND ADDRESSING CLIENT NEEDS

Police must also develop and practice these communication skills to effectively establish and address client needs in a way that respects the rights of all clients, including their rights to privacy and confidentiality.

Matters of a confidential nature in the possession of police should be kept confidential, unless the performance of duty or the needs of justice strictly require otherwise.[7]

Establishing and addressing client needs, requires police to first obtain an understanding of what the community expects or needs from them.

Generally, clients who approach a police officer in the street or at a station, are people who need assistance, require information or want to provide information.

[7] See International Human Rights Instrument titled 'Code of Conduct for Law Enforcement Officials', Article 4.

CLIENT SERVICE

These clients may not always present their needs in a calm, coherent or logical manner.

They may be:

- frightened, worried, sad or upset;
- physically, emotionally or mentally abused;
- hurt or sick;
- angry, abusive or hostile;

  or

- affected by alcohol and/or drugs.

The key to effective 'client service' is finding out what the clients really need.

Some of these perceived needs might include:

- 'responsiveness' – prompt attention/action;
- 'timeliness' – efficient service;
- 'reliability' – having confidence in police;

  and/or

- 'a long-term trusted relationship' – particularly important for the public who may need to call on police in cases of tragedy or family or personal crises.

However, members of the public also expect:

- 'sensitivity';
- 'understanding';
- 'helpfulness';

  and

- 'courtesy'

from police officers.

A client is satisfied when the service given meets or exceeds expectations, and is dissatisfied when their expectations exceed the service received.

[5.0] CLIENT SERVICE

[5.1] INTRODUCTION

The principles of 'client service' are:

- the attitude that the client is the focal point and reason for the organisation's existence;
- by adopting a 'Client Service' perspective, organisations become more efficient and effective;

  and

- the key to excellent service is finding out what the client wants.

The types of police-client interactions in service provision that are most likely to be experienced as part of daily station duties are:

- handling inquiries;
- handling complaints;
- handling problems and difficult clients;

  and/or

- handling appreciation.

[5.2] HANDLING INQUIRIES

Demonstrating appropriate communication skills and displaying a courteous and friendly manner whenever clients make inquiries, is one of the first steps in developing a partnership between police and community.

These interactions are opportunities for developing a more positive perception within the community of police officers and the services they provide.

When a client approaches a police officer with an inquiry, he or she should:

- smile and offer to help;
- ask questions to find out exactly what the client wants;

  and

- try to make positive suggestions, but if you do not know the answer, find it out.

[5.3] HANDLING COMPLAINTS

Clients define quality of service based on what they feel they should receive, in comparison to what they actually receive.

It is appropriate for all of us to make legitimate complaints when confronted with poor standards of service.

Such complaints should not be seen as trouble-making, but as timely feedback and an indicator of client satisfaction provision.

The information should be used to improve service effectiveness – not to punish individuals.

To improve, service providers need to know where they are failing to meet clients' expectations and acceptable standards, so that they can direct their efforts to improve those areas.

The real test of skills in client interactions is in dealing with complaints from clients about the services being provided.

These complaints may be justified.

Types of complaints received might allude to:

- lack of action by officers (little or no response or follow-up relating to previous inquiries);
- officers not 'doing their job' (not arresting obvious offenders);
- officers involved in corruption (undertaking or ignoring illegal activities);
- lack of police presence (not enough police patrols in the street or at markets);
- lack of or slow response by police (non-attendance or not attending promptly to calls);
- lack of proactive policing (not targeting areas of known or potential criminal activity);

  or
- lack of professionalism (police not dressed or behaving appropriately whilst on duty).

A police officer should not ignore such complaints, even if he or she may think that individual complaints are untrue or trivial.

Complaints are however usually a warning sign that something is not right.

Although there may be no evidence to justify a complaint, it is still an expression of a loss of trust and confidence in the police and this could indicate a general perception within the community.

[5.4] HANDLING PROBLEMS AND DIFFICULT CLIENTS

Whereas a complaint is usually a criticism of the services provided, a problem is more likely to be an issue that is perceived as important by the client.

When clients approach the police with a problem, they are usually seeking assistance in solving or resolving it.

Dealing with a problem is similar to handling an inquiry although the situation may be more urgent or require greater sensitivity and initiative on behalf of the officer attending to the client.

As mentioned earlier, police often interact with the community in situations that involve conflict or clients who are distressed in some way.

It is very common for police to be required to deal with persons who are angry or abusive or under the influence of alcohol and/or drugs.

These clients may be difficult to handle, and therefore police must use appropriate communication skills in executing their duty.

COMMUNITY POLICING

[1.0] INTRODUCTION

A major goal of the Bougainville Police Service and Royal Papua New Guinea Constabulary is to:

- develop;

  and

- foster

a strong and positive relationship between:

- police;

  and

- the community.

One of the main challenges facing police investigators is the need for them to:

- have a clear understanding and appreciation of their role as investigators of crime in the community;

- maintain their links with the community;

  and

- take appropriate steps to:

  - protect;

    and

  - preserve

  those links so that evidence and information is obtained freely and preserved to be presented to the courts.

Many cases that are filed are:

- dismissed;

  or

- struck out

due to the lack of attendance by:

- civilian witnesses;

  and

- police officers.

All police officers must maintain the necessary links with:

- the community;
- victims of crime;

  and

- those that report the commission of offences.

All investigators need to have a clear understanding of their role as agents of the community in:

- detecting and investigating crime;

  and

- prosecuting suspects.

A primary function of the Bougainville Police Service is:

- to serve the community;

  and

- preserve peace and good order in Bougainville.[8]

That primary function applies equally to the Royal Papua New Guinea Constabulary in the context of the rest of Papua New Guinea.

In carrying out that function the Bougainville Police Service shall[9], and the Royal Papua New Guinea Constabulary should, at all times:

- have respect for human rights[10];
- develop rehabilitatory and reconciliatory concepts of policing;

---

[8] See section 148(1) of the *Constitution of the Autonomous Region of Bougainville*.

[9] See section 148(2) of the *Constitution of the Autonomous Region of Bougainville*.

[10] See International Human Rights Instrument titled 'Code of Conduct for Law Enforcement Officials', Article 2.

- work in harmony and partnership with communities and encourage community participation in its activities;

  and

- support and work with traditional chiefs and other traditional leaders to resolve disputes and maintain law and order in communities.

Every policing organisation should be:

- representative of;

  and

- responsive and accountable

to the community as a whole.[11]

As policing organisations, the Bougainville Police Service and the Royal Papua New Guinea Constabulary have the responsibility of:

- protecting life and property;
- detecting offenders;
- maintaining law and order;

  and

- preventing crime.

As policing organisations move from:

- the traditional 'reactive' policing model, ie., apprehending offenders after an offence has been committed,

  to

- a more 'proactive' style of policing,

the focus has shifted from an emphasis on crime 'detection' to crime 'prevention' strategies.

[11] See International Human Rights Instrument titled 'Code of Conduct for Law Enforcement Officials', Preambular paragraph 8(a).

COMMUNITY POLICING

The 'proactive' approach of crime prevention involves more effective ways of solving ongoing problems to:

- help prevent crime;
- reduce fear of crime;

  and

- improve the quality of life within the community.

This shift in focus has important implications for the relationship between the police and the community.

This is because successful 'community policing' is:

dependent upon the community joining with the police in crime prevention and solution.

To more effectively undertake a preventative approach to solving crime, the police need to have a very good knowledge of the community that they must serve.

Police also need:

- the co-operation;

  and

- the support

of the community.

All police officers:

- are part of;

  and

- have a duty to serve

the community.[12]

The community is a valuable source of information, knowledge and skills that can be utilised by the police in a more co-operative partnership style of policing.

[12] See International Human Rights Instrument titled 'Code of Conduct for Law Enforcement Officials', Article 1.

COMMUNITY POLICING

The community may choose to provide valuable information that:

- may assist in the conduct of an investigation and apprehension of an offender;

  and

- may assist in crime prevention.

In order to gain this assistance from the community, police need to encourage:

- greater participation from community members;

  and

- a willingness to share the responsibility of crime prevention and control.

There needs to be regular liaison with community representatives.

This 'proactive' crime prevention strategy of developing a co-operative partnership between police and the community is known universally as 'Community Policing'[13].

'Community Policing' offers:

- police officers, as representatives of the Bougainville Police Service or the Royal Papua New Guinea Constabulary, the opportunity to promote and foster a positive image of the Bougainville Police Service and the Royal Papua New Guinea Constabulary within the community;

  and

- the Bougainville Police Service or the Royal Papua New Guinea Constabulary the means to:

  - advise the community about public safety activities;

    and

  - involve the community in these activities.[14]

---

[13] See International Human Rights Instruments titled 'Universal Declaration of Human Rights', Article 29(1); 'Code of Conduct for Law Enforcement Officials', Preambular paragraph 8(a); and 'United Nations Standard Minimum Rules for Non- custodial Measures', Preambular paragraphs 7 and 11(4) and Rule 1.2.

[14] See International Human Rights Instrument titled 'Code of Conduct for Law Enforcement Officials', Preambular paragraph 8(a).

[2.0] DEFINING COMMUNITY POLICING

[2.1] INTRODUCTION

The following are the main principles of 'community policing':

Partnership	Emphasises the creation of an effective working partnership between: • the community; and • the police.
Competent communities	The success of the police depends: • not only on the development of their own skills and capabilities, but also • on the creation of competent communities.
Actively helping	The role of the community: • is not just merely alerting the police to crime and other problems, but • to actively helping to keep their own community secure and free from crime. This may or may not involve police.
Working for the community	Police recognise that they work for: • the community, as well as • the law.

Consultation and information	Police seek wider consultation and more information from the community. Community priorities are taken seriously and acted upon.
Problem-solving	The same broad objectives that apply in: • problem-solving policing, also apply in • community policing (ie., crime detection, crime prevention, fear reduction and order maintenance).
On-going problems	It is recognised that crime can be caused by particular on-going problems in the community that: • generate; or • bring about a propensity or tendency for crime to occur.
Crime controlled by solving problems	Crimes can be controlled by solving problems and dealing with the underlying circumstances and conditions that lead to crime. Prevention is better than cure.
Community responsibility	The community itself and other organisations all have a part to play in dealing with: • community problems; and • preventing crime. In some instances police will play a proactive civic leadership role in directing community resources to a specific situation but ultimately the aim is to have communities take responsibility for their own circumstances.

Main Principles Of Community Policing[15]

[15] See Etter, B. and Palmer, M. (editors), 1995, 'Police Leadership in Australasia', The Federation Press, Australia.

Successful 'community policing' is:

dependent upon the community joining with the police in crime prevention and solution.

A key feature of successful community policing is police being visible and their physical presence of police personnel in the community. The presence of uniformed police officers stationed in the community makes communication and interactions between:

- police;

  and

- the community

more effective and deters crime.

[2.2] COLLABORATIVE EFFORT

'Community Policing' is a collaborative effort between the police and the community that:

- identifies problems of crime and disorder;

  and

- involves all elements of the community in the search for solutions to these problems.

With the police no longer the sole guardians of law and order, all members of the community become active allies in the effort to enhance the safety and quality of their community in which they live.

[2.3] PHILOSOPHY

'Community Policing' is not a separate policing program or function.

'Community Policing' is an ethos or philosophy to be embraced by all members of the Bougainville Police Service and the Royal Papua New Guinea Constabulary.

All police officers should adopt the principles of 'Community Policing' in:

- all aspects of their duties;

  and

- interactions with members of their community.

'Community Policing' must be integrated into the whole police structure, including policies and procedures.

[2.4] TRUST

'Community Policing' is established and built on close mutually beneficial ties between:

- police;

  and

- community members.

Getting communities actively involved is essential if crime is to be deterred.

In some communities, it will take time to break down barriers of apathy and mistrust so that meaningful partnerships can be forged.

'Trust' is the value that underlies and links the components of community partnership and problem-solving.

A foundation of 'trust' will allow police to form close relationships with the community that will produce solid achievements.

Without 'trust' between:

- police;

  and

- the community

effective policing is impossible.

[2.5] POSITIVE IMPACT

Effective 'Community Policing' has a positive impact on:

- 'reducing neighbourhood crime';
- 'helping to reduce fear of crime';

  and

- 'enhancing the quality of life in the community'.

[2.6] STRONG SELF-SUFFICIENT COMMUNITIES

'Community Policing' offers a way for law enforcement to encourage communities to get involved in their own:

- safety and security;

  and

- crime prevention.

Developing strong, self-sufficient communities is an essential step in creating an atmosphere in which serious crime will not grow and flourish.

[2.7] INNOVATION

'Community Policing' offers police the opportunity to:

- seek;

  and

- implement

innovative ways to:

- enhance performance;

  and

- maximise the use of resources.

[2.8] INTEGRATION

'Community Policing' initiatives allow police to get back to the principles upon which policing was founded, to integrate policing once again into the fabric of the community so that people come to the police for advice and assistance before a serious problem arises, and not after the fact.

[2.9] LONG-TERM COMMITMENT

'Community Policing' requires:

a long-term commitment by police to work with community members to reach mutually agreed-upon goals.

Forming lasting partnerships to eradicate the underlying causes of crime will take:

- effort;
- time;

  and
- patience

on the part of all involved.

[2.10] WIDE-RANGING BENEFITS

'Community Policing' has the following wide-ranging benefits:

- it brings police closer to the community;
- it makes effective use of skills and resources available within communities which assists police extend their limited resources;
- as police interaction with the community becomes more positive, productive partnerships will be formed;
- these partnerships will lead to greater satisfaction with police services and increased job satisfaction among officers;

  and
- reduced levels of crime will allow more police resources to be allocated to services that have the greatest impact on the quality of community life.

[3.0] COMMUNITY PARTNERSHIP

[3.1] INTRODUCTION

The foundations of a successful 'Community Policing' strategy are:

- the close;

  and

- mutually beneficial ties

between police and the community.

A community may encompass widely diverse cultures, values, and concerns.

A community consists of more than just the local government and the residents. Churches, schools, hospitals, social groups, private and public agencies, leaders in the community, and those who live and work in the area are also vital members of the community. In addition, those who visit for cultural or recreational purposes or provide services to the area are also concerned with the safety and security of the area.

Concerns and priorities will vary within and among communities.

Also, interest groups within communities can be in opposition to one another – sometimes in violent opposition.

These multiple and sometimes conflicting interests require police officers to function:

- not only as preservers of law and order,

  but also

- as skillful mediators.

Demands on police from one sector of the community can sometimes clash with the rights of another group within the community.

The police must:

- not only protect the rights of interest groups,

  but

- also work with all of the community members involved to find a way to preserve peace.

For this process to be effective, community members must:

- communicate their views and suggestions;

  and

- back up the negotiating efforts of the police.

In this way, the entire community:

- participates in the mediation process;

  and

- helps preserve order.

The police must encourage a spirit of co-operation that balances:

- the collective interests of all members;

  with

- the personal rights of individuals.

The conflicts within communities are as important as the commonalities.

Police must recognise the existence of both in order to build the co-operative bonds needed to:

- maintain order;
- provide a sense of security;

  and

- control crime.

Police must build lasting relationships that:

- encompass all elements of the community;

  and

- centre around the fundamental issues of:
    - public safety;

      and

    - quality of life.

The key to managing this difficult task is 'trust'.

[3.2] ESTABLISHING AND MAINTAINING MUTUAL TRUST

Establishing and maintaining 'mutual trust' is the central goal of community partnership.

Police recognise the need for co-operation with the community.

In 'Community Policing':

- the police become an integral part of the community culture;

  and

- the community assists in:

  - defining future priorities;

    and

  - allocating resources.

Community partnership means adopting a policing perspective that exceeds the standard law enforcement emphasis.

This wider outlook recognises the value of activities that contribute to the:

- orderliness;

  and

- well-being

of the community.

These activities could include:

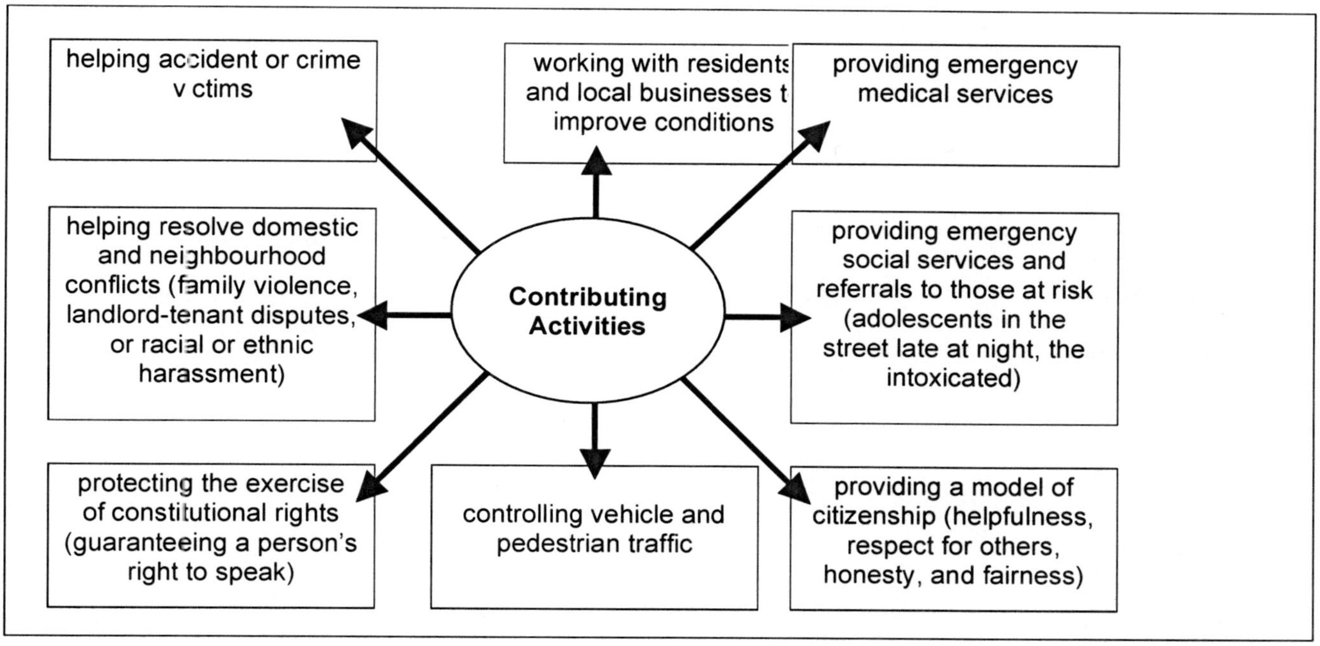

Police Activities Contributing To The Well-being Of The Community[16]

These services help develop 'trust' between the police and the community.

This 'trust' will:

- enable the police to gain greater access to valuable information from the community that could lead to the:
    - solution;

      and
    - prevention

  of offences;
- engender or produce support for needed crime-control measures;

  and
- provide an opportunity for officers to establish a working relationship with the community.

The whole police organisation must be involved in enlisting the co-operation of community members in promoting safety and security.

[16] See Community Policing Consortium's 'About Community Policing'.

COMMUNITY POLICING

Building 'trust' will not happen overnight; it will require ongoing effort.

But 'trust' must be achieved before police can:

- assess the needs of the community;

  and

- construct the close ties that will engender community support.

In turn, this co-operative relationship will deepen the bonds of 'trust'.

To build this 'trust' for an effective community partnership police must treat people with:

- respect;

  and

- sensitivity.

The use of unnecessary force and arrogance, aloofness, or rudeness at any level of the police will dampen the willingness of community members to:

- collaborate with;

  or

- support

the police.

'Community Policing' expands police efforts to:

- prevent crime;

  and

- control crime.

The community is no longer viewed by police as:

- a passive presence;

  or

- a source of limited information,

but as a partner in this effort.

Community concerns with crime and disorder thus become the target of efforts by:

- the police;

  and

- the community

working in tandem.

The close alliance forged with the community should not be:

- limited to:
  - an isolated incident;

    or

  - series of incidents;

  or

- confined to a specific timeframe.

The partnership between the police and the community must be:

- enduring;

  and

- balanced.

The police and the community must be collaborators in the quest to:

- encourage;

  and

- preserve

peace and prosperity.

Police can easily encourage this partnership by, for example:

- talking to local business owners to help identify their problems and concerns;
- offering advice on security within the home;

  and

- helping to organise and support regular community meetings.

In this police/community partnership, these types of social services will be acknowledged as being inextricably or inseparably linked to deterring crime and problem solving will become a co-operative effort.

The central goal of community partnership is:

- establishing;

  and

- maintaining

'mutual trust'.

[4.0] PROBLEM-ORIENTED POLICING

Problem solving is a broad term that:

- implies more than simply:
  - the elimination;

    and

  - the prevention

  of offences;

  and

- is based on the assumption that crime and disorder can be reduced in specified areas by:
  - carefully studying the characteristics or type and features of problems in that area;

    and then

  - applying the appropriate resources by the use of 'criminal intelligence'.

Identifying the underlying causes of crime and then working to reduce crime by attacking its causes is known as 'Problem-oriented Policing'.

'Problem-oriented policing' is a systematic approach to:

- identifying;
- analysing;

  and

- addressing

the causes of crime and associated community problems.

The theory behind 'Problem-oriented Policing' is simple:

- Underlying conditions create problems.

  These conditions might include:

  - the characteristics of the people involved (offenders, potential victims, and others);
  - the social setting in which these people interact;
  - the physical environments;

    and

  - the way the public deals with these conditions;

  and

- A problem created by these conditions may generate one or more incidents.

  These incidents, while stemming from a common source, may appear to be different.

  For example, social and physical conditions in a disused area of old and burnt down buildings may generate burglaries, acts of vandalism (eg., graffiti), intimidation of persons walking past by youths, and other incidents.

  These incidents, some of which come to police attention, are symptoms of the problems.

  The incidents will continue so long as the problem that creates them persists or remains.

Problem-solving involves a series of actions:

Initially recognising the existence of the problem

↓

Systematically analysing the problem to identify its possible causes

↓

Developing a response that focuses on the causes

↓

Assessing or measuring the effectiveness of the response

Series Of Actions Involved In Problem-Solving[17]

[5.0] COMMUNITY INVOLVEMENT IN PROBLEM-SOLVING

As police recognise the effectiveness of the problem-solving approach, there is a growing awareness that community involvement is essential for its success.

Determining the underlying causes of crime depends, to a great extent, on an in-depth knowledge of the community.

Therefore, community participation in:

- identifying priorities;

  and

- setting priorities

will contribute to effective problem-solving efforts by:

- the community;

  and

- the police.

[17] See Queensland Police Service, 2001, 'Guide to Problem Oriented and Partnership Policing'.

Co-operative problem-solving also:

- reinforces 'trust';
- facilitates the exchange of information or intelligence;

  and

- leads to the identification of other areas that could benefit from the mutual attention of:
  - the police;

    and

  - the community.

For this process to operate effectively the police need to:

- devote attention to;

  and

- recognise the validity of

community concerns.

The community and the police will not always agree on which specific problems deserve attention first.

Therefore, in addition to the serious crime problems identified by police, 'Community Policing' must also address the problems of significant concern to the community.

'Community Policing' allows community members to bring problems of great concern to them to the attention of the police.

Once informed of these community concerns, the police must work with community members to address them.

At the same time police must encourage community members to assist in solving the problems of concern to the police.

Solutions to problems range from:

- simple, inexpensive methods'

  to

- complex, long-term answers that will require significant investment of staff and resources.

COMMUNITY POLICING

Problem solving is limited only by the imagination, creativity, perseverance, and enthusiasm of those involved.

'Community Policing' allows solutions to be tailor-made or adapted to the specific concerns of each community.

The best solutions are those that:

- satisfy community members;
- improve safety;
- diminish or lessen anxiety or worry;
- lead to increased law and order;

  and

- strengthen the ties between the community and police.

ETHICS AND ACCOUNTABILITY

[1.0] INTRODUCTION

People must feel free to live their lives knowing that they have the protection of the laws of the country.[18]

Breakages of these laws must be dealt with effectively by:

- the police;

  and

- the judicial system.[19]

Upholding the 'Rule of Law' is of paramount importance to:

- peace;
- security

  and

- freedom.[20]

For criminals to run free and exert power through force and intimidation is to deny ordinary people the freedom to live their lives peacefully, and is therefore a denial of democracy.[21]

Both the Bougainville Police Service and Royal Papua New Guinea Constabulary must strive to be a police service of excellence that is:

- trusted by the community;

  and

- accountable for their actions.[22]

---

[18] See Solomon Islands Human Development Report 2002 -- Building a Nation, Volume 1, Main Report, page 26.

[19] See Solomon Islands Human Development Report 2002 -- Building a Nation, Volume 1, Main Report, page 26.

[20] See Solomon Islands Human Development Report 2002 -- Building a Nation, Volume 1, Main Report, page 26.

[21] See Solomon Islands Human Development Report 2002 -- Building a Nation, Volume 1, Main Report, page 26.

[22] The Code of Ethics of the Royal Papua New Guinea Constabulary is Appendix 1.

All police officers must demonstrate this by displaying appropriate behaviour by being:

- 'Honest';
- 'Fair';
- 'Respectful';
- 'Open';

  and
- 'Accountable'.

All police officers must discharge their duty professionally:

- without favour;

  and
- with honour.

All officers should not commit a disciplinary offence.[23]

The people of Papua New Guinea rightly expect that all police officers will uphold the law whilst being ethical at all times, especially considering the powers which they hold to detain, arrest, search and seize.[24]

Police officers should:

- understand;

  and
- be able to apply

ethical standards in dealing with the community's expectations on the reported crime and investigations in order to avoid compromising their work.

[23] See section 20 of the *Police Act 1998*.

See also: Appendix 2.

[24] Refer also to the chapter titled 'Police Powers'.

ETHICS AND ACCOUNTABILITY

Police officers should at all times:

- respect the law;

  and

- obey the law.[25]

Police officers must always respect the human rights[26] of all persons whom they deal with.[27]

Human rights derive from the inherent dignity of the human person.[28]

All citizens have the same rights, privileges, obligations and duties, irrespective of race, tribe, place of origin, political opinion, colour, creed, religion[29] or sex.[30]

There should be no discrimination shown to a victim on grounds of race, colour, sex, language, religion, political or other opinion, national or social origin, property, birth or other status. Their religious beliefs and moral precepts should be respected.[31]

---

[25] See International Human Rights Instrument titled 'Code of Conduct for Law Enforcement Officials', Article 8.

A police officer is required to obey the orders of the Court, see section 274 of the *District Courts Act* (Ch. 40) and section 146 of the *Police Force Act* 1998.

[26] The community may also provide information that can assist in crime prevention.

[27] See section 148(2)(a) and Part 14 of the *Constitution of the Autonomous Region of Bougainville.*

See also: International Human Rights Instrument titled 'Code of Conduct for Law Enforcement Officials', Article 2.

[28] See International Human Rights Instrument titled 'International Declaration of Human Rights', Preamble and Article 1.

[29] See section 45 of the *Constitution of the Independent State of Papua New Guinea.*

[30] See section 55(1) of the *Constitution of the Independent State of Papua New Guinea.*

[31] See International Human Rights Instruments titled 'Convention on the Elimination of All Forms of Discrimination against Women'; 'United Nations Declaration on the Elimination of All Forms of Racial Discrimination'; 'International Convention on the Elimination of Racial Discrimination'; 'Declaration on the Elimination of All Forms of Intolerance and of Discrimination based on Religion or Belief'; 'Declaration on Race and Racial Prejudice' and 'Declaration on the Rights of Persons Belonging to National or Ethnic, Religious and Linguistic Minorities'.

An officer must prove his or her:

- personal;

  and

- professional

integrity by his or her actions as a police officer.

If an officer complies with:

- the policy, practices, procedures and values of the Bougainville Police Service and Royal Papua New Guinea Constabulary;

  and

- the law

then that officer will be acting ethically.

[2.0] PROFESSIONALISM

So what is professionalism?

Police officers are expected to at all times fulfil the duty imposed upon them by law, by:

- serving the community;

  and

- protecting all persons against illegal acts, consistent with the high degree of responsibility required by their profession.[32]

The police officer of the future must emerge as a responsible professional who:

- is self-regulating in his or her personal conduct;

  and

- accepts accountability as an important personal challenge.[33]

---

[32] See International Human Rights Instrument titled 'Code of Conduct for Law Enforcement Officials', Article 1.

[33] See Palmer in Etter, B. and Palmer, M. (editors), 1995, 'Police Leadership in Australasia', The Federation Press, Australia, page 5.

An officer is expected to monitor his or her own performance standards to ensure that he or she consistently serves as a role model for:

- other officers;

  and

- the community as a whole.

An officer will be held accountable for his or her behaviour.

Police work is not rote; it is varied, unpredictable, and full, for better or worse, of surprises that cannot be covered by precise rules.[34]

Police work by its very nature requires considerable freedom of action, and a high degree of individual discretion and judgment, often in situations where little or no direct supervision is possible.[35]

Corruption can be minimised only by taking all reasonable steps to ensure that:

- discretion;

  and

- judgment

are exercised:

- soundly;

  and

- within acceptable boundaries.[36]

Accountability should not be automatically related to punishment, and neither should unethical behaviour.[37]

---

[34] See Etter, B. and Palmer, M. (editors), 1995, 'Police Leadership in Australasia', The Federation Press, Australia, page 159.

[35] See Etter, B. and Palmer, M. (editors), 1995, 'Police Leadership in Australasia', The Federation Press, Australia, page 160.

[36] See Etter, B. and Palmer, M. (editors), 1995, 'Police Leadership in Australasia', The Federation Press, Australia, page 160.

[37] See Etter, B. and Palmer, M. (editors), 1995, 'Police Leadership in Australasia', The Federation Press, Australia, page 5.

Accountability is not an incursion or hindrance, but a necessity for all organisations, particularly those which are taxpayer funded and especially because of:

- the nature of police work;

  and

- the great powers that police exercise.[38]

Professional knowledge of:

- the policies, practices, procedures and values of the Bougainville Police Service and Royal Papua New Guinea Constabulary;

  and

- the law

is a police officer's personal and professional acceptance of the responsibilities of being 'accountable' for his or her actions.

An officer must constantly demonstrate his or her:

- understanding;

  and

- commitment

by correctly applying:

- the policies, practices, procedures and values of the Bougainville Police Service and Royal Papua New Guinea Constabulary;

  and

- the law.

---

[38] See Queensland Police Service Review, 1996, 'Report on the Review of the Queensland Police Service', (Sir M. Bingham, chairperson), Queensland Government, Brisbane, page 261.

Refer also to the chapter titled 'Police Powers'.

It is generally accepted that 'accountability' of police officers is to:

- the community[39];

  and

- their respective police organisation.

Police officers have a personal responsibility for accountability as regards:

- their efficient, effective and ethical use of resources;

  and

- their ethical behaviour:
  - on the job;

    and

  - off the job.

Though public scrutiny and constant emphasis on 'accountability' and 'ethical behaviour' may seem like an intrusion into the private lives of officers, it also signifies the concept of policing as a 'profession'.

[3.0] POLICE CULTURE

So what is culture?

> It is a 'perception'.[40]

So what is organisational culture?

> It is a system of shared meaning within an organisation that determines, in large degree, how employees act.[41]

In every organisation, there are systems or patterns of values, symbols, rituals, myths, and practice that have evolved over time.[42]

---

[39] See Hunter in Etter, B. and Palmer, M. (editors), 1995, 'Police Leadership in Australasia', The Federation Press, Australia, page 5.

[40] See Robbins, S., 1994, 'Management', 4th edition, Prentice-Hall, USA, page 71.

[41] See Robbins, S., 1994, 'Management', 4th edition, Prentice-Hall, USA, page 71.

[42] See Robbins, S., 1994, 'Management', 4th edition, Prentice-Hall, USA, page 71.

Collectively, groups develop patterns of behaviour which may become ritualistic; symbols and symbolic behaviours (or meanings associated with particular behaviours) which are peculiar to them; their own language and jargon; and stories, legends and traditions.[43]

These features help to establish meanings and beliefs and they are transmitted -- as culture is a communicative phenomena -- through formal and informal socialisation processes.[44]

There is no doubt that each policing organisation has its own culture, and some say:

- for better;

  and

- for worse.

In some sections within a policing organisation there may be a tendency for officers to be unethical.

Common sense is, however, the lifeblood of the police culture.[45]

In police organisations, common sense is:

> the accumulated wisdom of line-officer culture, carrying the wisdom, history, and traditions of the department.[46]

Remember, policing is about applying ‘common sense’.

To act ethically is to:

> act in the ‘right’ manner in the circumstances.

A police officer cannot blame cultural influences for acting unethically.

---

[43] See Fulop, L. and Linstead, S., 1999, ‘Leading and managing’, ‘Management: A Critical Text’, MacMillan Education Australia Pty Ltd, Australia, page 100.

[44] See Fulop, L. and Linstead, S., 1999, ‘Leading and managing’, ‘Management: A Critical Text’, MacMillan Education Australia Pty Ltd, Australia, page 100.

[45] See Crank, P., 1998, ‘Understanding Police Culture’, Anderson Publishing Co., USA, page 164.

[46] See Crank, P., 1998, ‘Understanding Police Culture’, Anderson Publishing Co., USA, page 164.

[4.0] ETHICS

So what is ethics?

Ethics is the principles of 'right' behaviour.[47]

Ethical behaviour is directed at improving the welfare of:

- individuals;

  and

- society

as a whole.[48]

It is generally agreed that a wide variety of psychological and sociological influences determine the ethical values of an individual.[49]

These include attitudes, perceptions, motivations, personality, family, peer group and situational factors.[50]

Ethics are the rules or standards of conduct any society imposes in respect of the rights and interests of its members recognising the fundamental moral principles that underpin every:

- decision;

  and

- action

a member may make.

---

[47] See Viljoen, J., 1994, 'Strategic Management', 2nd edition, Addison Wesley Longman Australia Pty Ltd, Australia, page 98.

[48] See Viljoen, J., 1994, 'Strategic Management', 2nd edition, Addison Wesley Longman Australia Pty Ltd, Australia, page 98.

[49] See Viljoen, J., 1994, 'Strategic Management', 2nd edition, Addison Wesley Longman Australia Pty Ltd, Australia, page 98.

[50] See Viljoen, J., 1994, 'Strategic Management', 2nd edition, Addison Wesley Longman Australia Pty Ltd, Australia, page 98.

ETHICS AND ACCOUNTABILITY

In the work environment ethical principles can be used to provide guidance in situations where:

- there are no specific policies, practices or procedures in place;

  or

- matters are unclear.

Such principles help determine what is:

- right;

  and

- proper.

Irrespective of what occurs an officer is required to always act 'ethically'.

All officers play a vital and integral role in the provision of policing services to the community and are expected to provide these services in a manner that promotes the public confidence.

In doing so, an officer should conduct himself or herself in a professional and therefore, ethical manner and aspire to the principles of:

- fairness;
- impartiality;
- diligence;
- integrity;

  and

- efficiency.

Personal and professional integrity must engender:

- confidence;

  and

- respect

from the community.

In relation to the conduct of a police officer who is off-duty, at least this much is patently clear; a police officer's private life is never above public scrutiny.[51]

An officer is expected to behave ethically whilst:

- working;

  and

- off-duty.

Though this public scrutiny and constant emphasis on 'accountability' and 'ethical behaviour' may seem like an intrusion into the private lives of officers, it also signifies the concept of policing as a 'profession'.

Accountability should not automatically be related to punishment.

There is a need for police to feel a sense of pride and professionalism in:

- their work;

  and

- their organisation.[52]

Despite the Bougainville Police Service and Royal Papua New Guinea Constabulary setting a high standard of ethical behaviour there will be some officers who are lacking in ethical values.[53]

In some cases unethical behaviour is premeditated.[54]

If an officer chooses to act unethically then he or she will be dealt with accordingly.

---

[51] See Moses, D, 1999, 'Beyond the call of duty – Misconduct of a private nature', The Queensland Police Union Journal, November.

[52] See Palmer, in Etter, B. and Palmer, M. (editors), 1995, 'Police Leadership in Australasia', The Federation Press, Australia, page 5.

[53] See Gellerman in Viljoen, J., 1994, 'Strategic Management', 2nd edition, Addison Wesley Longman Australia Pty Ltd, Australia, page 101.

[54] See Gellerman in Viljoen, J., 1994, 'Strategic Management', 2nd edition, Addison Wesley Longman Australia Pty Ltd, Australia, page 101.

Training in how to:

- recognise ethical issues;

  and

- how to deal with ethical dilemmas

can help create the right culture in an organisation.[55]

In any given situation if an officer is uncertain as to what is the ethical way of dealing with the situation, then he or she should apply:

the SELF Test[56].

---

[55] See Viljoen, J., 1994, 'Strategic Management', 2nd edition, Addison Wesley Longman Australia Pty Ltd, Australia, page 105.

[56] See Appendix 3.

[1.0] INTRODUCTION

When an offence has been committed it is the responsibility of the Bougainville Police Service and the Royal Papua New Guinea Constabulary to conduct a thorough investigation.

The initial objective of the investigating officer must be:

to determine whether an offence has actually been committed.

When it has been established that an offence has been committed[57], the next objectives are to establish:

- the identity of the offender[58];

  and

- his or her whereabouts.

The initial action taken by an investigating officer at the scene of an offence, referred to as the 'crime scene', may determine the outcome of the investigation, depending on the circumstances of the commission of the offence, and particularly whether there is a reliance on the admissibility of forensic evidence.

Appropriate action can ensure the success of an investigation whereas incorrect action can result in failure.

An investigation must:

- be conducted:

  - competently;
  - thoroughly;
  - promptly;

    and

---

[57] If no offence has actually been committed and the incident involves the death of a person or a fire involving substantial destruction then the investigating officer should conduct a coronial investigation.

Refer also to the text titled 'Injia on Coronial Proceedings in Papua New Guinea and the Pacific'.

[58] Refer also to the section titled 'Identification Evidence' in the chapter titled 'Evidence' in the text titled 'Injia on Criminal Practice and Procedure in Papua New Guinea and the Pacific'.

- impartially[59];

and

- serve to identify victims[60]; recover evidence[61]; discover witnesses[62]; discover cause, manner, location and time of the offence; and identify[63] and apprehend offenders.[64]

Investigation is an art, rather than a science.

It must therefore be considered in terms of principles and experience, rather than just inflexible rules and theories.

However,

- investigatory activities shall be conducted lawfully with due cause;

  and

- arbitrary or unduly intrusive investigatory activities must not be applied.[65]

---

59 Refer also to the chapter titled 'Ethics And Accountability'.

See also: International Human Rights Instrument titled 'Principles on the Effective Prevention and Investigation of Extralegal, Arbitrary and Summary Executions', Principle 9.

60 Refer also to the chapters titled 'Victims Of Crime' and 'Client Service'.

61 Refer also to the chapter titled 'Evidence' in the text titled 'Injia on Criminal Practice and Procedure in Papua New Guinea and the Pacific'.

62 Refer also to:

- the chapter titled 'Witnesses'; and
- the chapter titled 'Witnesses' in the text titled 'Injia on Criminal Practice and Procedure in Papua New Guinea and the Pacific'.

63 Refer also to:

- the chapter titled 'Forensic Evidence'; and
- the section titled 'Identification Evidence' in the chapter titled 'Evidence' in the text titled 'Injia on Criminal Practice and Procedure in Papua New Guinea and the Pacific'.

64 See International Human Rights Instrument titled 'Principles on the Effective Prevention and Investigation of Extralegal, Arbitrary and Summary Executions', Principle 9.

65 See International Human Rights Instruments titled 'Code of Conduct for Law Enforcement Officials', Article 4; 'Body of Principles for the Protection of All Persons under Any Form of Detention or Imprisonment', Principles 21, 23 and 36; and 'Principles on the Effective Prevention and Investigation of Extralegal, Arbitrary and Summary Executions', Principles 9, 10 and 11.

Offences do not just happen, but rather are committed by people.

No two people are the same, and no two criminals are the same.

A wide variety of people commit offences for an equally wide variety of reasons.

Depending on the complexity of an investigation it may be necessary to conduct the investigation in accordance with an 'Investigation Plan'.[66]

It should not be forgotten that the vast majority of investigations are solved as a result of painstaking investigation, with perhaps, a little bit of luck.

It is often possible for an investigating officer to create his or her own luck by means of a combination of preparation and opportunity. It is in this sense that his or her awareness of the appropriate 'avenues of inquiry' provides the opportunity to achieve a result which otherwise would not be possible.

Upon being satisfied that an offence has been committed, an investigating officer must then decide whether to institute proceedings[67] by way of:

- making an arrest[68];
- applying for and executing a warrant of arrest;

  or
- applying for and serving a summons.

Proceedings however should not be instituted, unless a decision has been made to prosecute the offender.[69]

[2.0] THE INVESTIGATOR

The investigating officer is the person who is responsible for conducting an investigation into a particular offence.

---

[66] Refer also to the chapter titled 'Investigation Plan'.

[67] Refer also to the section titled 'Institution Of Proceedings' in the chapter titled 'Charges' in the text titled 'Injia on Criminal Practice and Procedure in Papua New Guinea and the Pacific'.

[68] Refer also to the section titled 'Power To Arrest' in the chapter titled 'Police Powers'.

[69] Refer also to the section titled 'Institution Of Proceedings' in the chapter titled 'Charges' in the text titled 'Injia on Criminal Practice and Procedure in Papua New Guinea and the Pacific'.

PRINCIPLES OF INVESTIGATION

The approach of an investigating officer must be:

- completely 'objective';

  and

- as much concerned with the exculpation of an innocent person, as with a conviction of a guilty person.

It is the duty of an investigating officer to determine the truth of the matter under inquiry by:

- collecting;

  and

- evaluating

all of the available admissible evidence[70].

An investigating officer seeks to establish evidence of four facts:

- Whether an offence has actually been committed[71];

  and if so:

- The identity of the offender[72];
- The whereabouts of the offender;

  and

- A nexus or connection between the offender and the offence.

---

[70] Refer also to the chapter titled 'Evidence' in the text titled 'Injia on Criminal Practice and Procedure in Papua New Guinea and the Pacific'.

[71] If no offence has actually been committed and the incident involves the death of a person or a fire involving substantial destruction then the investigating officer should conduct a coronial investigation.

Refer also to the text titled 'Injia on Coronial Proceedings in Papua New Guinea and the Pacific'.

[72] Refer also to the section titled 'Identification Evidence' in the chapter titled 'Evidence' in the text titled 'Injia on Criminal Practice and Procedure in Papua New Guinea and the Pacific'.

[3.0] INVESTIGATION CONFIDENTIALITY

Incidents have occurred where a Case File has been mislaid, stolen or otherwise interfered with.[73]

Confidentiality and care in handling of sensitive information is to be exercised at all times.[74]

An investigating officer is responsible for the security of all evidence under his or her control.

Under no circumstances is investigatory information to be made accessible to a suspect/offender, unless otherwise then in accordance with:

- the law;

  or

- relevant policy.

Instances when:

- the confidentiality of the identity of an informer[75];

  or

- the security of investigatory information

have not been maintained should be reported to enable a discipline investigation to be conducted.

An officer who knowingly fails to disclose the existence of any relevant evidence that is within his or her knowledge in relation to a criminal charge commits a disciplinary offence.[76]

---

[73] Refer also to the chapter titled 'Ethics And Accountability'.

[74] See International Human Rights Instrument titled 'Code of Conduct for Law Enforcement Officials', Article 4.

[75] As regards the law in relation to the protection of informers, refer to the section titled 'Search Warrant' in the chapter titled 'Police Powers'.

[76] See section 20(1)(z) of the *Police Act 1998*.

[4.0] INVESTIGATION DEFINED

An investigation is a search for the truth:

- in the interests of justice;

  and

- in accordance with the law.

In order to arrive at the truth as to the commission of an offence there needs to be the collection of evidence[77], ie., 'induction', which in turn permits logical conclusions to be drawn, ie., 'deductions'.

An investigation is:

> an objective assessment of an incident with a view to determining whether any offence has been committed.

The evidence on which this assessment is based must be obtained within the limits of established rules of law and procedure, referred to as the 'rules of evidence'.[78]

An investigation is concerned with the modus operandi or method used in the commission of an offence. Since this involves:

- the use of physical things;

  and

- the application of personal technique,

an examination of the physical evidence might identify the offender as certainly as if he or she left his or her signature at the crime scene.[79]

Initial action at a crime scene requires the investigating officer to apply:

- his or her intelligence;
- his or her ability to reason;

  and

- his or her experience

---

[77] Refer also to the chapter titled 'Evidence' in the text titled 'Injia on Criminal Practice and Procedure in Papua New Guinea and the Pacific'.

[78] Refer also to the chapter titled 'Evidence' in the text titled 'Injia on Criminal Practice and Procedure in Papua New Guinea and the Pacific'.

[79] Refer also to the chapter titled 'Forensic Evidence'.

in the investigation of the incident.[80]

Unlike mistakes made during the later stages of an investigation, errors in initial action at a crime scene cannot be rectified.

However, errors will be minimised if the investigating officer remains alert to:

- the fact that errors may be made;

  and

- the transitory nature of some evidence.[81]

Even with experienced investigating officers, there is a compelling urge to seek the suspect/offender, rather than to proceed with the more mundane task of examining the crime scene as comprehensively as possible.[82]

Without a thorough examination of the crime scene being conducted the investigating officer may not be able to obtain all of the available evidence concerning the commission of an offence.

Depending on the circumstances of the offence the desire to quickly interview the suspect/offender[83] must be resisted.

It can also be a distinct disadvantage to interview the suspect/offender before the collection of all the available evidence.

---

[80] Refer also to the chapter titled and 'Incident Management'.

[81] Refer also to the section titled 'Exhibit Handling Procedure' in the chapter titled 'Exhibits'.

[82] Refer also to the chapter titled and 'Incident Management'.

[83] Refer also to:

- the chapter titled 'Interviewing Suspects'; and
- the section titled 'Confessional Evidence' in the chapter titled 'Evidence' in the text titled 'Injia on Criminal Practice and Procedure in Papua New Guinea and the Pacific'.

[5.0] INTRODUCTION TO EVIDENCE[84]

Evidence consists of:

- the testimony of witnesses[85];

  and

- physical exhibits[86], including:
  - documentary evidence[87];

    and

  - forensic evidence[88],

that may be legally admitted in a court in order to:

- prove;

  or

- disprove

the facts under investigation.

---

[84] As regards the law in relation to the admissibility of evidence, refer to the chapter titled 'Evidence' in the text titled 'Injia on Criminal Practice and Procedure in Papua New Guinea and the Pacific'.

[85] Refer also to:

- the chapter titled 'Witness Statements'; and
- the chapter titled 'Witnesses' in the text titled 'Injia on Criminal Practice and Procedure in Papua New Guinea and the Pacific'.

[86] Refer also to the chapter titled 'Exhibits'.

[87] Refer also to:

- the section titled 'Handwriting Evidence' in the chapter titled 'Forensic Evidence'; and
- the section titled 'Documentary Evidence' in the chapter titled 'Evidence' in the text titled 'Injia on Criminal Practice and Procedure in Papua New Guinea and the Pacific'.

[88] Refer also to:

- the chapter titled 'Forensic Evidence'; and
- the chapter titled 'Evidence' in the text titled 'Injia on Criminal Practice and Procedure in Papua New Guinea and the Pacific'.

An investigating officer has recourse to numerous sources of evidence in the course of an investigation, including:

- examination of the crime scene[89];
- examination of exhibits[90];
- interviewing of witnesses[91];
- collection of information from informers;
- inspection of official records;
- search of suspects, premises and vehicles[92];

  and
- interrogation of suspects[93].

[6.0] INITIAL ACTION AT A CRIME SCENE

It is important that initial action at a crime scene should be taken to:

- preserve the crime scene in its original state;

  and
- prevent contamination of the crime scene.[94]

---

89 Refer also to the chapter titled 'Incident Management'.

90 Refer also to the chapter titled 'Exhibits'.

91 Refer also to:

- the chapter titled 'Witness Statements'; and
- the chapter titled 'Witnesses' in the text titled 'Injia on Criminal Practice and Procedure in Papua New Guinea and the Pacific'.

92 Refer also to the section titled 'Power To Search' in the chapter titled 'Police Powers' in the text titled 'Injia on Criminal Practice and Procedure in Papua New Guinea and the Pacific'.

93 Refer also to:

- the chapter titled 'Interviewing Suspects'; and
- the section titled 'Confessional Evidence' in the chapter titled 'Evidence' in the text titled 'Injia on Criminal Practice and Procedure in Papua New Guinea and the Pacific'.

94 Refer also to the chapter titled 'Incident Management'.

Unless this action is taken, an investigating officer cannot observe the crime scene as it was at the time of the commission of the offence.

The routes:

- to;

  and

- from

should also be examined thoroughly and methodically at the first opportunity.

The investigating officer may not be the first officer to arrive at the crime scene.

If other officers are already present the investigating officer should ascertain the following:

- who is in charge?, ie., the First Response Officer/Forward Commander[95];
- how many police are in attendance?;
- what has been discovered about the offence?;
- what action has been already taken?;
- is the crime scene adequately protected from contamination and guarded?;
- have appropriate and/or specialist groups been notified?;
- has action been taken to locate, retain and isolate witnesses?;

  and

- has any suspect/offender been isolated from other people at the crime scene and kept under supervision?

[95] Refer also to the chapter titled 'Incident Management'.

However, in some situations, a crime scene may never be visited. If an offender confesses to the commission of an offence[96] that has not been reported, particularly if a considerable time period has elapsed since it was committed, it may be pointless or impracticable to visit the crime scene. Such situations may arise when an offender admits to committing an offence against a person unknown. Where there is a complainant, an attempt should be made to:

- visit and inspect the crime scene;

  and

- corroborate the confession.

[7.0] PEOPLE AND THINGS

[7.1] INTRODUCTION

The approach to an investigation should be based on a logical assessment of the:

- 'people'.

  The 'people' includes the victims and witnesses who may know something about the offence, as well as the criminal who knows all about it;

  and

- the 'things' involved in the commission of the offence.

  The 'things' includes the means of committing the offence.

[7.2] THE PEOPLE

[7.2.1] INTRODUCTION

All members of the community must be treated in a:

- fair;
- equitable;

  and

[96] Refer also to:

- the chapter titled 'Interviewing Suspects'; and
- the section titled 'Confessional Evidence' in the chapter titled 'Evidence' in the text titled 'Injia on Criminal Practice and Procedure in Papua New Guinea and the Pacific'.

- non-discriminatory manner,

whether they are a:

- victim[97];
- witness;

  or
- suspect.[98]

In the performance of their duty, a police officer should:

- respect and protect human dignity;

  and
- maintain and uphold the human rights of all persons.[99]

All citizens have the same rights, privileges, obligations and duties, irrespective of race, tribe, place of origin, political opinion, colour, creed, religion[100] or sex.[101]

There should be no discrimination shown to any person on grounds of race, colour, sex, language, religion, political or other opinion, national or social origin, property, birth or other status. The religious beliefs and moral precepts of such persons should be respected.[102]

---

[97] Refer also to the chapters titled 'Victims Of Crime' and 'Client Service'.

[98] Refer also to the chapter titled 'Ethics And Accountability'.

[99] See section 148(2)(a) and Part 14 of the *Constitution of the Autonomous Region of Bougainville*.

See also: International Human Rights Instrument titled 'Code of Conduct for Law Enforcement Officials', Article 2.

[100] See section 45 of the *Constitution of the Independent State of Papua New Guinea*.

[101] See section 55(1) of the *Constitution of the Independent State of Papua New Guinea*.

[102] See International Human Rights Instruments titled 'Convention on the Elimination of All Forms of Discrimination against Women'; 'United Nations Declaration on the Elimination of All Forms of Racial Discrimination'; 'International Convention on the Elimination of Racial Discrimination'; 'Declaration on the Elimination of All Forms of Intolerance and of Discrimination based on Religion or Belief'; 'Declaration on Race and Racial Prejudice'; and 'Declaration on the Rights of Persons Belonging to National or Ethnic, Religious and Linguistic Minorities.'

Eliciting facts from people, whether that person is a victim, witness or suspect, is an inexact process requiring:

- skills;
- patience;

  and
- an understanding of human nature.

It must be remembered that evidence derived from people will have varying degrees of reliability, borne of human error, uncertainty and imperfection.

Human memory is not infallible.

People may have varying degrees of assimilation, be prejudiced or simply mistaken.

That is why it is fundamentally important to obtain statements from:

- witnesses;

  and
- victims

as soon as possible after the commission of an offence.

Every effort must be made to obtain confirmation of:

- the statements of witnesses;

  and
- the admissions and denials made by suspects/offenders

by independent means.

[7.2.2] VICTIMS AND WITNESSES

Victims[103] and witnesses should be the subject of interviews in which the investigating officer seeks to elicit facts and information within their knowledge.

However, no person can be required to answer a question of a police officer.[104]

---

[103] Refer also to the chapters titled 'Victims Of Crime' and 'Client Service'.

[104] See sections 32(2)(c) and 49 of the *Constitution of the Independent State of Papua New Guinea*.

Witnesses (including victims) should always be:

- separated from each other so that they do not talk to each other, prior to being interviewed;

  and

- interviewed as soon as possible after the commission of an offence in order to obtain their statements.[105]

[7.2.3] SUSPECTS

Suspects should be the subject of interrogation[106], based on known facts, in order to determine their degree of involvement in the commission of the offence.

Suspects should be:

- separated from each other and other persons so that they do not talk to any witness or co-accused;

- searched according to the law[107], if necessary, for possible 'exhibits' and weapons;

  and

- secured so that they do not escape, after being lawfully arrested or detained[108].

---

[105] Refer also to:

- the chapter titled 'Witness Statements'; and

- the chapter titled 'Witnesses' in the text titled 'Injia on Criminal Practice and Procedure in Papua New Guinea and the Pacific'.

[106] Refer also to:

- the chapter titled 'Interviewing Suspects'; and

- the section titled 'Confessional Evidence' in the chapter titled 'Evidence' in the text titled 'Injia on Criminal Practice and Procedure in Papua New Guinea and the Pacific'.

[107] Refer also to the section titled 'Power To Search' in the chapter titled 'Police Powers'.

[108] Refer also to:

- the section titled 'Power To Arrest' in the chapter titled 'Police Powers'; and

- the section titled 'Institution Of Proceedings' in the chapter titled 'Charges' in the text titled 'Injia on Criminal Practice and Procedure in Papua New Guinea and the Pacific'.

[7.3] THE THINGS

An investigating officer must appreciate the potential evidential value of the physical things involved in the commission of an offence.[109]

An investigating officer must understand:

- what physical evidence is;
- how it is to be collected and preserved[110];
- how to obtain the best value from the information it affords;

  and
- how to interpret the information so obtained.

Physical evidence:

- is factual evidence;
- is not subject to adverse influences affecting human recollection;

  and
- always tells the same story.

At most crime scenes the offender makes contact with physical things.

Accordingly, there may be:

- contamination of the crime scene by the offender;

  or
- a mutual exchange of traces between:
  - the offender;

    and
  - the environment of the crime scene.

---

[109] Refer also to the section titled 'Exhibit Handling Procedure' in the chapter titled 'Exhibits'.

[110] Refer also to the chapter titled 'Forensic Evidence'.

If an investigating officer adopts the theory that when a person:

- enters;

  and/or

- leaves

an environment that person:

- brings into;

  and/or

- carries away from

the crime scene traces such as hairs, fibres, dust, etc. which may connect the offender with the offence, the investigating officer will be much more mindful of the necessity to adopt this action.

The principle that every contact leaves its traces is known as:

the 'principle of exchange'.[111]

Fingerprints, footmarks, tool-marks, bloodstains, glass fragments, hairs and soil are examples of physical traces that can provide evidence against an offender.

Physical evidence includes any material, whether solid, liquid or gaseous, weapon used, a signature obtained and the contents of a bottle. So too, do microscopic fragments of dust, fibres and other traces that may still be available even though the offender has attempted to conceal that evidence.

A vital phase of an investigation is:

- the search of the crime scene;

  and

- the examination of physical evidence found there.

It is essential that contamination of a crime scene by:

- humans;

  or

- a natural agency, such as rain,

should be prevented, if possible.

[111] Refer also to the chapter titled 'Forensic Evidence'.

Prompt attention at a crime scene will ensure the preservation of physical evidence, thereby increasing the prospects of solving the offence.

The full benefit of physical evidence can often be realised only after expert examination or analysis. Therefore, an investigating officer must know who the appropriate experts are and how, when and where to enlist their aid.[112] However, an investigating officer must not expect the impossible of the expert who can do no more than evaluate the physical material submitted for examination.

There will be occasions on which expert examination of physical evidence can prove certain facts beyond any doubt through the employment of exact sciences.

However, such an examination cannot be made unless an investigating officer:

- finds the physical evidence;

  or

- enables it to be found in the first place.

It must be remembered that the expertise of science and technology are aids to, rather than substitutes for, investigation.

[8.0] FURTHER AVENUES OF INQUIRY

[8.1] INTRODUCTION

The potential 'avenues of inquiry' open to an investigating officer are practically unlimited.

However, their availability and development depend largely on the personal ingenuity of the individual investigating officer.

It is feasible for an investigating officer to:

- develop permanent contacts through avenues of inquiry that are always accessible;

  and

- create opportunities for making specific inquiries from casual contacts as the occasion requires.

Such contacts occur as a result of the investigating officer's ability to use the knowledge that he or she has acquired in the course of his or her experience.

[112] Refer also to the chapter titled 'Forensic Evidence'.

It has been said that any investigating officer is only as good as his or her 'criminal intelligence[113]', and while this is a self-evident truth, there is a tendency to interpret the term 'criminal intelligence' as implying only that information that is received from criminal sources.[114]

[8.2] PROTECTION OF AN INFORMER

An investigating officer who can avail himself or herself of the benefit of information from an 'informer' is fortunate indeed, and often produces dramatic results.

An 'informer' is a person who is not a member of the Bougainville Police Service or Royal Papua New Guinea Constabulary who informs police of facts relating to:

- the proposed commission of offences and the criminals involved;

  or

- the identity of persons involved in the commission of offences already committed.

There is a rule of law that the identity of informers may not be disclosed in most legal proceedings, unless ordered by the court in very strict circumstances.

Individuals give information they know but it may be hearsay[115] and inadmissible in a court because it is information based on what they were told, and not what they saw themselves occur. Such information may well lead to the obtaining of other evidence which can be used. Some individuals will be able to give information which will be admissible evidence but choose not to, and merely give sufficient information that leads the police to make other inquiries which does not produce admissible evidence. Information in either of these categories may be given willingly and openly. Some information will be given anonymously.[116]

Some individuals will give it on a condition that they are not identified. Many individuals will give information where nothing is explicitly stated about any condition of or desire for confidentiality of the identity of the informer.[117]

---

[113] Refer also to the chapter titled 'Criminal Intelligence'.

[114] Refer also to the chapter titled 'Community Policing'.

[115] The 'Hearsay Rule' states that a witness must only give evidence of what he or she saw and not what he or she was told, subject to a number of exceptions.

As regards the law in relation to 'Hearsay Evidence', refer to the chapter titled 'Evidence' in the text titled 'Injia on Criminal Practice and Procedure in Papua New Guinea and the Pacific'.

[116] See *Mason* (2000) 12 A Crim R 266 at 271.

[117] See *Mason* (2000) 12 A Crim R 266 at 271.

The rationale of the rule as it applies to police informers is plain. If their identity were liable to be disclosed in a Court:

- these sources of information would dry up;

  and

- the police would be hindered in their duty of preventing and detecting crime.[118]

So the public interest in preserving the anonymity of police informers has to be weighed against the public interest that information that might assist a court to ascertain facts relevant to an issue upon which it is required to adjudicate should be withheld from that court.[119]

No police officer is to disclose the identity of an 'informer':

- to a member of the public;

- to any other officer of the Bougainville Police Service or Royal Papua New Guinea Constabulary, unless there is a reason for such disclosure;

  or

- unless directed by a Court.

Such orders by a Court should only be made if it is demonstrated that there is good reason to think that disclosure of the informer's identity may be of substantial assistance to the accused person in answering the charge/s against him or her.

[8.3] GENERAL KNOWLEDGE

There are certain 'avenues of inquiry' open to an investigating officer by means of which he or she can obtain information directly on application as a matter of routine. Some of these avenues of inquiry exist through the records systems of the Bougainville Police Service, Royal Papua New Guinea Constabulary and other government departments. Other avenues of inquiry are to be found in public records and directories and through a general knowledge of business practice and social customs of the community.

It is essential that an investigating officer should have a thorough understanding of the potential of these avenues of inquiry.

---

118 See *D v National Society for the Prevention of Cruelty in Children* [1978] AC 171, per Lord Diplock at 218.

119 See *D v National Society for the Prevention of Cruelty in Children* [1978] AC 171, per Lord Diplock at 218.

It must be remembered that the ability to exploit or use these avenues of inquiry depends largely on:

- the personality of the investigating officer;

  and

- the manner in which the information is sought.

A pleasant approach invites co-operation.

It frequently happens that when a contact in a particular organisation realises that the investigating officer is interested in certain developments, he or she will contact the investigating officer spontaneously when similar situations occur.

Thus an effective liaison is established.

Assistance from other officers should be sought in appropriate circumstances.

When a suspect is being sought, an investigating officer should consider carefully his or her background, occupation, family, associates and places frequented.

[8.4] DOOR TO DOOR INQUIRIES

The value of 'door to door inquiries' should not be overlooked.

This is an important investigative tool which has proved its worth again and again.

It is the process by which officers go from house to house in the vicinity of the offence, seeking potential witnesses and/or informers.

Witnesses and informers are often reluctant to come forward voluntarily and their information will never be obtained, unless the police seek them out.

The occasions on which a house to house canvass is employed will depend on the nature of the offence.

However, when it has been decided to make such a canvass, it is essential that it should cover every house:

- within sight or hearing of the crime scene;

  and

- along the route which the offender may have taken in going to and coming from the crime scene.

In conducting the canvass, the investigating officer must make comprehensive notes of their progress in order to prevent duplication or omissions.

[9.0] LEGAL BACKGROUND TO AN INVESTIGATION

Investigations occur within a legal framework that governs investigative procedure.

The following two traditional common law principles operate in favour of a person suspected of committing an offence:

- Presumption of Innocence[120];

  and

- Right to Silence.[121]

The law not only presumes that every person is innocent of any offence until the contrary is proven 'beyond reasonable doubt'[122] by the prosecution, but also that every person is entitled to the 'right to silence'.

As a result, having established that an offence has been committed, the investigation must be able to prove that the offender committed the offence 'beyond reasonable doubt[123]' and, if necessary, in the absence of any admission or confession from the offender.

This is an extremely difficult undertaking which can only be achieved by:

- the proof of the existence of 'physical' evidence;

  and/or

- the proof of 'circumstantial evidence[124]';

  and

---

[120] See section 37(4)(a) of the *Constitution of the Independent State of Papua New Guinea*.

[121] See section 32(2)(c) of the *Constitution of the Independent State of Papua New Guinea*.

Refer also to:

- the chapter titled 'Interviewing Suspects'; and
- the section titled 'Confessional Evidence' in the chapter titled 'Evidence' in the text titled 'Injia on Criminal Practice and Procedure in Papua New Guinea and the Pacific'.

[122] Refer also to the chapter titled 'Proof Of Issues' in the text titled 'Injia on Criminal Practice and Procedure in Papua New Guinea and the Pacific'.

[123] Refer also to the chapter titled 'Proof Of Issues' in the text titled 'Injia on Criminal Practice and Procedure in Papua New Guinea and the Pacific'.

[124] Refer also to the section titled 'Circumstantial Evidence' in the chapter titled 'Evidence' in the text titled 'Injia on Criminal Practice and Procedure in Papua New Guinea and the Pacific'.

- the evidence of witnesses[125].

But the only means of proving some offences may be by obtaining a confession from the offender.

However, in accordance with section 42(2) of the *Constitution of the Independent State of Papua New Guinea* a person who has been arrested or detained[126]:

- shall be permitted whenever practicable to communicate without delay and in private with a member of his or her family or a personal friend, and with a lawyer of his or her choice (including the Public Solicitor if he or she is entitled to legal aid);

  and

- shall be given adequate opportunity to give instructions to a lawyer of his or her choice in the place in which he or she is detained.[127]

Successful offences are secret offences. The circumstances of the commission of a successful offence are such that it remains either undetected or unreported. There may be little or no physical evidence of its commission.

Other than through the discovery of an offence during its commission, an investigating officer is dependent upon a report of an offence to initiate an investigation.

The absence of confessional evidence does not necessarily preclude the conviction of the offender. A case based solely on 'circumstantial evidence'[128] can be just as compelling as a case based solely on 'confessional evidence'[129]. Whereas admissions or confessions can be denied, physical evidence left by an offender at a crime scene cannot be.

---

[125] Refer also to:

- the chapter titled 'Witness Statements'; and
- the chapter titled 'Witnesses' in the text titled 'Injia on Criminal Practice and Procedure in Papua New Guinea and the Pacific'.

[126] See also: section 18(2) of the *Arrest Act* (Ch. 339).

Refer also to the section titled 'Power To Arrest' in the chapter titled 'Police Powers'.

[127] Refer also to the section titled 'Right To Legal Representation' in the chapter titled 'Rights Of An Accused Person' in the text titled 'Injia on Criminal Practice and Procedure in Papua New Guinea and the Pacific'.

[128] Refer also to the section titled 'Circumstantial Evidence' in the chapter titled 'Evidence' in the text titled 'Injia on Criminal Practice and Procedure in Papua New Guinea and the Pacific'.

[129] Refer also to the section titled 'Confessional Evidence' in the chapter titled 'Evidence' in the text titled 'Injia on Criminal Practice and Procedure in Papua New Guinea and the Pacific'.

The law requires that any admission or confession made by an offender must be made in compliance with the law which includes being voluntary.

This means in the exercise of the free choice to:

- speak

  or

- be silent.

The onus is on an investigating officer to prove that the confessional evidence was obtained in compliance with the law.[130]

It is therefore important that an investigating officer complies with the law when interrogating a suspect.[131]

[10.0] NOTE-TAKING

An investigating officer is expected to record notes in relation to all investigations.

The following information should be recorded:

- reports of offences;
- details in relation to any investigation conducted and arrests made;
- details of incidents attended, such as crime scenes, fires, drownings and other accidental deaths;
- details of particular importance provided in briefings;

  and

- details of property handed over by members of the public.

Full and precise notes should be progressively maintained throughout an investigation. These should commence with the initial particulars of the report of the offence. The investigating officer's time of arrival at an incident/crime scene and the sequence of his or her activities should be recorded.

---

130 Refer also to the section titled 'Confessional Evidence' in the chapter titled 'Evidence' in the text titled 'Injia on Criminal Practice and Procedure in Papua New Guinea and the Pacific'.

131 Refer also to the chapter titled 'Interviewing Suspects'.

The notes should detail the incident/crime scene, including diagrams, measurements and other relevant conditions, with particular attention to the relative position of any exhibit.

Such notes provide a valuable record of the development of the investigation and will assist in the preparation of the Case File and can assist in giving evidence in court.[132]

[132] Refer also to the section titled 'Witness Refreshing Memory' in the chapter titled 'Witnesses' in the text titled 'Injia on Criminal Practice and Procedure in Papua New Guinea and the Pacific'.

TRAFFIC ACCIDENT INVESTIGATION

[1.0] INTRODUCTION

A traffic accident occurs when a vehicle operated by a driver or rider impacts with a stationary object, another vehicle, animal or person.[133]

When injury is caused to a person or an animal or damage is caused to a vehicle then police should conduct an investigation.[134]

[2.0] FACTORS THAT MAY CAUSE A TRAFFIC ACCIDENT

A traffic accident may occur for a number of reasons, including:

- an act or omission by the driver;
- a defect in a motor vehicle;

  or
- an unexpected occurrence.

[3.0] INITIAL RECORDING OF A TRAFFIC ACCIDENT

An entry should be made in the Station Occurrence Book, including:

- the location of the traffic accidence;
- whether any person has been injured or killed;
- whether there is an obstruction to traffic;

  and
- whether the person reporting the traffic accident is:
  - involved in;

    or
  - a witness to the traffic accident

  and their full name and address and mobile telephone number.

[133] As regards the law in relation to offences involving traffic accidents, refer to the chapter titled 'Traffic Offences' in the text titled 'Injia on Criminal Offences in Papua New Guinea and the Pacific'.

[134] See section 24 of the *Motor Traffic Act* (Ch. 243).

[4.0] ATTENDANCE AT THE TRAFFIC ACCIDENT SCENE

[4.1] INTRODUCTION

A police officer should, as far as possible, always attend the scene of a traffic accident for the purpose of conducting an investigation.[135]

[4.2] INITIAL DUTIES

The initial duties upon arrival at the scene of a traffic accident are:

- attend to the welfare of any injured persons;
- attend to any deceased person;
- identify the drivers of the vehicles concerned and passengers;

  and
- identify witnesses.

[4.3] NOTEBOOK ENTRY

An entry in an official police notebook in relation to a traffic accident should contain:

- the location and time of traffic accident;
- a brief statement or version of the drivers involved;
- a brief statement or version of all witnesses, including the passengers of the vehicles involved;
- any question asked to clarify:
  - anything arising out of their statement;

    or
  - any other circumstances in relation to the traffic accident;

  and
- a sketch plan of the traffic accident scene.

[135] Refer also to the chapter titled 'Principles Of Investigation'.

[4.4] SKETCH PLAN

A sketch plan of a scene of a traffic accident is done to create a clear and accurate image for the court as to the following:

- the point of impact of the collision;
- the location of the vehicle/s, including full details as the make, type and registration number;
- the direction of the vehicle/s after the point of impact;
- measurement of any skid marks;
- measurement of the width of the road;
- road markings;
- measurements to fixed objects in close proximity of the traffic accident scene from the vehicle/s;

  and

- measurements to the location of any injured/deceased as a consequence of the traffic accident.

The sketch plan should not include the direction of the vehicle/s prior to the point of impact, unless:

- the officer preparing the sketch plan witnessed the accident;

  or

- it is obvious from the scene of the accident.

If that information is provided by another person to the investigating officer then such information is 'hearsay evidence[136]' and is inadmissible. In those circumstances the sketch plan would have to be tendered through the witness to the accident.

[136] The 'Hearsay Rule' states that a witness must only give evidence of what he or she saw and not what he or she was told, subject to a number of exceptions.

As regards the law in relation to 'Hearsay Evidence', refer to the chapter titled 'Evidence' in the text titled 'Injia on Criminal Practice and Procedure in Papua New Guinea and the Pacific'.

INVESTIGATION PLAN

[1.0] INTRODUCTION

It is imperative that the investigator who is responsible for the overall management of an investigation, and therefore the implementation of the 'Investigation Plan[137]', understands what is to be investigated.

The goals of an investigation are:

- To determine whether an offence has actually been committed[138];

  and if so:

- The identity of the offender[139];

- The whereabouts of the offender;

  and

- A nexus or connection between the offender and the offence.

The complexity of an Investigation Plan is dictated by the complexity of the investigation to be conducted.

Therefore, not all investigations will require the development of a written Investigation Plan.

However, all investigations required some degree of planning.

Obviously,

- the seriousness of an offence;

  and/or

---

137 See Appendix 4.

138 If no offence has actually been committed and the incident involves the death of a person or a fire involving substantial destruction then the investigating officer should conduct a coronial investigation.

Refer also to:

- the chapter titled 'Coronial Proceedings'; and
- the text titled 'Injia on Coronial Proceedings in Papua New Guinea and the Pacific'.

139 Refer also to the section titled 'Identification Evidence' in the chapter titled 'Evidence' in the text titled 'Injia on Criminal Practice and Procedure in Papua New Guinea and the Pacific'.

- whether an offence is based on 'circumstantial evidence[140]', ie., no witnesses to the offence and no eyewitness identification of an offender,

will necessarily impact on the complexity of an investigation and therefore, the need for a written Investigation Plan.

In some situations the officer responsible for the management of an investigation should ideally attend the crime scene.

Upon arrival at the crime scene that officer is expected to:

- take control of the crime scene;

  and

- commence the management of the investigation.[141]

Investigation planning is the first step in the investigation process.

Planning is however a continuous process.

Planning alone is no guarantee of success and success depends on effective implementation of the Investigation Plan.

All Investigation Plans need to be managed competently particularly as regards the management functions of:

- organising;
- leading;

  and

- controlling.

[2.0] PLANNING

Planning can be defined as:

determining in advance what needs to be done in order to achieve the goals of an investigation.

---

[140] Refer also to the section titled 'Circumstantial Evidence' in the chapter titled 'Evidence' in the text titled 'Injia on Criminal Practice and Procedure in Papua New Guinea and the Pacific'.

[141] Refer also to the chapters titled 'Principles Of Investigation' and 'Incident Management'.

INVESTIGATION PLAN

An Investigation Plan is devised to achieve:

- **Direction**

  A need to determine:

  - what are the goals of the investigation;

    and

  - how the goals of the investigation are to be achieved.

- **Uniform Effort**

  Enables all persons involved in an investigation to have a clear understanding of:

  - the goals of the investigation;
  - their role in the Investigation Plan;

    and

  - what they must do as a team in order to have success in the investigation.

  The investigation team can therefore work together in order to achieve the goals of the investigation in a coordinated manner.

- **Control**

  An Investigation Plan ensures that an investigation is heading in the correct direction.

  However, the officer responsible for the management of an investigation in accordance with the Investigation Plan is expected to provide appropriate leadership to the investigation team.

The process of planning for an investigation can be summarised in the following steps:

- Determine the Investigation Goals;
- Develop an Investigation Plan;
- Implement the Investigation Plan;

  and

- Review the Investigation Plan.

[3.0] DETERMINE THE INVESTIGATIONS GOALS

Planning begins with defining what is to be achieved.

The goals of an investigation are:

- To determine whether an offence has actually been committed[142];

  and if so:

- The identity of the offender[143];
- The whereabouts of the offender;

  and

- A nexus or connection between the offender and the offence.

The goals of an investigation should be included in any Investigation Plan, and must be:

- **Specific**

  The goals need to be clearly defined.

  There should be no misunderstanding as to what are the goals.

- **Measurable**

  All investigators need to know:

  - how the investigation team is progressing in achieving the goals;

    and

  - at what stage the investigation is at.

---

[142] If no offence has actually been committed and the incident involves the death of a person or a fire involving substantial destruction then the investigating officer should conduct a coronial investigation.

Refer also to:

- the chapter titled 'Coronial Proceedings'; and
- the text titled 'Injia on Coronial Proceedings in Papua New Guinea and the Pacific'.

[143] Refer also to the section titled 'Identification Evidence' in the chapter titled 'Evidence' in the text titled 'Injia on Criminal Practice and Procedure in Papua New Guinea and the Pacific'.

- **Achievable**

  All goals need to be able to be achieved.

- **Realistic**

  All goals must be realistic whilst taking into account any perceived constraints.

- **Timelines Set**

  Timelines must be set to achieve each of the set investigation tasks and therefore, the goals.

[4.0] DEVELOP AN INVESTIGATION PLAN

The current situation needs to be assessed before any future activity should be commenced.

In order to determine how an investigation should be conducted it is necessary to conduct an initial analysis as to:

- how the offence was committed;

  or

- what incident or circumstances needs to be investigated.

  This is referred to as the 'Background Information' in an Investigation Plan.

The best way to develop an Investigation Plan is to have a meeting with the investigation team in order to discuss:

- what should be the goals of the investigation;

  and

- how the goals should be achieved.

At such a meeting,

- the investigation tasks should be determined in order to achieve the goals.

  Each investigation task is a key stage of an Investigation Plan;

- the approximate time period to complete each of the investigation tasks should be determined;

  and

- the investigation tasks should then be prioritised by asking oneself:

  'In what order should the investigation tasks be done?'.

This process will form the basis of an Investigation Plan.

The Investigation Plan then needs to be checked by working backwards through each of the investigation tasks.

The investigation tasks for most investigations will be:

- Identify the offence(s);
- Obtain statements;
- Attain admissible evidence;
- Identify the offender(s);
- Interview the offender(s);
- Prepare the Case File and submit it to the prosecution;

  and
- Present the evidence in court.

Some of the considerations that need to be assessed during the development of an Investigation Plan include:

- **Offence(s)**

  All investigators should have a clear understanding of the offence(s) to be investigated.

  Sometimes at an early stage of an investigation the actual offence(s) may not be known, such as a specific fraud offence.

  Furthermore, an investigation may need to be conducted in order to determine whether an offence has actually been committed.

- **Urgency**

  The urgency or importance of an investigation needs to be determined.

  Issues that should be taken into consideration include:

  - the seriousness of the offence under investigation;
  - the possible loss of evidence;

and

- the possible difficulty in apprehending an offender, if the investigation is postponed.

- **Resource Implications**

  The resource implications of conducting an investigation need to be determined and properly planned.

  The availability of staff, finance and vehicles will need to be determined.

- **Complexity**

  It may be difficult to initially determine the complexity of an investigation.

  Depending on the circumstances of the commission of an offence the assistance of forensic experts may be needed.

- **Establishing Time-frames**

  The time-frame for each investigation task needs to be determined.

  Such time-frames must be based on facts, and not just assumptions.

- **Risk Management**

  This is an important facet of an Investigation Plan.

  All potential risks need to be identified.

  Such risks will include:

  - safety of officers in conducting the investigation;
  - safety of witnesses;

    and

  - risks associated with the obtaining of information and/or evidence.

  The probability and likely impact of each risk on the investigation then needs to be determined.

  The appropriate course of action to address such risks then needs to be determined and implemented.

  All risks should then be monitored during the course of the investigation.

There is no magic formulae for the right amount of detail in an Investigation Plan.

However, a good guide is to:

> 'Never spend more time on the Investigation Plan than it would take to fix the problem if there were no plan'.

[5.0] IMPLEMENT THE INVESTIGATION PLAN

[5.1] TASK ALLOCATION

In order to implement an Investigation Plan it is necessary to allocate the investigation tasks.

Task allocation needs to be:

- effective;
- accountable;

  and
- efficient.

The following must be considered when investigation tasks are allocated:

- the officer understands the task to be achieved;
- that the officer has the appropriate:
  - skills;
  - experience;

    and
  - knowledge

  to achieve the allocated task;

  and
- there should be enough time to accomplish the allocated task.

[5.2] MANAGEMENT OF INVESTIGATION DATA

Depending on the complexity of an investigation a large quantity of information will be generated.

All of such information needs to be managed correctly.

Quality control is vital.

All incoming information needs to be analysed.

An Information Management System must:

- ensure that investigation tasks that are assigned to investigators are recorded;
- ensure that the results obtained from the conduct of the investigation into those specific investigation tasks is recorded (progress reports);

  and

- ensure that all important information is not overlooked.

All investigators must understand the importance of sharing information obtained during the course of an investigation.

Confidential information should only be shared with the officer responsible for the management of the investigation.

That officer would then be responsible for determining who else should be aware of the confidential information.

[5.3] INVESTIGATION TEAM MEETINGS

An issue to consider when an investigation team is investigating an offence is:

'How will the overall progress of the investigation be monitored?'

It may be necessary to conduct meetings in order to ensure that the investigation team is aware of the progress of the investigation against the Investigation Plan.

[6.0] REVIEW AN INVESTIGATION PLAN

Flexibility is fundamentally important.

An Investigation Plan should be constantly re-evaluated, and if necessary modified, throughout an investigation.

If necessary the goals of an investigation may need to be changed before proceeding with re-planning.

If a certain avenue of inquiry is closed during the execution of an Investigation Plan it should be flexible enough to change direction in order to achieve the goals, if necessary.

A rigid Investigation Plan must be avoided.

A review should be conducted upon the achievement of a goal to ensure that all investigation tasks have been undertaken.

There should be an ongoing circular process of:

- information collection;
- investigation;

  and
- review.

Upon completion of an investigation a Final Review should be conducted which addresses the lessons learnt:

- What was done well?;
- What could have been done better?;

  and
- What went wrong and why?

Such a review should involve all participants in the investigation process.

Strategies or recommendations for future improvement should be identified.

[1.0] INTRODUCTION

It is of utmost importance to the success of an investigation that the officer who arrives first at the scene makes no errors, whether by:

- commission;

  or

- omission.

The actual 'incident scene' is the place from which all leads will emanate as to how the incident occurred.

The incident scene is:

> the area in the immediate vicinity of where the incident occurred.

The incident scene provides the investigating officer with a starting point in determining whether the incident occurred as a consequence of the commission of a criminal offence, and is therefore it is be initially treated as a 'crime scene'.

It is important to determine:

- what caused the incident under investigation;

  and

- whether criminal conduct was involved.[144]

If there is the possibility that a criminal offence was committed then the incident scene is in fact a crime scene and consideration should be given as whether there are any 'secondary crime scenes'.

A secondary crime scene is:

> a location where there may be evidence connecting the offenders with the offence, other than the crime scene.

---

[144] If no offence has actually been committed and the incident involves the death of a person or a fire involving substantial destruction then the investigating officer should conduct a coronial investigation.

Refer also to:

- the chapter titled 'Coronial Proceedings'; and

- the text titled 'Injia on Coronial Proceedings in Papua New Guinea and the Pacific'.

INCIDENT MANAGEMENT

The officer with the most service who arrives in the first police vehicle at an incident scene is referred to as:

the 'First Response Officer'.

It is important that the initial action taken by the First Response Officer is to:

- secure and preserve the incident/crime scene in its original state;

  and

- prevent contamination of the scene by humans or otherwise.

The deciding factors in safeguarding an incident/crime scene are:

- the likelihood that the offender has left evidence;

  and

- the likelihood that this evidence can be recovered.

Each case must be decided individually.

It can happen that a comparatively serious incident may occur at a location where effective safeguarding of the incident/crime scene may be impossible. It also may not be possible to secure the incident/crime scene early enough to prevent evidence from being destroyed.

In difficult conditions the First Response Officer is often faced with problems that put to a severe test his or her ability to:

- analyse quickly a situation;

  and

- take the appropriate steps.

But if the First Response Officer follows the basic rules of always anticipating the worst and as a consequence takes extensive, rather than minimum precautions, he or she should be able to avoid the most serious errors.

Depending on the circumstances upon arrival of a supervising officer that officer is responsible for assuming control/command/coordination of the incident, referred to as:

the 'Forward Commander'.

Upon arrival that officer takes over the responsibilities of the First Response Officer.

Upon taking command of an incident/crime scene as the 'Forward Commander' an officer needs to:

- take command;
- ensure that communication centre is advised as to who is the Forward Commander at the incident/crime scene;
- obtain a briefing from the First Response Officer;

  The First Response Officer should be in a position to accurately brief the Forward Commander regarding the incident as required;
- assess the incident/crime scene.
- co-ordinate the response;

  and
- maintain effective communications with the communications centre.

[2.0] RESPONSIBILITIES OF A FIRST RESPONSE OFFICER

The principle responsibilities of a First Response Officer at an incident/crime scene are:

- take command of the scene;
- secure and preserve the scene;
- assess the scene;
- take action to protect life and property;

  and
- maintain effective communications with the communications centre.

Once an officer has taken charge of an incident/crime scene, that officer should remain in charge until he or she is relieved by a senior officer.

The action taken by the First Response Officer may dictate what physical evidence is preserved.

In order to preserve the incident/crime scene the First Response Officer should take action that will provide the minimum disturbance to the physical evidence at the incident/crime scene.

The 'keep your hands in your pockets' approach is good, but it is better to limit any access to the incident/crime scene to the bare minimum.

Disturbance of a minor degree may be unavoidable in order for the First Response Officer to:

- make an assessment of the incident/crime scene;

  and

- ensure that any injured persons are provided with medical treatment.

Similarly should there be evidence which is in danger of being destroyed by its nature, location or weather conditions, then the First Response Officer may take steps to protect that evidence (eg., to move broken glass outside the point of entry out of the rain).

The First Response Officer may also be the investigating officer, and therefore responsible for conducting the investigation.

[3.0] INITIAL REPORT

It is important, to remember that on receiving the initial report of an incident, whether:

- in person;

  or

- on the telephone,

sufficient details should be recorded at the time from the person making the report to enable the attending officers to take any essential action before proceeding to the incident/crime scene.

Confusion can arise if sufficient basic particulars are not:

- obtained;

  and

- recorded

at the outset.

The following basic information is required:

- nature of the incident;
- any person injured or killed;
- exact location;
- when committed;
- any offender, if so, description and whether that person is still at the incident/crime scene;
- name, address and mobile telephone number of the person reporting the incident;

  and
- date and time of the report of the incident received.

If the person reporting the incident is on the telephone, he or she should be asked to await the arrival of the police and not to touch anything. If the caller wishes to remain anonymous the officer should try to obtain all the particulars that he or she can. Experience proves that anonymous callers rarely call again. The officer should keep calm because people reporting incidents may be frightened or excited.

Upon receipt of information it needs to be assessed so that an appropriate response is determined.

The importance of patrols being adequately informed about the situation that they are being tasked to attend (or happen up) is self evident. However, often they arrive at an incident with the barest of details.[145]

There are obviously a number of reasons why information is not available. However, it is important that dispatchers [communication staff and who ever receives the initial report] and officers attending an incident scene endeavour to seek as much information as possible about a situation prior to engaging with suspects or people at the incident scene. This may mean that dispatchers are encouraged to draw more information from the callers and attending police officers are encouraged to request more detail from dispatchers.[146]

---

[145] See Australasian Centre for Policing Research, 1998, 'National minimum guidelines for incident management, conflict resolution and use of force', Report Series No. 132.1, page 25.

[146] See Australasian Centre for Policing Research, 1998, 'National minimum guidelines for incident management, conflict resolution and use of force', Report Series No. 132.1, page 25.

[4.0] RESPONDING TO AN INCIDENT

All officers should acknowledge receipt of jobs when received over the radio and advise the communication centre of their arrival at the incident/crime scene.

A reduction in the interval between:

- call-time;

  and

- response-time

increases the prospects of:

- solving any offence;

  and

- saving lives and property.

The most appropriate route to the incident/crime scene should be followed in order to minimise response time.

Prompt attendance may result in:

- saving lives and property;
- the offender being located at or near the incident/crime scene;
- witnesses being located at the incident/crime scene before they have had time to leave or to discuss the event with other witnesses;
- prevention of access to the incident/crime scene by unauthorised persons;
- prevention of loss or destruction of evidence through interference or removal by persons at the incident/crime scene;

  and

- prevention of contamination.

[5.0] PROCEEDING TO AN INCIDENT/CRIME SCENE

Whilst proceeding to an incident/crime scene en-route hazards need to be recognised and negotiated to minimise risk.

An officer should consider, from the nature of the original report:

- whether there is an offender;
- whether the offender is armed, and if so, what with;

  and
- whether that person is likely to be on foot, in a vehicle or carrying anything which might identify him or her.

If the physical description of the offender has been supplied an officer should be on the alert for any person answering that description.

Local knowledge of the area might permit a prediction of the route an offender would likely take in fleeing the incident/crime scene.

[6.0] APPROACHING AN INCIDENT/CRIME SCENE

The manner in which the incident/crime scene is approached will depend on the nature of the report received.

An officer should always consider:

- his or her safety;

  and
- the safety of other officers

whenever approaching an incident/crime scene.

Sometimes it is better to avoid the direct approach by parking police vehicles away from the front of residential incidents or, in other environments, parking away from the centre of the incident.[147]

This will maximise the safety of approach and provide:

- a secure observation and (initial) command post;

  and
- an escape route.[148]

---

[147] See Australasian Centre for Policing Research, 1998, 'National minimum guidelines for incident management, conflict resolution and use of force', Report Series No. 132.1, page 27.

[148] See Australasian Centre for Policing Research, 1998, 'National minimum guidelines for incident management, conflict resolution and use of force', Report Series No. 132.1, page 27.

There is ample evidence in the reports of operations that have 'gone wrong' that patrols have driven to the centre of activity only to be attacked as they have exited the car.[149]

As a result they have:

- reduced the opportunity for a low use of force option;

  and

- increased the risk of injury to themselves.[150]

Officers will also invariably attend incidents that are still in progress. In such circumstances it is very important that such incidents are resolved without any person being injured or any life lost.

It may be possible to enlist assistance in covering the front and rear of the premises if an incident is still in progress.

[7.0] ASSESSING AN INCIDENT/CRIME SCENE

The four bas c concepts used in making an assessment of an incident/crime scene are as follows:

AIM ⇨	What must be achieved?
FACTORS ⇨	What circumstances, facts or influences will contribute to the result?
OPTIONS ⇨	What are the possible ways of achieving the aim?
PLAN ⇨	What is the best action to take to achieve the aim?

Assessing the Situation

[149] See Australasian Centre for Policing Research, 1998, 'National minimum guidelines for incident management, conflict resolution and use of force', Report Series No. 132.1, page 27.

[150] See Australasian Centre for Policing Research, 1998, 'National minimum guidelines for incident management, conflict resolution and use of force', Report Series No. 132.1, page 27.

INCIDENT MANAGEMENT

When approaching an incident/crime scene an officer should, as quickly as possible, try to assess the situation in terms of determining:

- how to effectively deal with the situation;

  and

- any potential risks or threats.

This assessment is the basis of any appropriate action.

An officer should ask himself or herself the following questions:

- What has happened?;
- Has a criminal offence been committed?;
- What now needs to be done in order of priority?;
- Has any person been injured? and if so, What are the extent of the injuries?;
- Has any person been killed?;
- What is the location of the offender?;
- Is the offender armed?, if so, What with?;
- Is there the potential of any person being injured or killed?;
- What further assistance is needed?;

  and

- Is the offender affected by drugs or alcohol?

The initial assessment of an incident/crime scene needs to be carried out promptly.

An incident/crime scene may need to be continually assessed in order to determine whether the incident is being dealt with as effectively and efficiently as possible.

In that regard consideration must be given as to whether:

- additional resources are needed;

  and

- the incident can be dealt with better.

Whenever there is the potential for a person to be seriously injured or killed, it is important to act cautiously.

Hazards or potential hazards at an incident/crime scene need to be:

- assessed and minimized or controlled;

  and

- monitored continuously and any changes need to be acted upon urgently, depending on:

  - the nature of the hazard;

    and

  - the potential of such a hazard to impact on any person's safety in the vicinity of the scene.

When entering an incident/crime scene an officer must:

- proceed with extreme caution;

  and

- concentrate his or her attention on what needs to be undertaken at that time.

Depending on the circumstances nothing at the incident/crime scene should be moved, unless absolutely necessary because the incident/crime scene must, as far as possible, be intact when the investigating officer arrives. It may be necessary to recover or to move an object in a public area because it may be disturbed by onlookers. Before an object is moved its location must be noted. The exact location of an object may turn out to be of vital importance to the case. Its position can be marked on a rough sketch.

Under no circumstances should any officer walk around the incident/crime scene and satisfy his or her curiosity by touching things. There are actual cases recorded where the First Response Officer toured the incident/crime scene leaving his or her fingerprints on a variety of objects. Such carelessness cannot be tolerated. Nor should any officer use the toilet, turn on water, smoke, or use towels at an incident/crime scene. The offender may have used the bathroom and towels to wipe himself/herself or weapons which may have been bloodstained. There is also a possibility that blood may be caught in the sink trap.

All officers should clearly understand that they will be called later to account for every move they made in an incident/crime scene.

This is necessary for the investigating officer to get a clear picture of the original condition of the incident/crime scene.

It sometimes happens that the relatives of a deceased person may attempt to clean up the premises. Such persons would like everything to be in proper order when the police arrive, or they may be trying to conceal the true situation. If such rearranging is in progress upon the arrival of the First Response Officer then that officer should ask that it be stopped. If it has already been accomplished or if the First Response Officer suspects that such is the case, that officer should make detailed inquiries in order to establish the original conditions at the incident/crime scene. It is often possible to recover undamaged objects which may have been thrown in the garbage.

If the initial assessment of the incident/crime scene indicates the possibility of an offence being committed then the incident scene is to be treated as a 'crime scene'.

Consideration must also be given as to whether there is a 'secondary crime scene'.

[8.0] INCIDENT PLAN – MAJOR INCIDENT

Depending on the complexity of the incident, it is the responsibility of the First Response Officer to develop the initial Incident Plan based on available information.

When confronted with an incident the First Response Officer must:

- constantly assess the incident;
- formulate an Incident Plan;

  and
- act on that plan.[151]

Any Incident Plan needs to include:

- an assessment of the incident, including any potential hazards/threats;
- an assessment of resources needed to effectively deal with the incident;

  and
- strategies and tactics to deal effectively with the incident, including securing and preserving the incident/crime scene.

[151] See Australasian Centre for Policing Research, 1998, 'National minimum guidelines for incident management, conflict resolution and use of force', Report Series No. 132.1, page 26.

- Consideration of the possible options, together with their various advantages and disadvantages, will lead to a preferred option.
- The preferred option then serves as a basis for an Incident Plan. The plan must be clear, definite, practical and tactically sound.
- The Incident Plan must then be communicated. This is best achieved by the verbal delivery of the plan – by issuing orders or instructions in the form of a briefing.

INCIDENT CONTROL

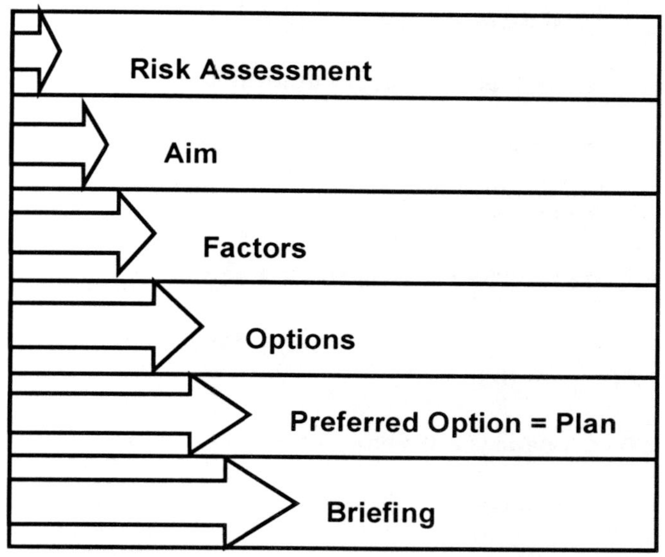

Communicating Incident Plan

In order to adopt best practice as the officer in command of an incident/crime scene, the First Response Officer needs to implement the Incident Plan by:

- taking charge of the incident/crime scene by showing leadership;
- delegating tasks to officers clearly, accurately and in a timely manner;
- deploying appropriate available equipment and material to deal with the incident;

  and
- taking action to protect life and property in relevant circumstances.

A briefing is vital to the success in dealing with a major incident.

A briefing can take five to ten minutes (or longer) for complex tasks, or be as short as 30 seconds for a simple task.

Orders and instructions must:

- be accurate;
- be brief and clear;
- contain all necessary information;
- be capable of being acted upon;

  and

- be received in time to be acted upon.

The success of any Incident Plan depends largely on all people taking part being fully informed on all aspects of the plan.

When conducting a briefing a First Response Officer should:

- present orders in a logical and detailed fashion;
- use the SMEAC system.

  The most efficient and effective method of issuing orders or instructions is by means of the acronym SMEAC.

  SMEAC is a logical sequence of conveying intentions and/or plan to others;

- if possible, read from a prepared layout (ensure pages are in sequence);
- present the orders clearly and concisely at slow speed – speak out (project his or her voice), but use simple and jargon-free language;
- reinforce his or her messages using body language and whatever visual aids are available (e.g. use a whiteboard or at scene, draw a mud map);
- allow time for those being briefed to write down important information;
- synchronise watches before taking questions;
- take questions in an orderly fashion;
- ask questions to check understanding;

  and

- conclude the briefing with a statement that the orders are to proceed, i.e. the next step is to begin.

	STANDS FOR	MEANING	WHAT TO CONSIDER
S	Situation	What has happened (the big picture)	• Details of the incident • Life and property • Location • Weather • Resource deployment
M	Mission	The aim	• Incident objectives
E	Execution	How the aim is to be accomplished (This may change as more information becomes available)	• Sectorisation • Strategies and tactics • Contingencies
A	Administration and logistics	What support (and coordination) will be provided and how	• Location of staging areas • Incident control and operation points
C	Command and communications	Who will be in control and how the communication system will work	• Incident management structure • Communication plan • Radio channels

Sequence Of SMEAC

Apart from using SMEAC, a First Response Officer should also consider the following when planning a briefing:

- who should and will be there – ensure the right people are present;
- the need to obtain supplementary or supporting documents, e.g. maps, planning documents (i.e. sector or logistics plans, resource summary, etc.);

  and

- the location of the briefing – away from danger and noise.

As the Incident Plan is implemented regular SITREPs need to be provided to the communication centre.

The Incident Plan needs to be continually monitored and reviewed by the First Response Officer in light of any additional information.

Any major changes in the implementation of the Incident Plan need to be communicated to relevant personnel and the communication centre.

[9.0] SECURING AND PRESERVING AN INCIDENT/CRIME SCENE

[9.1] INTRODUCTION

In order to determine what has occurred or what is occurring it may be necessary to secure and preserve the incident/crime scene and any secondary crime scene.

The purpose of preserving a crime scene is:

to ensure that any admissible evidence is not lost.

A plan and strategies must be in place to preserve the crime scene as first observed by using appropriate methods of preserving such evidence. This is critical for an effective investigation, and therefore successful prosecution of the offender.

The preservation of evidence at a crime scene is important considering the date of a trial may be some months or years away from the date of the commission of the offence.

Photographs of a crime scene should be taken.

For the safety and security of the public and in order to establish a safe and effective operational environment, it is at times necessary to isolate and contain an incident.

Isolation and containment are necessary to:

- separate and protect the public from the incident;

  and

- preserve the continuity of any evidence at the scene.[152]

As soon as possible after arriving at the incident/crime scene it is the responsibility of the First Response Officer to ensure that the scene is protected and therefore, preserved in its original state.

[9.2] SECURING AN INCIDENT/CRIME SCENE

As soon as possible after arriving at the incident/crime scene, the First Response Officer must take steps to protect it from the curious.

[152] Refer also to the section titled 'Continuity Of Possession' in the chapter titled 'Exhibits'.

The First Response Officer will sometimes have to use some ingenuity because sufficient personnel to block unauthorised entry may not be immediately available. If the incident/crime scene can be closed off by simply locking a door, the solution is given. But usually, curious onlookers must be kept outside an area that cannot be restricted by a closed door.

Techniques which can be utilised to secure an incident/crime scene may include:

- posting guards;
- setting up cordons using crime scene tape or rope;
- placing vehicles across roads or paths;

  or

- using markers or signs.

Effective isolation and containment of an incident/crime scene may require some form of inner and outer cordon (also referred to as 'inner and outer perimeters' and 'hot and cold zones').

A cordon is an imposed barrier, either manufactured or natural, which is used to:

- keep things in;

  and/or

- keep things out.

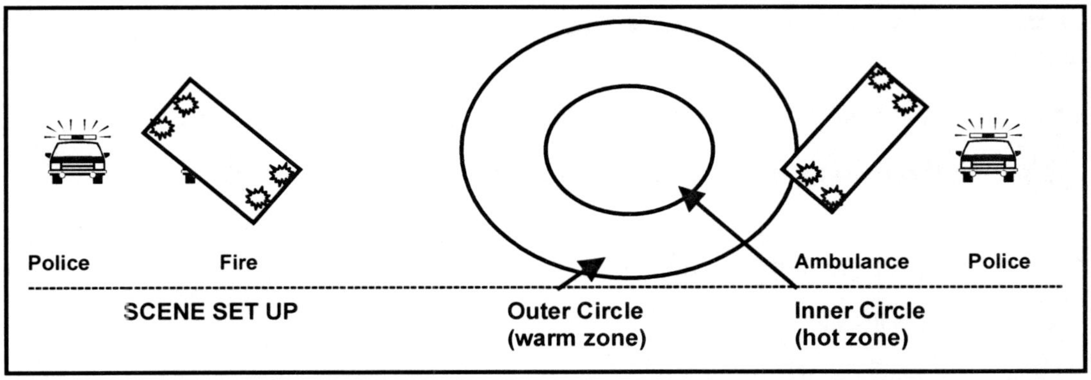

Example of a Cordon

Depending on the incident, the First Response Officer may need to establish inner and outer cordons and a Forward Command Post.

The Forward Command Post may be a police vehicle, but it must have radio communication and is usually positioned just inside the 'outer cordon'.

The 'inner cordon' focus is inward and enables the fire service or police to focus on the primary emergency.

It invariably excludes all people who are not members of the fire service or police.

For safety, unauthorised people are excluded from:

- entering;

  or

- remaining

inside the 'outer cordon'.

Not just major incidents require cordons. As an example, an officer may be faced with an individual sitting in a car threatening to commit suicide. Blocking the street or car park to the public is, in effect, a form of cordon.

A First Response Officer may initially lack the resources to establish two cordons to the extent required. As additional personnel arrive and in liaison with the communication centre a priority is to separate the community from the incident as soon as it is safe to do so in order to protect life and property.

The extent of the protective measures must be decided on in each individual case.

As a general rule:

> if the scene is indoors the area barricaded should include the incident/crime scene and, where possible, the offender's entry and exit paths.

The protective measures at an incident/crime scene should be taken as early as possible thereby preventing valuable or even vital evidence from being destroyed.

It is further essential that the barricaded area is made extensive enough from the start.

Experience has often shown that a sufficient area is not protected soon enough.

The protection of the incident/crime scene means that no person including officers should not walk around aimlessly inside or immediately outside the incident/crime scene.

The First Response Officer should arrange:

- for an officer to remain at the incident/crime scene, whenever possible, to safeguard it.

  That officer should only leave the supervision of an incident/crime scene to a member of the public in exceptional circumstances;

  and

- for the CID to be contacted, if necessary.

If an examination of an incident/crime scene cannot be properly undertaken because of darkness or other cause, sufficient police officers should remain to safeguard the area and prevent unauthorised intrusion.

[9.3] CRIME SCENE LOG

If there is the suspicion that an offence has been committed and the circumstances warrant that the incident/crime scene be secured the First Response Officer is to commence a Crime Scene Log to record the entry of persons to a incident/crime scene including:

- name and rank;
- date of entry;
- time of entry;

  and
- reason for entry.

Such information is to be provided to the investigating officer upon his or her arrival.

The use of a Crime Scene Log is a particularly useful tool because it:

- records important facts which may be crucial in later aspects of the crime scene examination;

  and
- serves to discourage unwanted visitors (usually other unnecessary police officers) who do not have a legitimate business at an incident/crime scene.

[9.4] PRESERVING AN INCIDENT/CRIME SCENE

It is imperative that every effort should be taken to prevent contamination of an incident/crime scene.

Contamination results in the loss, deterioration or destruction of evidence.

Preserving an incident/crime scene means taking whatever action is practicable under the circumstances to protect any evidence and its area of origin.

Contamination occurs:

- through the actions of humans;

  or

- by natural circumstances, such as rain.

Contamination by natural agencies can be prevented by protecting an incident scene (or the relevant parts of it) from the elements. It might be possible to rig a covering over parts of a scene of a murder, for example, in order to protect such parts from the weather. Footprints, tyremarks and other impressions can also be protected by covering them appropriately.

Contamination by humans is a different hazard and the one that is the most difficult to prevent. People exhibit extreme curiosity at an incident/crime scene and are likely to interfere with vital evidence, and not necessarily intentionally, unless measures are taken to prevent their intrusion. Even experienced investigating officers have been known to handle weapons and exhibits at incident/crime scenes out of mere curiosity.

It is imperative that the First Response Officer should control the movements of the people there. All officers who have no business at an incident/crime scene should be refused entry.

The basic rule is:

> those persons found at an incident/crime scene on arrival should be kept there and those who are off the scene should be kept off.

No person should be allowed to move any article:

- in an incident/crime scene;

- from an incident/crime scene;

  or

- into an incident/crime scene.

Where witnesses or suspects have been detained at an incident/crime scene, the First Response Officer should ensure that they do not touch anything without his or her permission.

Similarly, the First Response Officer should ensure that such persons do not contaminate the incident/crime scene by introducing alien objects such as cigarette butts, matches and the like.

As a general rule:

> the fewer people present at the incident/crime scene the less the risk there is of contamination.

[10.0] INJURED PERSON AT AN INCIDENT/CRIME SCENE[153]

If an injured person is at an incident/crime scene first aid should be provided immediately to that person even though valuable evidence may be unavoidably destroyed.

All other considerations must yield when a human life can be saved.

When a medical practitioner, health extension officer, nurse or ambulance personnel arrive the First Response Officer should without in any way interfering in their work, instruct them how to enter the incident/crime scene so as to not to disturb it needlessly. A First Response Officer should further observe the actions of the medical personnel and note what objects they moved, where they walked, and so on.

If a seriously injured person who has been the victim of violence is moved to an ambulance, a police officer should accompany the victim. An alert officer may hear an important word or accusation that might be a key to solving an offence or explaining what occurred.

The police officer who attends the hospital or doctor's surgery should arrange for the correct removal and custody of the clothing of the victim. Too often when a hospital is contacted for the purpose of obtaining the victim's garments, it may be incinerated or at best wadded into an almost hopeless mess after being cut or ripped from the victim's body.

[11.0] DEAD PERSON AT AN INCIDENT/CRIME SCENE

If the First Response Officer is able to establish certain signs of death, ie., no pulse, marked rigour mortis, odour, lividity or beginning decomposition, the rule is:

> do not touch or remove the body of the deceased person until a detailed examination can be made.

---

[153] Refer alsc to the section titled 'Caring For Victims At An Incident/Crime Scene' in the chapter titled 'Victims Of Cr me'.

[1.0] INTRODUCTION

Victims are persons who, individually or collectively, have suffered harm, including:

- physical or mental injury;
- emotional suffering;
- economic loss;

  or

- substantial impairment of their fundamental rights,

through acts or omissions that are in violation of criminal laws, including those laws proscribing criminal abuse of power.[154]

A criminal act of violation is never an isolated event. It affects everything in the victim's experience. But, it does not only affect the person who has been violated (the primary victim). Family members, work colleagues, friends and other victims may also be adversely affected. These people may then be classified as victims of crime and may include:

- individuals financially or psychologically dependent on the primary victim (e.g. spouse, child, parent);
- persons financially or psychologically dependent on an accused person in prison (eg. spouse, child, parent);

  and

- all members of the community who have their freedom[155] and basic rights restricted[156] and no longer feel safe and secure within their community.

Each victim is an individual and each person reacts differently to an offence, regardless of the severity of the offence.

What may be a trivial offence to one person may be a traumatic ordeal to another.

Providing a service to the public does not only include solving an offence or charging an offender; police must also take care of the victim in need of assistance.

The care of victims of crime is an essential part of operational policing.

---

[154] See International Human Rights Instrument titled 'Declaration of Basic Principles of Justice for Victims of Crime and Abuse of Power, Principle 1.

[155] See section 32(2) of the *Constitution of the Independent State of Papua New Guinea*.

[156] See Division 3 of Part III of the *Constitution of the Independent State of Papua New Guinea*.

Victims are never to be treated as merely a cold statistic because they are human beings with emotions. If a particular victim is argumentative, abrupt and/or rude it is not good practice to argue with the victim because he or she may be upset and/or scared. It is best to be patient at all times.

The mere fact that a victim has approached a police officer means that he or she has confidence in the Bougainville Police Service or the Royal Papua New Guinea Constabulary in investigating their complaint, rather than relying on the unlawful actions of wantoks. This should never be forgotten when speaking to a victim.

No pressure, physical or mental should be exerted on a witness or victim in attempting to obtain information.[157]

However, no victim can be required to provide a statement, and if a victim decides not to provide a statement then their decision must be respected.[158]

It may be necessary to attend the home of a victim in order to obtain a statement.

A victim should not be required to attend a police station before their complaint is investigated.

A female victim of a sexual offence should be interviewed by a female police officer.

All victims:

- should be treated with:
    - compassion[159];
    - respect for their dignity[160];

---

[157] See International Human Rights Instruments titled 'Declaration on the Protection of All Persons from Enforced Disappearance', Article 13(3); and 'Principles on the Effective Prevention and Investigation of Extralegal, Arbitrary and Summary Executions', Principle 15. On the basic duties of law enforcement officials with regard to all persons (including victims, witnesses and suspects) whether conducting investigations or otherwise, see 'Code of Conduct for Law Enforcement Officials', Article 2. 'The Convention Against Torture and Other Cruel, Inhuman or Degrading Treatment or Punishment' includes a special provision in Article 13, that in cases of allegation of torture witnesses be protected against ill – treatment or intimidation. For more specific information regarding the rights of victims to appropriate treatment and sensitivity, see 'Declaration of Basic Principles of Justice for Victims of Crime and Abuse of Power' Principles 4, 5 and 6(d).

[158] See sections 32(2)(c) and 49 of the *Constitution of the Independent State of Papua New Guinea*.

[159] See International Human Rights Instruments titled 'Declaration of Basic Principles of Justice for Victims of Crime and Abuse of Power', Principle 4 and 'Principles on the Effective Prevention and Investigation of Extralegal, Arbitrary and Summary Executions', Principle 15.

[160] See International Human Rights Instruments titled 'Declaration of Basic Principles of Justice for Victims of Crime and Abuse of Power', Principle 4 and 'Principles on the Effective Prevention and Investigation of Extralegal, Arbitrary and Summary Executions', Principle 15.

- courtesy;

  and

- due respect for their personal rights, dignity, and physical and mental well-being.

All citizens have the same rights, privileges, obligations and duties, irrespective of race, tribe, place of origin, political opinion, colour, creed, religion or sex.[161]

There should be no discrimination shown to a victim on grounds of race, colour, sex, language, religion, political or other opinion, national or social origin, property, birth or other status. Their religious beliefs and moral precepts should be respected[162];

- should be interviewed with sensitivity;

- are entitled to be compensated[163], depending on the nature of the offence and within the legal framework provided by the law.

  An investigating officer is expected to ensure that all relevant compensation details are placed before the court at the time of sentencing;

  and

- are entitled to receive the necessary material, medical, psychological and social assistance through governmental, voluntary and community-based means.[164]

  However, the reality is that such assistance is not always possible in Papua New Guinea.

---

[161] See section 55(1) of the *Constitution of the Independent State of Papua New Guinea.*

[162] See International Human Rights Instruments titled 'Convention on the Elimination of All Forms of Discrimination against Women'; 'United Nations Declaration on the Elimination of All Forms of Racial Discrimination'; 'International Convention on the Elimination of Racial Discrimination'; 'Declaration on the Elimination of All Forms of Intolerance and of Discrimination based on Religion or Belief'; 'Declaration on Race and Racial Prejudice' and 'Declaration on the Rights of Persons Belonging to National or Ethnic, Religious and Linguistic Minorities'.

[163] See International Human Rights Instrument titled 'Declaration of Basic Principles of Justice for Victims of Crime and Abuse of Power', Principles 8-13.

Refer also to the section titled 'Compensation Order' in the chapter titled 'Sentencing Options' in the text titled 'Injia on Sentencing in Papua New Guinea and the Pacific'.

[164] See International Human Rights Instrument titled 'Declaration of Basic Principles of Justice for Victims of Crime and Abuse of Power', Principles 14 and 15.

VICTIMS OF CRIME

An investigating officer should:

- keep the victim informed of the outcomes of the investigation and prosecution of any offender[165];
- provide proper assistance to victims throughout the legal process;
- avoid any unnecessary delay in the investigation and prosecution of cases;

  and

- take measures to minimise inconvenience to a victim, protect their privacy, when necessary, and ensure their safety, as well as that of their families and witnesses on their behalf, from intimidation and retaliation.[166]

  Alleged victims of torture or ill-treatment, witnesses and their families should be protected from violence, threats of violence or any other form of intimidation that may arise pursuant to the investigation.[167]

  Therefore, if necessary an investigating officer should apply to either:

  - have bail refused to the offender so that he or she is remanded in custody;

    or

  - have a bail condition imposed that requires the offender not to contact any witness and then monitor compliance.[168]

Every situation must be looked at on an individual basis and the victim should be treated accordingly.

---

165 See International Human Rights Instrument titled 'Declaration of Basic Principles of Justice for Victims of Crime and Abuse of Power, Principle 6(a).

166 See International Human Rights Instrument titled 'Declaration of Basic Principles of Justice for Victims of Crime and Abuse of Power', Principle 5.

167 See International Human Rights Instrument titled 'Principles on the Effective Investigation and Documentation of Torture and Other Cruel, Inhuman or Degrading Treatment or Punishment', Principle 3.

168 Refer also to:

- the section titled 'Bail' in the chapter titled 'Case File'; and
- the section titled 'Right To Bail' in the chapter titled 'Rights of an Accused Person' in the text titled 'Injia on Criminal Practice and Procedure in Papua New Guinea and the Pacific'.

[2.0] THE PHYSICAL IMPACT

Some of the physical reactions as a consequence of being a victim of crime may not occur immediately, but after the danger has passed. They may also recur at a later stage, when memories of the crime return.

Such reactions may persist for some time after the crime has occurred.

Physical injuries arising from victimisation may not always be immediately apparent. The most frequent injuries experienced in assault cases are facial. Victims may suffer a range of physical damage, including abrasions and bruises; broken nose, cheekbone and jawbone; and damage to, or loss of, teeth. Other injuries will be associated with assaults involving knives or firearms.

Physical injuries may be a permanent effect of the crime, and there is evidence that this has a negative effect on long-term psychological recovery, since the physical scars serve as a constant reminder of the crime.

[3.0] THE PSYCHOLOGICAL IMPACT

The experience of being a victim of crime affects different people in different ways. What may seem disastrous to one person is not necessarily so to another. While some people are less resilient than others and, when exposed to traumatic events may develop Post-traumatic Stress Disorder (PTSD), others do not.

People vary widely in their ability to cope with becoming a victim, as they do with all crises.

People have widely different:

- personality attributes;
- social skills;

  and
- other resources,

all of which may bear on their ability to cope in the aftermath of victimisation.

In the aftermath of a traumatic experience, the degree and quality of social support received by the victim is of particular importance to their subsequent adjustment. Family and friends of the traumatised victim can help their loved ones, not by judging their response to what has happened, but by being there for them and with them in their torment.

Although most victims of serious crime suffer emotional turmoil, some victims have more difficulty coping with the chaos than others. Some victims may take longer to restructure their lives, while others seem unable to resume a functional life. There is a need for research to:

- identify victims in the high-risk category;

  and

- devise early and intensive interventions to lower their risk of long-term debilitation.

[4.0] DO'S AND DON'TS OF VICTIM CARE

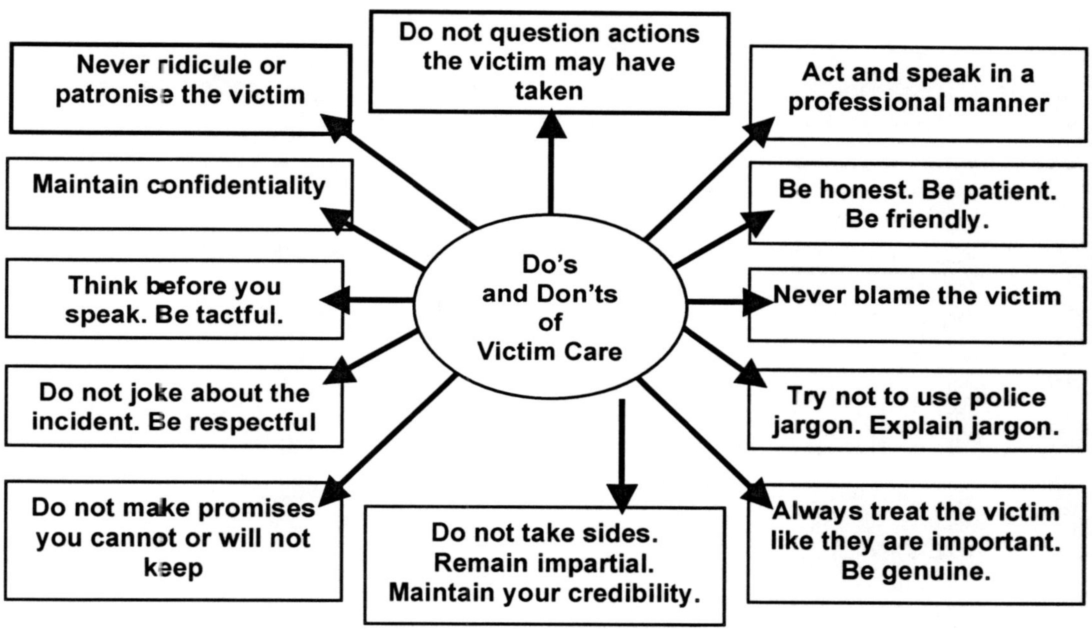

Do's And Don'ts Of Victim Care[169]

[5.0] CARING FOR VICTIMS AT AN INCIDENT/CRIME SCENE

As the 'First Response Officer' at an incident/crime scene, an officer needs to:

- speak to the person in need of care in a calm, caring and reassuring manner, especially considering that such a person will be under a great deal of stress and maybe discomfort;

[169] See NSW Police Service, 1995, 'Volunteers in Policing'.

- make an initial assessment as to the extent and nature of the assistance required;
- take appropriate action where possible to prevent further injury to the person in need;
- offer what medical attention and comfort that can be provided at the time;
- arrange for additional medical attention in appropriate circumstances, such as arranging for an ambulance to attend.

  Upon arrival of the ambulance the officer should provide whatever assistance that is necessary.

  However, an officer may need to convey the person to a hospital, a doctor or another place offering medical attention;
- advise the person in need of care as to what assistance is being arranged so as to try to keep that person calm and relaxed as possible;

  and
- arrange for the close relatives of the person in need of care to be advised of
  - what has occurred;

    and
  - where the person in need of care is being conveyed to, if possible.

[6.0] VICTIM SUPPORT

An investigating officer is expected to provide advice to a victim as to who is able to provide them support as a consequence of being the victim of a crime, such as churches and non-government organisations.

[7.0] VICTIM IMPACT STATEMENT[170]

The position of the victim is in fact given special consideration by the law. Section 21A of the *Criminal Code* (Ch. 262) requires the Court to consider any victim impact statement[171] that may have been prepared by the victim of crime.

---

[170] As regards the law in relation to a 'Victim Impact Statement', refer to the text titled 'Injia on Sentencing in Papua New Guinea and the Pacific'.

[171] See Appendix 5.

VICTIMS OF CRIME

An investigating officer is to ensure that a Victim Impact Statement is prepared whenever:

- harm has been done;

  or

- loss suffered by a victim

arising from the commission of an offence.

In a case where the victim is dead, ill or incapable of giving evidence, 'victim' includes the relatives of the deceased.[172]

Section 21A states:

> '(1) For the purposes of determining the sentence to be imposed on an offender, the court shall consider any statement that may have been prepared in accordance with Subsection (2) of a victim of the offence describing the harm done to, or loss suffered by, the victim arising from the commission of the offence.
>
> (2) A statement referred to in Subsection (1) must be –
>
> (a) prepared in writing in the form and in accordance with the procedures established for that purpose; and
>
> (b) filed with the court.
>
> (3) A statement of the victim of an offence prepared and filed in accordance with Subsection (2) does not prevent the court from considering any other evidence concerning any victim of the offence for the purpose of determining the sentence to be imposed on the offender.
>
> (4) For the purposes of this section, "Victim", in relation to any offence –
>
> (a) means the person to whom harm was done or who suffered physical or emotional loss as a result of the commission of the offence; and
>
> (b) where the person described in Paragraph (a) is dead, ill or otherwise incapable of making a statement referred to in Subsection (1), includes the spouse or any other relative of that person, anyone who has in law or fact the custody of that person or is responsible for the case (sic. The word "care was intended) or support of that person or any dependent of that person'.

---

[172] See *Steven Loke Ume, Charles Patrick Kaona and Greg Wawa Kovoa v The State* [2006] PGSC 9, (2006) SC836.

[8.0] PAYMENT OF COMPENSATION[173]

Compensation for:

- physical;

  and

- non-physical

injury to a person wrongfully inflicted by another person is widely practised in many Papua New Guinea traditional societies. Compensation for injury or damage to personal property is also widely practised in traditional societies in Papua New Guinea. Indeed compensation for personal injury and injury to personal property is a universal principle.[174]

However in *The State v William Muma*[175] Injia J (as he then was) stated:

> 'Whilst it is true that compensation was paid to harmonise the differences between the accused and the victim's relatives caused by the offence, the victim was not really compensated for the wrong done to her. She was too young to recognise and appreciate the efforts made between the two sides to normalise their relationship'.[176]

No officer is to participate in or sanction in any way community compensation negotiations and payments designed to shield offenders of violent crimes from facing criminal prosecution. The payment of compensation as a form of punishment is the exclusive jurisdiction of the National Court and District Court as provided for by the *Criminal Law (Compensation) Act 1991*. Compensation arises to be considered by the Court after conviction when sentence is considered.

If a compensation agreement derails any criminal proceedings not instigated or otherwise approved by a victim then an investigation is to be conducted in order to determine whether a criminal offence has been committed.

---

[173] Refer also to:

- the section titled 'Compensation Order' in the chapter titled 'Sentencing Options' in the text titled 'Injia on Sentencing in Papua New Guinea and the Pacific'; and

- the section titled 'Payment Of Compensation' in the chapter titled 'Mitigating Factors' in the text titled 'Injia on Sentencing in Papua New Guinea and the Pacific'.

[174] See *Manu Kovi v The State* (2005) SC789.

[175] [1995] PNGLR 161, [1995] PGNC 76, [1995] N1371.

[176] As regards the victim of sexual offence, see also: *The State v Gidingeng Yaking (No. 2)* [2006] PGNC 98; *The State v Kenneth Peter* (2002) N2336 and *The State v Alexander Junior Nara (No. 2)* (2007) N3214, [2007] PGNC 86.

The payment of compensation does not excuse an accused person from his or her criminal liability because under no circumstances should compensation be a substitute for a penalty.[177]

If the accused person plays no meaningful part in the:

- organisation;

  and

- payment

of compensation it should not operate in his or her favour.[178]

This is because the whole basis of the criminal justice system and any penalty imposed is dependent on the accused person's culpability[179], and the accused person is the only one that is personally responsible for his or her actions.[180]

The payment of compensation can restore a victim to his or her position before the commission of the offence.[181]

But compensation can be taken into account as a mitigating factor only when there is appropriate evidence confirming, the payment of any compensation, including:

- the amount paid;
- when;

---

[177] See *Joe Giamur v The State* (2006) SC884; *Kepa Wanege v The State* (2004) SC742, [2004] PGSC 22; *Baune Bernard Olmi v The State* (2004) SC872, [2004] PGSC 43; *Sakarowa Koe v The State* (2004) SC739, [2004] PGSC 33; *The State v Rex Lialu* [1988-89] PNGLR 499; *Acting Public Prosecutor v Nitak Mangilonde Taganis of Tambitanis* [1982] PNGLR 299, [1982] PGSC 6; *The State v Paul Potape Huliya* (2005) N2872, [2005] PGNC 77; *The State v Alice Wilmot* (2005) N2857, [2005] PGNC 105; *The State v Darius Taulo* (2001) N2034; *The State v Abel Airi* (2000) N2007; *The State v Nickson Pari (No. 2)* (2001) N2033; *The State v Henry Idab* (2001) N2172; *The State v Jim Paupa* (1973) No 765; *The State v Lossy Karapus* (2009) N3640, [2009] PGNC 59; *The State v Eddie John Naopa* (2003) N2411; *The State v Jimmy Ketu (No. 2)* (2007) N3394, [2007] PGNC 153; *The State v Martin Muru* [2007] PGNC 117; *The State v Henry Idab* (2001) N2172; *The State v Moki Lepi (No. 3)* (2004) N2734 and *The State v Gibson Haulai* (2004) N2555.

[178] See *Kepa Wanege v The State* (2004) SC742, [2004] PGSC 22; *The State v Darius Taulo* (2001) N2034; *The State v Eddie John Naopa* (2003) N2411 and *The State v Wilmot* (2005) N2857, [2005] PGNC 105.

[179] See *The State v Abel Airi* (2000) N2007.

[180] See *The State v Nickson Pari (No. 2)* (2001) N2033.

As to the involvement of the family of an accused person in paying compensation, see *The State v Allan Nareti and Amstrong Kupe* (2004) N2582 and *The State v Dobi Ao (No. 2)* (2002) N2247.

[181] See *The State v Oa Seseka* (1990) N921.

- by whom;

  and

- to whom.[182]

In the circumstances in which an accused person does not wish to make a submission as to the amount of compensation it is appropriate for a Court to assess quantum on the basis of:

- the evidence[183];

  and/or

- a submission from the prosecution[184].

An investigating officer is to provide all relevant information regarding compensation.[185]

A Court also has the power to award a payment of customary compensation as a form of punishment under the *Criminal Law (Compensation) Act 1991*.[186]

[9.0] PROPERTY ORDERS

[9.1] STOLEN GOODS[187]

[9.1.1] STATUTORY PROVISIONS

Section 21 of the *Goods Act* (Ch. 251) states:

'(1) Subject to this Part, where goods are sold by a person who –

(a) is not the owner; and

(b) does not sell them under the authority or with the consent of the owner,

---

182 See *Sakarowa Koe v The State* (2004) SC739, [2004] PGSC 33 and *The State v Steven Mul Mangi (No. 2)* (2005) N2993, [2005] PGNC 12.

183 See *R v O'Rourke* [1990] 1 NZLR 155.

184 See *R v Gray* [1993] NZCA 356/93.

185 See Appendix 6.

186 The law in relation to such an order is examined in the section titled 'Compensation Order' in the chapter titled 'Sentencing Options'.

187 See also: section 132(2) of the *District Courts Act* (Ch. 40).

the buyer acquires no better title to the goods than the seller had unless the owner of the goods is precluded by his conduct from denying the seller's authority to sell.

(2) This Part does not affect –

(a) the provisions of Part III. or any enactment enabling the apparent owner of goods to dispose of them as if he were the true owner of the goods; or

(b) the validity of a contract of sale under–

(i) a special, common law or statutory power of sale; or

(ii) an order of a court'.

Section 24(1) states:

'Where goods have been stolen and the offender is convicted, the property in the goods stolen revests in the person who was the owner of the goods or his personal representative, notwithstanding any intermediate dealing with them'.

[9.1.2] GENERAL PRINCIPLES

Section 21 of the *Goods Act* (Ch. 251) provides that a seller, who is not the owner or is not selling with the owner's consent or authority, confers no better title on the buyer than he or she had himself or herself, unless the owner is stopped by his or her conduct from denying the seller's authority to sell. This general rule is subject to several exceptions, the most important of which are set out in sections 22, 23, 24 and 25 of that Act.[188]

When property has been stolen then the ownership of that property remains with the rightful owner, irrespective of whether the thief sells the property to another person.

In such circumstances the prosecutor should apply to the Court for an order as to a return of the property to the complainant.

[9.2] FRAUDULENTLY OBTAINED GOODS

[9.2.1] STATUTORY PROVISION

Section 24(2) of the *Goods Act* (Ch. 251) states:

'Notwithstanding any other enactment, where goods have been obtained by fraud or other wrongful means not amounting to larceny the property in the goods does not revest in the person who was the owner of the goods or his personal representative by reason only of the conviction of the offender'.

[188] See *Shem Pake v Daniel Tulapi and Jimmy Arete* (2003) N2375.

[9.2.2] GENERAL PRINCIPLE

When an accused person obtains property by means of a fraud or other wrongful means not amounting to 'Stealing' the ownership in the property transfers from the rightful owner to the accused person.

In such circumstances the prosecutor should apply for compensation to an equal value of the property.

[10.0] SEXUAL OFFENCE VICTIM[189]

[10.1] INTRODUCTION

The law in relation to an offence of a sexual nature reflects the morals and present standards of the community.

The evidence in many sexual cases often relates to sordid and disgusting details of abnormal sexual behaviour that is usually done in circumstances of secrecy.

An offence of a sexual nature is not a crime of passion, it is a crime involving an abuse of power.

The public is encouraged to report any offence of a sexual nature, and victims of such offences are to be treated with:

- respect;
- compassion;
- dignity;

  and
- confidentiality.[190]

---

[189] As regards the law in relation to offences of a sexual nature, refer to the chapter titled 'Sexual Offences' in the text titled 'Injia on Criminal Offences in Papua New Guinea and the Pacific'.

[190] See International Human Rights Instrument titled 'Declaration of Basic Principles of Justice for Victims of Crime and Abuse of Power', Principle 4.

[10.2] INVESTIGATION

[10.2.1] RECEIPT OF COMPLAINT

An officer who receives a complaint involving the alleged commission of a sexual offence should:

- record the following information at that time:
    - the personal details of both the accused person, if known and the victim, including:
        - full name;
        - date of birth;
        - address;

          and
        - contact telephone number;
    - the presence, extent and cause of any injuries;

      and
    - the need for medical attention;

  and
- complete an entry in the Station Occurrence Book.

The complainant or victim should then be advised what will be the initial response of the police.

If the complaint is made by the victim it is referred to as the 'Fresh Complaint'.

[10.2.2] INITIAL RESPONSE

On arrival at the scene of an offence of a sexual nature the First Response Officer[191] is to:

- depending on the circumstances treat the scene as a 'crime scene';

[191] The term 'First Response Officer' refers the officer who arrives first at a Crime Scene with the highest rank or most length of service if the officers are of the same rank.

- attend to the safety and well-being of the victim as a priority, and therefore it may be necessary to arrange for medical treatment to be provided to the victim whether at the scene or a hospital, but subject to the consent of:
    - the victim;

      or

    - a parent[192] of the victim, depending on the age and maturity of the victim;
- where possible, arrange for an officer to stay with the victim at all times and preferably be of the same sex as the victim;
- attend to the wishes of the victim if the victim wishes to have a family member or friend present for support;

  and

- arrange for a female officer to attend the crime scene if the victim is a female, if necessary.

[10.2.3] INVESTIGATING OFFICER

The OIC, CID should appoint an experienced officer from the CID of the same sex as the victim to conduct the investigation into all offences of a sexual nature.

An Investigating Officer should:

- explain to the victim the criminal justice process, and their role in it;
- allow the victim to decide as to whether there is to be a prosecution of the offender, depending on the age and maturity of the victim;
- arrange for a medical examination of the victim to be conducted, only if considered applicable and subject to obtaining the consent of the victim;
- conduct a preliminary interview with the victim in private prior to any medical examination;
- attend the medical centre in order to support the victim, subject to obtaining the consent of the victim;

[192] A 'parent' is not necessarily only a mother or father, but may include a person who has parental responsibility, such as a step-parent.

- arrange a change of clothing for the victim, if the victim's clothing has been damaged or may otherwise be used as evidence, but subject to obtaining the consent of the victim;
- arrange for support to be given to the victim by a relevant NGO in compliance with relevant referral protocol/s, subject to obtaining the consent of the victim;
- conduct a thorough interview with a victim in private and with only officers of the same sex as the victim present when the victim is prepared to do so.

  Irrespective, the number of persons present is to be strictly limited;

  and
- conduct the interview at the location where the victim feels most comfortable, and therefore, not necessarily at a police station.

If the victim is intellectually disabled or mentally impaired then a close relative or friend is to be requested to attend.

[10.2.4] CHILD VICTIM

If the victim of a sexual offence is a child the Investigating Officer is to:

- arrange for a parent or a person responsible for the welfare of the child[193], if a parent is unavailable, to attend when a child is being interviewed;
- advise the parent or a person responsible for the welfare of the child, if a parent is unavailable, that a detailed statement needs to be taken;
- ask the child who he or she would like present whilst the statement is being taken;
- find out from the child in his or her own words for what he or she calls his or her private parts;
- be extremely sensitive to the welfare of the child whilst the statement is being taken;

  and
- request permission from the child depending on his or her age and maturity and/or a parent or a person responsible for the welfare of a child, if a parent is unavailable, to be examined by a medical practitioner, health extension officer or nurse, if there is the possibility of evidence being obtained.

[193] A 'child' is a person apparently under the age of eighteen years.

[10.2.5] QUESTIONING OF A VICTIM

An officer involved in the investigation of a sexual offence is to display a:

- sympathetic;

  and

- supportive

attitude towards the victim.

Equally important is the need for members to recognise the trauma that a victim may have experienced which will include a range of emotions and reactions.

The immediate reaction to the commission of a sexual offence will vary from victim to victim. It is not unusual for victims to appear calm and composed. This in itself may be a sign that the victim:

- is numbed or struggling to regain a sense of control;

  or

- is already forcing himself or herself to blank out their emotional reaction to the offence.

Other reactions and emotions possibly experienced by a victim include fear, anger, shame, guilt, self blame, embarrassment, helplessness, anxiety, powerlessness, mood swings, confusion and disorientation.

A victim may be severely traumatised which will make him or her very vulnerable.

Considering that the victim:

- will be in crisis;
- may still be in danger;

  and

- may not be thinking rationally

consideration is to be given to their safety.

An officer should never assume based solely on the reactions displayed by a victim that an offence did not take place.

An Interviewing Officer must:

- be sure to 'listen actively';

  and

- talk in a way that supports the victim's feelings and statements.

A statement that is;

- detailed;

  and

- accurate statement

is to be taken with the consent of the victim.[194]

The Investigating Officer is to be extremely sensitive to the welfare of the victim whilst the statement is being taken.

The statement must describe what occurred in the words of the victim. Questions must be kept short, and leading questions[195] are to be avoided.

An Investigating Officer is to ensure that any question asked:

- avoids any suggestion;

  or

- provides an answer.

The basic questions of investigation are:

- What happened?;
- Where did it happen?;
- When did it happen?;
- How did it happen?;
- Why did it happen?;

---

[194] See sections 32(2)(c) and 49 of the *Constitution of the Independent State of Papua New Guinea*.

[195] A 'leading question' is a question that puts words or ideas in the mouth of the witness before the witness actually says it.

and

- Who did it?

[10.2.6] EXAMINATION OF THE BODY OF THE OFFENDER

Depending on the circumstances of the case an examination of the body of an offender may be conducted by a medical practitioner[196], but not a health extension officer or nurse, unless otherwise with consent.

The taking of blood and hair samples has been held to amount to an examination of a person.

[10.2.7] WITHDRAWAL OF A COMPLAINT

Under no circumstances should an officer encourage a victim to withdraw his or her complaint, particularly in relation to a sexual offence.

[10.3] SUSPECT WITNESS[197]

Historically, at common law certain categories of witnesses were regarded as unreliable, and the common law required a Court to warn itself about the dangers of relying on such evidence where it was uncorroborated.[198]

The Courts will not lightly accept the unsupported evidence of a disputable or unsavoury witness where such evidence is the only evidence implicating an accused person.[199]

The categories of suspect witnesses at common law include[200]:

- a victim in a sexual offence case;

---

196 See section 22 of the *Arrest Act* (Ch. 339).

197 As regards the law in relation to a 'Suspect Witness', refer to the chapter titled 'Witnesses' in the text titled 'Injia on Criminal Practice and Procedure in Papua New Guinea and the Pacific'.

198 See *Bromley v R* (1989) 168 CLR 79, per Brennan J at 324.

See also: *Pollitt v R* (1992) 174 CLR 558 at 599 and *Jenkins v R* [2004] HCA 57.

199 See *Vetrovec v R* [1982] 1 SCR 811 at 831.

200 The categories of suspect witnesses at common law may not be closed, see *B v R* (1992) 175 CLR 599 at 616 and *Bromley v R* (1986) 161 CLR 315, per Gibbs CJ at 319.

See however, *Carr v R* (1988) 165 CLR 314 at 319.

and

- a child of tender years.

At common law, children were traditionally seen as unreliable witnesses.[201]

However, there is currently a substantial body of psychological research indicating that children, even very young children, give reliable evidence, including in respect of a child's ability to recall stressful events.[202]

[10.4] BAIL

If an accused person is to be granted bail then the prosecution should seek a no contract condition with the victim and other witnesses to called by the prosecution, depending on the circumstances of the offence.[203]

---

[201] See *Kendall v R* [1962] SCR 469.

See also: Australian Law Reform Commission, 2005, 'Uniform Evidence Law', Report 112, NSWLRC Report 102 and VLRC Final Report, paragraph 16.79 and Ontario Law Reform Commission, 1991, 'Report on Child Witnesses', section 3.

However, current research findings indicate that the evidence of children is not inherently unreliable and that children are not therefore a class of witnesses as to whom it is unsafe to rely, see The Law Reform Commission Of Western Australia, 1991, 'Evidence of Children and other Vulnerable Witnesses Report', Project No 87, paragraph 2.44 and New Zealand Law Commission, 'The Evidence of Children and Other Vulnerable Witnesses', Preliminary Paper 26.

[202] Refer to the subsection titled 'Child Of Tender Years' in the section titled 'Suspect Witness' in the chapter titled 'Witnesses' in the text titled 'Injia on Criminal Practice and Procedure in Papua New Guinea and the Pacific'.

[203] Refer also to:

- the section titled 'Bail' in the chapter titled 'Case File'; and
- the section titled 'Right To Bail' in the chapter titled 'Rights Of An Accused Person' in the text titled 'Injia on Criminal Practice and Procedure in Papua New Guinea and the Pacific'.

[1.0] INTRODUCTION[204]

Clearly the prosecution is expected to present the strongest possible case. That requires statements to be taken from all possible witnesses who are able to give 'material evidence'. Evidence is 'material' if it is relevant to an issue in the case.[205] Therefore, investigating officers should not rely solely on 'confessional evidence[206]'.

An investigating officer needs to:

- take command of an incident[207];

  and

- communicate an enthusiastic attitude towards successful investigation.

A potential witness needs to feel his or her efforts will be:

- worthwhile;
- appreciated;

  and

- likely to be acted upon by the investigating officer.

A professional and positive image displayed by an investigating officer inspires confidence and respect, and this is likely to result in the co-operation of those able to contribute to the investigation, as they will feel it be a worthwhile exercise.[208]

---

[204] As regards the law in relation to witnesses, refer to the chapter titled 'Witnesses' in the text titled 'Injia on Criminal Practice and Procedure in Papua New Guinea and the Pacific'.

[205] See *R v Reading JJ; ex parte Berkshire County Council* [1996] 1 Cr App R 239.

See also: *R v Bishop* (1980) 54 FLR 1.

[206] Refer also to:

- the chapter titled 'Interviewing Suspects'; and
- the section titled 'Confessional Evidence' in the chapter titled 'Evidence' in the text titled 'Injia on Criminal Practice and Procedure in Papua New Guinea and the Pacific'.

[207] Refer also to the chapters titled 'Principles Of Investigation' and 'Incident Management'.

[208] Refer also the chapter titled 'Client Service' and 'Victims Of Crime'.

WITNESSES

It is the responsibility of an investigating officer to take down statements from civilian witnesses in order to ensure that all elements of the charge preferred against an offender can be proven 'beyond reasonable doubt[209]'.

However, no victim or a witness can be required to provide a statement, and if any victim or witness decides not to provide a statement then their decision must be respected.[210]

Prior to taking a statement from a witness an investigating officer needs to be properly prepared.

A statement should be taken as soon as possible after the commission of an offence, thereby reducing the potential of their recollection being influenced by the recollection of other witnesses.

Depending on the circumstances of the offence it may be prudent to accompany a witness back to a crime scene prior to taking his or her statement.

It is advisable on occasions, for an investigating officer to wait until he or she has gained some understanding of the commission of the offence by:

- reading all available information, such as statements from other witnesses;
- talking to any other police officer who may have been involved in the investigation;
- visiting the crime scene;

  and
- examining any physical evidence

prior to interviewing witnesses.

This practice enables the investigating officer to:

- have an understanding of the commission of the offence;
- be in a better position to decide whether a witness is being truthful;

  and
- obtain an insight into what type of a witness he or she is dealing with.

Not all witnesses or victims tell the truth. It is always best practice to compare statements in order to determine the truth as to what actually happened.

---

[209] Refer also to the chapter titled 'Proof Of Issues' in the text titled 'Injia on Criminal Practice and Procedure in Papua New Guinea and the Pacific'.

[210] See sections 32(2)(c) and 49 of the *Constitution of the Independent State of Papua New Guinea*.

Furthermore, a statement is not to be taken from a juvenile[211], unless:

- consent has been obtained from a parent of the juvenile;
- is at a reasonable time when the juvenile is not tired;

  and
- the juvenile is in company of a parent, an adult close friend or relative.

A witness may:

- have nothing to gain personally by becoming a witness;
- have to give up a significant amount of their personal time by being interviewed and providing a statement;
- have to give evidence in the presence of the accused person's wantoks[212];
- have to face the accused person and his or her wantoks after the court proceedings are finalised;

  and
- feel responsible for any subsequent punishment by the court.

When considering these issues it is surprising that most people, if approached correctly, are still willing to involve themselves in the criminal justice process. However, much depends upon the manner of the investigating officer in their initial encounter with a witness as it will greatly influence their willingness or otherwise to co-operate.

Respect must be shown whenever speaking to members of the public whether the person is:

- a victim;

  or
- a witness.

---

[211] ie., a person under the age of 18 years.

[212] As regards the evidence of a 'Vulnerable and Intimidated Witness', refer to the chapter titled 'Witnesses' in the text titled 'Injia on Criminal Practice and Procedure in Papua New Guinea and the Pacific'.

WITNESSES

Victims[213] and witnesses are to be treated with:

- compassion;

  and

- respect for their dignity.[214]

In the performance of their duty, a police officer shall:

- respect and protect human dignity;

  and

- maintain and uphold the human rights of all persons.[215]

All citizens have the same rights, privileges, obligations and duties, irrespective of race, tribe, place of origin, political opinion, colour, creed, religion[216] or sex.[217]

There should be no discrimination shown to a witness on grounds of race, colour, sex, language, religion, political or other opinion, national or social origin, property, birth or other status. Their religious beliefs and moral precepts should be respected.[218]

---

213 Refer also to the chapter titled 'Victims Of Crime'.

214 See section 148(2)(a) and Part 14 of the *Constitution of the Autonomous Region of Bougainville.*

See also: International Human Rights Instrument titled 'Code of Conduct for Law Enforcement Officials', Article 2; 'Declaration of Basic Principles of Justice for Victims of Crime and Abuse of Power', Principle 4 and 'Principles on the Effective Prevention and Investigation of Extralegal, Arbitrary and Summary Executions', Principle 15.

215 See section 148(2)(a) and Part 14 of the *Constitution of the Autonomous Region of Bougainville.*

See also: International Human Rights Instrument titled 'Code of Conduct for Law Enforcement Officials', Article 2.

216 See section 45 of the *Constitution of the Independent State of Papua New Guinea.*

217 See section 55(1) of the *Constitution of the Independent State of Papua New Guinea.*

218 See International Human Rights Instruments titled 'Convention on the Elimination of All Forms of Discrimination against Women'; 'United Nations Declaration on the Elimination of All Forms of Racial Discrimination'; 'International Convention on the Elimination of Racial Discrimination'; 'Declaration on the Elimination of All Forms of Intolerance and of Discrimination based on Religion or Belief'; 'Declaration on Race and Racial Prejudice' and 'Declaration on the Rights of Persons Belonging to National or Ethnic, Religious and Linguistic Minorities.'

WITNESSES

All members of the community must be treated in a:

- fair;
- equitable;

  and
- non–discriminatory manner.

Whilst a statement should be taken from a witness as soon as possible after the commission of an offence, the circumstances of the offence must be taken into account. It is not best practice to interview a person who is visibly upset, unless there is no other option. Such persons should always be given sufficient time to try to calm down and relax. Unless relaxed it may be very difficult for a witness to remember all of the important facts. The danger in this of course, is that if the witness is given time to reflect, he or she may decide to say nothing.

Each case must be judged on its individual merits.

Names and addresses of all potential witnesses should still be obtained immediately.

Since much of the evidence in any investigation is available only through the examination of witnesses, an investigating officer must consider:

- the perception of witnesses;
- the time to interview;
- the place to interview;

  and
- the manner of the interview.

In other words, an investigating officer must decide:

- when;
- where;

  and
- how

an interview will be conducted in order to obtain the best possible results.

WITNESSES

A witness should not be interviewed with other witnesses present.

Witnesses should be requested not to talk to the media, but rather contact the appropriate representative of the Bougainville Police Service or the Royal Papua New Guinea Constabulary.

Alleged victims of torture or ill-treatment, witnesses and their families should be protected from:

- violence;
- threats of violence;

  or

- any other form of intimidation

that may arise pursuant to the investigation.[219]

Therefore, if necessary an investigating officer should apply to either:

- have bail refused to the offender so that he or she is remanded in custody;

  or

- have a bail condition imposed that requires the offender not to contact any witness, and then monitor compliance.[220]

Witnesses should be advised that if an accused person, a friend of an accused person or a member of an accused person's family tries to influence them not to give evidence then they should advise the investigating officer.

---

[219] See International Human Rights Instrument titled 'Principles on the Effective Investigation and Documentation of Torture and Other Cruel, Inhuman or Degrading Treatment or Punishment', Principle 3.

[220] Refer also to:

- the section titled 'Bail' in the chapter titled 'Case File'; and
- the section title 'Right To Bail' in the chapter titled 'Rights Of An Accused Person' in the text titled 'Injia on Criminal Practice and Procedure in Papua New Guinea and the Pacific'.

If an accused person attempts to interfere with the witnesses to be called by the prosecution then he or she should:

- be charged with an offence as specified in Division 5 of Part III of the *Criminal Code* (Ch. 262) which are offences relating to the administration of justice[221];

  and

- be remanded in custody until the completion of the case.

All witnesses should be kept up-to-date as to the current status of their case by the investigating officer.

Witnesses should also be requested to rehearse what they can recall at regular intervals because over time the memory of a witness will fade. This is particularly important when a trial may not be conducted for some months or years after the date of the incident.

[2.0] PREPARATION FOR INTERVIEW

An investigating officer should try to gain as much background information as possible prior to obtaining statements from witnesses.

Whilst the time available will vary, the time that is invested in preparation and planning will vastly improve both the confidence of the investigating officer and in the long term, save time.

An investigating officer who is knowledgeable will be in control of the situation and much more likely to gain the maximum amount of relevant information.

In order to be properly prepared to obtain a statement from a witness, an investigating officer should:

- read all available information, such as statements from other witnesses;
- talk to any other police officer who may have been involved in the investigation;
- if necessary and practicable, visit the crime scene;
- evaluate all related 'circumstantial evidence[222]';

  and

[221] As regards the law in relation to offences against the administration of justice, refer to the chapter titled 'Administration Of Justice Offences' in the text titled 'Injia on Criminal Offences in Papua New Guinea and the Pacific'.

[222] Refer also to the section titled 'Circumstantial Evidence' in the chapter titled 'Evidence' in the text titled 'Injia on Criminal Practice and Procedure in Papua New Guinea and the Pacific'.

- examine any related physical evidence.

An investigating officer should have the best possible understanding of the investigation and witnesses prior to the interview.

[3.0] WHO TO INTERVIEW

In almost every investigation, it will be desirable to question every person thought to have information before the investigation is completed.

An investigating officer must never assume that all witnesses to the commission of an offence will come forward and volunteer information.

The investigating officer must try to:

- locate the witnesses;

  and

- attempt to induce the witnesses to tell what they know.

In a search for the truth, the whole truth cannot be revealed unless all of the available witnesses to the incident have been thoroughly interviewed.

In order to try to find witnesses the value of a 'door to door inquiries' should not be overlooked.

When known witnesses are interviewed and questioned, they should be queried about the identity of other witnesses who may have information into the commission of the offence.

[4.0] TIMING OF THE INTERVIEW

The timing of an interview with a witness is an important factor and, when there is a choice, an investigating officer should try to arrange a time that is also suitable to the witness.

All statements should be recorded 'as soon as possible' after the commission of an offence whilst the incident is still fresh in the memory of the witness.

There is a natural tendency for a witness to discuss his or her experience with others. This often results in the witness, consciously or unconsciously, embellishing or modifying his or her story to agree with the accounts of other witnesses, or with what he or she has read or heard in the media.

It may not always be possible to interview a witness immediately after an incident. The emotional or physical condition of a witness may be such that an immediate interview would be pointless or of little use to an investigating officer. The danger of this is of course that if the witness is given time to reflect, he or she may decide to say nothing.

The human memory of an event becomes more and more vague or uncertain with the passage of time until the witness forgets almost everything about the occurrence.

Witnesses are more likely to volunteer information immediately after the commission of an offence than they are after a considerable lapse of time. Therefore, statements should be obtained at the first practicable opportunity.

Witnesses should be requested not to speak to any other potential witness as to what they saw.

[5.0] LOCATION OF THE INTERVIEW

Before undertaking an interview, consideration should be given to the environment in which it is to be conducted.

The goal of obtaining accurate, factual and relevant information can be best achieved after an investigating officer has made an effort to provide an environment in which the process can evolve naturally.

The more a witness feels comfortable in his or her surroundings, the more likely he or she will be able to concentrate upon the demanding task of disclosing all the information that he or she has relating to the matter under investigation.

However, often an investigating officer will have to conduct an interview in less than an ideal situation.

Irrespective, the investigating officer who does not at least try to create the best possible environment for an interview will fail in their role as a competent investigator.

Wherever possible, witnesses should be interviewed in privacy.

Obviously, a witness is more likely to communicate personal details or private suspicions to an investigating officer in the absence of an audience.

Witnesses should therefore be interviewed in a room or area in which no other person can hear.

An investigating officer should endeavour to create the situation whereby he or she can have freedom from interruption and therefore give the witness his or her undivided attention.

A victim should not be required to attend a police station before their complaint is investigated.

At times, an investigating officer may have no choice but to interview a witness at the crime scene, in a hospital ward, in the witness's place of employment, or in some other environment that is not of the investigating officer's choice.

Whatever the circumstances, it is essential that a reasonable degree of privacy should exist.

Sometimes, it is advisable to take a witness to the crime scene. This has the effect of placing the witness in familiar surroundings and stimulating his or her recollection of events. It has the added advantage of enabling the investigating officer to understand the conditions under which the witness made his or her observation.

[6.0] MANNER OF INTERVIEW

[6.1] INTRODUCTION

The manner of the interview will depend on the type of matter under investigation and the witness, including:

- the age of the witness;
- the mental capacity of the witness;
- the maturity of the witness;
- the emotional state of the witness;
- the fears and other safety concerns of the witness;
- whether the witness is related to the offender;
- whether the witness is tired;
- whether the witness is adversely affected by alcohol or a drug;

  and
- the attitude of the witness.

  The attitude of a witness may depend on many factors, including:

  - what type of witness the witness is;

    and
  - the attitude and behaviour of the investigating officer.

An investigating officer must adapt himself or herself to:

- the situation;

  and

- the type of witness being dealt with.

Questions should be:

- asked in a conversational tone of voice;

  and

- expressed in simple terms.

Every effort should be made to establish a pleasant relationship with the witness.

An investigating officer should therefore be patient, but persistent.

An investigating officer should remember that it may be the first experience of the witness in an investigation.

The conduct of an investigating officer:

- will leave a lasting impression on the witness;

  and

- may influence his or her future attitude in relation to assisting the police.

Furthermore, an investigating officer needs to be:

- **Impartial**

  Impartiality, complete neutrality and open mindedness must be displayed by an investigating officer.

  An investigating officer should never declare his or her own personal:

  - standards;
  - feelings;

    or

  - attitude

  to a witness.

An investigating officer should never allow his or her judgment to be clouded by:

- emotion;

  or

- bias;

and

- **Firm**

  Firmness is not arrogance.

  Witnesses should be treated professionally, and not treated as though they are criminals.

[6.2] PERCEPTION

Perception is the process of receiving knowledge, through the sense organs, ie., sight, smell, hearing, taste and touch.

Perception requires mental interpretation of the knowledge received by the sensory organs. Therefore, people remember things from knowledge obtained through their sense organs.

Whilst a witness will rely on their perception when recounting what they observed, it is important that an investigating officer not only hears, but also 'listens actively' to a witness.

[6.3] LISTEN ACTIVELY

There is little point in conducting an interview if an investigating officer fails to listen to what the witness is saying.

Total concentration is required, but often an investigating officer is:

- thinking about the next question;
- jumping to conclusions;

  or

- filtering out information that appears to be irrelevant.

All too often people say they are listening when they really are only hearing.

Hearing is passive.

A person does not have to do anything to hear.

Sometimes a person:

- is not even aware of;

  or

- does not take any notice of

some of the words or sounds that he or she is hearing.

But listening is active.

Listening is a complex and demanding task which requires the investigating officer's:

- concentration;

  and

- analysis

throughout the whole of the interview.

It is a valuable skill, as it:

- allows the investigating officer to interpret the information being provided;

  and

- contributes towards successful management of the conversation.

Listening actively enhances the evidential value of the interview, and, as important evidential facts emerge the investigating officer is more likely to identify their importance.

Listening actively requires:

- concentration on what is being said;
- understanding what is being said;
- remembering what has been said;

  and

- comparing what has been said.

An investigating officer:

- should listen intently to everything that is said and compare it with what is already known;
- should use appropriate body language and facial expressions in order to show that they are interested and paying attention;
- must listen carefully and make notes, especially about issues that need to be clarified;

  and

- will not accomplish their task of taking a statement from a witness competently if he or she fails to identify a significant remark and explore it.

It also helps if an investigating officer develops empathy with the witness or victim. This means putting himself or herself in the position of the witness.

An investigating officer should try to develop an understanding of the feelings and attitude of the witness, rather than making hasty judgments.

[7.0] COMMENCEMENT OF INTERVIEW

Prior to the commencement of an interview an investigating officer should:

- introduce himself or herself and other persons present and their roles during the course of the interview;
- explain the purpose of the interview.

  The reasons for interviewing a witness are to:

  - ascertain exactly what has happened;
  - determine the involvement of the parties concerned;

    and

  - make an informed decision as to what action should be taken;
- explain how the interview will be conducted.

  The structure of the interview should enable the investigating officer to:

  - ask the witness to give his or her account of the matter under investigation;

and

- then ask questions that may be necessary to enlarge upon the account and to clarify it;

- explain what is required of the witness.

  The witness will be required to:

  - concentrate totally upon what has occurred;

    and

  - provide an accurate, factual and unbiased account of it.

  The witness should be advised as follows:

  - concentrate on the incident;
  - be ready to work hard to recall what happened;
  - take as much time as necessary;
  - do not try to hurry and speak slowly;
  - try to recall everything that they can remember in as much detail as possible.
  - do not miss anything, no matter how immaterial it may seem, as every piece of information is vital;
  - be prepared to go over the incident several times to assist the recall process;

    and

  - feel free to ask questions at any stage if they are unsure of anything;

- remember that a witness may feel insecure, stressed and uncomfortable in providing information;

- discuss any fears or other safety concerns of the witness and what the police can do to assist;

  and

- briefly 'set the scene' by asking the witness to recreate the events in their own mind by recalling:
    - where they were;
    - what they were doing;

      and
    - what was occurring

  immediately before the incident.

[8.0] INITIAL ACCOUNT

In any investigation an investigating officer seeks the answers to questions concerning the matter under investigation.

The basic questions of investigation are:

- What happened?;
- Where did it happen?;
- When did it happen?;
- How did it happen?;
- Why did it happen?;

  and
- Who did it?

A witness should be allowed to tell his or her story:

- in his or her own words;
- in his or her own way.
- in his or her own time;

  and
- without interruption.

The aim is obtain the maximum amount of relevant factual detail from the witness's version of what had occurred.

The usual way of achieving this is by putting a brief open-ended question to the witness in order to encourage an extended response.

The question should be so worded as to direct the witness to what information is required and invite him or her to tell the investigating officer everything they know in relation to it.

An example of such a question is as follows:

> 'I understand that you witnessed an event in the Buka Market yesterday afternoon in which a person was assaulted. Can you tell me what happened?

There is no doubt that this will probably result in the witness introducing much irrelevant detail. However, it will give the investigating officer an opportunity to determine the witness's value.

Once the witness has exhausted his or her account of the event, he or she should then be asked specific questions by the investigating officer in order to clarify issues. At this stage, completely irrelevant details can be excluded and the relevant information assembled to present a coherent account of the event.

[9.0] RECORDING OF A STATEMENT

Upon the initial account of a witness being obtained the statement of the witness should then be recorded.

It is fundamentally important that all information provided by a witness is:

- accurately recorded;

  and

- as comprehensive as possible.

The quality of a statement of a witness and the evidence that it contains is vital to the prosecution case, and ultimately reflects the level of professionalism of the investigating officer.

An investigation is reliant upon high-quality witness statements that will often determine the direction of an investigation and ultimately the difference between success and failure in establishing the facts surrounding an incident under investigation.

WITNESSES

A statement from a witness:

- is to be recorded on a 'Witness Statement'[223];
- must contain what the witness can recall;
- must be a record as to what the witness will tell the court as to what he or she can then recall;
- should be as thorough as possible;
- must contain what the witness knows, and not what he or she has been told by anyone else, subject to the 'Hearsay Rule[224]';
- should be expressed in the first person;
- should be in a clear and straight-forward narrative form;
- should follow the chronological sequence of the events or matters;
- should, as far as possible, be in the actual words of the witness;
- should, as far as possible, include the actual words spoken at the time of the incident;
- should contain only such material facts as the witness is able to give from their own knowledge;
- should not contain police expressions;

  and

- must outline their relationship, if any, with:
  - the accused person;

    and

  - all other civilian witnesses.

  The best civilian witness in a case is the independent witness, ie., a witness who does not know the complainant or the accused person.

---

[223] See Appendix 7.

[224] The 'Hearsay Rule' states that a witness must only give evidence of what he or she saw and not what they were told, subject to a number of exceptions.

As regards the law in relation to 'Hearsay Evidence', refer to the chapter titled 'Evidence' in the text titled 'Injia on Criminal Practice and Procedure in Papua New Guinea and the Pacific'.

It is very important that if a witness knows:

- the complainant;

  or

- the accused person

then that fact should be explained in the statement.

Irrelevant details should not be included in a statement of a witness, such as information that is based on 'hearsay', unless it is subject to an exception to the Hearsay Rule.

An investigating officer should avoid asking any 'leading question' that might suggest the desired answer to the witness when initially obtaining their version as to what happened.

A 'leading question' is a question that suggests that something happened.

For example:

'Did you see ... happen?'

However, the investigating officer should be careful to ask the witness specific questions to clarify details stated by the witness which are of importance.

Witnesses will often:

- answer only the actual questions put to them by the investigating officer;

  and

- neglect to volunteer any other information.

A witness should not be asked to write out his or her own statement.

A statement from a witness should be written in the language understood by the witness.

Upon completion the statement should be read over to the witness in the language in that the statement is recorded or otherwise understood by the witness.

It may be necessary to use the services of an interpreter for this purpose.

A witness should also be given an opportunity to read his or her statement, if able to do so.

Each page of the statement is to be consecutively numbered (1, 2, 3, 4, etc) and the witness should sign it, or if illiterate place an appropriate mark, at the bottom of each page.

WITNESSES

Prior to signing or attesting his or her mark, a witness should be asked if his or her statement is true and correct. If not, deletions, alterations and additions must be allowed and these must also be initialled or marked by the witness. All deletions and alterations are to be marked with a line horizontally through the relevant words and initialed by the witness.

All statements, whether that of a police officer or civilian witness, should end with the following endorsement[225]:

> 'I .... certify that this statement is true to the best of my knowledge and belief. I make it knowing that if it is tendered in evidence I will be liable to prosecution if I have knowingly stated anything that is false or misleading in any particular.'
>
> ....
> (Signature)
>
> Date ....

When an interpreter is used to interpret a statement he or she should make an additional endorsement on the statement certifying that he or she has read or interpreted the statement to the witness before the witness signed it as follows:

> I ... (full name) of ... (address), ... (occupation), hereby certify that I can read and understand and am fluent in the ... language (language used in the written statement) and the ... language (language understood by the person making the statement) and I have read and interpreted the contents of this statement to ... (name of person making statement) in the ... language (language understood by the person making the statement) and the said ... (person making the statement) seemed to fully understand the contents of this document before he or she signed it.
>
> ....
>
> (Signature of Interpreter/Person reading document)
>
> Date ....[226]

There is the need for such an endorsement if the statement of the witness is in the English language and he or she does not understand that language.[227]

---

[225] Whilst this endorsement is required in relation to committal proceedings [see section 94(1A) of the *District Courts Act* (Ch. 40)] it should be included on all statements, including those for summary matters.

[226] Whilst such an endorsement is only required in relation to statements that are tended in committal proceedings [see *The State v Kai Wabu* [1994] PNGLR 498, [1994] PGNC 146] it should be used for all statements of witness when the services of an interpreter is used.

[227] See *The State v Kai Wabu* [1994] PNGLR 498, [1994] PGNC 146 and *The Matter of an Application pursuant to Section 155(4) of the Constitution; Richard Liri and Philip Kit Kinomen v The State* (2006) N3110, [2006] PGNC 120.

When a witness has finished giving their version, and it has been recorded, it should be compared with:

- the accounts of other witnesses;

  and

- the findings of the crime scene examination as contained in any forensic[228] or expert[229] evidence.

The importance of the role of scientific examination to:

- corroborate;

  or

- contradict

the evidence of witnesses is often overlooked.

If a witness was not taken back to the crime scene, consider going back to the scene to check that everything described can actually be seen from where the witness said they were.

If discrepancies are found between:

- the accounts of witnesses;

  and

- the forensic or expert evidence

then another statement, referred to as an 'Addendum Statement' should be obtained solely for the purpose of clarification, if necessary, and not in any attempt to change the evidence of the witness.

The original and addendum statements are to be included together in the Case File.

---

228 Refer also to the chapter titled 'Forensic Evidence'.

229 Refer also to the section titled 'Expert' in the chapter titled 'Opinion Evidence' in the text titled 'Injia on Criminal Practice and Procedure in Papua New Guinea and the Pacific'.

[10.0] TYPES OF WITNESSES

[10.1] INTRODUCTION

The types of witnesses that an investigating officer may encounter include:

- Impartial Witnesses;
- Biased Witnesses;
- Unfriendly Witnesses;
- Untruthful Witnesses;
- Unwilling Witnesses;
- Nervous Witnesses;
- Child Witnesses;
- Female Witnesses;
- Husbands And Wives;
- Expert Witnesses;

  and
- Negative Witnesses.

[10.2] IMPARTIAL WITNESS

An 'impartial witness' has nothing to gain and nothing to lose as a result of the investigation and is therefore, the ideal witness.

Such witnesses are usually persons with a sense of civic responsibility and generally make the best witnesses because of their absence of vested interest in the outcome of the case.

[10.3] BIASED WITNESS

Unlike an impartial witness, a 'biased witness' is a person who has a definite interest in the outcome of an investigation and may modify his or her recollection of the facts accordingly.

The reason for this bias may not be immediately apparent, but can be due to any of a number of emotional motives.

An investigating officer must constantly analyse the evidence of all witnesses for any indication of bias.

An investigating officer should never be reluctant to cross-examine a suspected biased witness about the reason for his or her prejudice.

Once an investigating officer has exposed a witness's bias, the investigating officer may be able to convince him or her to be a reliable and thus valuable witness.

[10.4] UNFRIENDLY WITNESS

An 'unfriendly witness' is a person who is hostile towards:

- an investigating officer;

  or

- the investigation.

Generally an unfriendly witness is:

- a relative;
- a friend;

  or

- an associate

of the offender.

Such witnesses may try to deliberately mislead an investigation.

The only way to cope with an unfriendly witness is by a display of complete impartiality.

An investigating officer should always endeavour to obtain a signed statement from an unfriendly witness.

Such a statement may be used to lessen the 'weight[230]' that a Court could give to the evidence of an unfriendly witness if there is an inconsistency between:

- the contents of the statement;

  and

- his or her sworn evidence.

---

[230] Refer also to the section titled 'Weight' in the chapter titled 'Evidence' in the text titled 'Injia on Criminal Practice and Procedure in Papua New Guinea and the Pacific'.

[10.5] UNTRUTHFUL WITNESS

An 'untruthful witness' is not necessarily an unfriendly witness.

There are those witnesses who try to help so much that they invent facts that they think will please an investigating officer.

An untruthful witness may readily adopt any suggestion advanced by an investigating officer or simply tell a lie.

If an investigating officer succeeds in exposing an untruthful witness, he or she should endeavour to establish the reason for the untruthfulness.

If the witness, in fact, knows nothing, an investigating officer should obtain a signed statement to that effect.

Such a statement may be used to lessen the 'weight[231]' that a Court could give to the evidence of an unfriendly witness if there is an inconsistency between:

- the contents of the statement;

  and

- his or her sworn evidence.

[10.6] UNWILLING WITNESS

Unwillingness may arise from a variety of reasons.

A witness may be unwilling because of a dislike of the police or court proceedings.

Such a witness may:

- have been involved in court proceedings previously and wants to avoid inconvenience or embarrassment;

  or

- have an aversion to the publicity that is likely to arise.

In any case of unwillingness, an investigating officer should try to:

- establish the reason for the unwillingness of the witness;

  and

---

231 Refer also to the section titled 'Weight' in the chapter titled 'Evidence' in the text titled 'Injia on Criminal Practice and Procedure in Papua New Guinea and the Pacific'.

- endeavour to remove the cause, if possible.

An appeal to emotion or reason, depending on the type of person, may remove the cause.

[10.7] NERVOUS WITNESS

An investigating officer must encourage the 'nervous witness' to tell his or her story by displaying:

- confidence;

  and

- consideration

when talking to that particular witness.

It is not best practice to question a 'nervous witness' on the basic facts of the incident, without first gaining his or her confidence.

A nervous witness must be allowed to tell his or her own story in his or her own way. The account of what happened can then be probed politely and conversationally by the investigating officer.

[10.8] CHILD WITNESS

Depending on their age, children often make extremely good witnesses.[232]

Children are capable of observing accurately and recalling faithfully what they have observed.

However, some children are inclined to be suggestive and easily influenced.[233]

A statement is not to be taken from a child, unless:

- consent has been obtained from a parent or a person responsible for the welfare of the child;

- is at a reasonable time when the child is not tired;

  and

[232] Refer also to the subsection titled 'Child Of Tender Years' in the chapter titled 'Witnesses' in the text titled 'Injia on Criminal Practice and Procedure in Papua New Guinea and the Pacific'.

[233] Refer also to the subsection titled 'Child Victim' in the section titled 'Sexual Offence Victim' in the chapter titled 'Victims Of Crime'.

- the child is in company of a parent or a person responsible for the welfare of the child.

[10.9] FEMALE WITNESS

The questioning of a 'female witness' should be conducted with due courtesy and propriety.

Some women and girls may decline to discuss an event, such as a sexual offence, with a male investigating officer and it will be necessary to enlist the assistance of a female police officer.

[10.10] HUSBAND AND WIFE[234]

An investigating officer should not make the mistake of neglecting to obtain a signed statement from the husband or wife of a suspect.

Experience has shown that the spouse of an offender is more likely to provide a statement immediately after the commission of an offence then after a period of time in which they may change their mind.

Furthermore, they may be forced not to provide a statement.

Such a statement may be used to lessen the 'weight[235]' that a Court could give to the evidence of an unfriendly witness if there is an inconsistency between:

- the contents of the statement;

  and

- his or her sworn evidence.

[10.11] EXPERT WITNESS[236]

An investigating officer should remember that although an expert might be highly qualified and skilled in his or her own area of expertise, he or she may be ignorant of the law.

[234] Refer also to the section titled 'Competency And Compellability' in the chapter titled 'Witnesses' in the text titled 'Injia on Criminal Practice and Procedure in Papua New Guinea and the Pacific'.

[235] Refer also to the section titled 'Weight' in the chapter titled 'Evidence' in the text titled 'Injia on Criminal Practice and Procedure in Papua New Guinea and the Pacific'.

[236] Refer also to the section titled 'Opinion Evidence' in the chapter titled 'Evidence' in the text titled 'Injia on Criminal Practice and Procedure in Papua New Guinea and the Pacific'.

If an investigating officer intends to call an 'expert witness' there must be evidence in their statement outlining:

- his or her academic qualifications;
- his or her experience;
- the 'facts' upon which his or her 'opinion' is based.

  An expert must be given sufficient facts and details to enable him or her to apply his or her own experience to prove an opinion;

  and
- the reasons for his or her conclusion/s.

[10.12] NEGATIVE WITNESS

Frequently, an investigating officer will encounter a person who says that they:

- saw nothing;
- heard nothing;

  and
- will say nothing

despite the fact that it is obvious that he or she must have observed something.

In these circumstances, it is important to obtain a signed statement from the witness to that effect which is referred to as a 'Negative Statement'.

Such a statement may be used to lessen the 'weight[237]' that a Court could give to the evidence of an unfriendly witness if there is an inconsistency between:

- the contents of the statement;

  and
- his or her sworn evidence.

---

[237] Refer also to the section titled 'Weight' in the chapter titled 'Evidence' in the text titled 'Injia on Criminal Practice and Procedure in Papua New Guinea and the Pacific'.

[1.0] INTRODUCTION

Interrogation is a vital part of an investigation and one of the essential tools of an investigating officer.

The purpose of interviewing a suspect is to:

- try to ascertain the truth of the matter under investigation;
- gather information;

  and
- obtain admissible evidence.

Therefore, an investigating officer must comply with the law.[238]

In respect to some investigations the only available evidence occurs as a direct result of interrogation. Physical evidence, such as forensic evidence[239], has compelling 'probative value[240]', but where such evidence simply does not exist, the only prospect of a conviction is as a consequence of confessional evidence being obtained by pure interrogation.

The admissibility of confessional evidence may be challenged on the following grounds:

- voluntariness, ie., whether the accused person did exercise a free choice to speak or be silent.

  It is illegal to try to obtain a confession by means of force, an act of torture or cruel, inhuman or degrading treatment.

  Under such circumstances any confession would be ruled to be inadmissible by a Court because all confession evidence must be proved to have been taken voluntarily.
- non-compliance with the Judges Rules;
- non-compliance with section 42(2) of the *Constitution of the Independent State of Papua New Guinea*, ie., whether an accused person was given the right to communicate without delay and in private with a member of his or her family or a personal friend and a legal representative of his or her own choice;

  and/or

---

[238] Refer also to the section titled 'Confessional Evidence', refer to the chapter titled 'Evidence' in the text titled 'Injia on Criminal Practice and Procedure in Papua New Guinea and the Pacific'.

[239] Refer also to the chapter titled 'Forensic Evidence'.

[240] Refer also to the section titled 'Weight' in the chapter titled 'Evidence' in the text titled 'Injia on Criminal Practice and Procedure in Papua New Guinea and the Pacific'.

- behaviour that otherwise resulted in the confessional evidence being obtained:
    - improperly;

      or
    - unfairly.

In order to determine the admissibility of confessional evidence a Court may conduct a voir dire proceedings[241].

During the course of such a proceedings evidence must be given by all officers involved in the taking of the confessional evidence.

A suspect should be transported to a police station for questioning, and not questioned elsewhere.

The prosecution is expected to present its strongest possible case.

An investigating officer should not rely solely on a 'Voluntary Statement'[242], rather than conducting a comprehensive investigation, including the conduct of a Record of Interview.[243]

An investigating officer is expected to conduct a 'Record of Interview' with a suspect, in addition to asking for a 'Voluntary Statement'.

The importance of trying to conduct a Record of Interview is that in a Voluntary Statement the suspect will only tell the investigating officer what he or she wishes to say, and not all the information that should be obtained if a thorough investigation is being conducted.

Whilst it is not unconstitutional or unfair to:

- conduct a 'Record of Interview';

  and
- take a 'Voluntary Statement'[244]

---

[241] Refer also to the section titled 'Confessional Evidence' in the chapter titled 'Evidence' in the text titled 'Injia on Criminal Practice and Procedure in Papua New Guinea and the Pacific'.

[242] See Appendix 8.

[243] See Appendix 9.

[244] See Rule 4 of the *Judges Rules*.

each case must be assessed on its merits[245], including whether the initial confessional evidence was obtained unlawfully[246].

Prior to the conducting of a 'Record of Interview' and the taking of a 'Voluntary Statement' a suspect must be:

- advised of his or her rights under the *Constitution of the Independent State of Papua New Guinea*;

  and

- cautioned in compliance with the *Judges Rules*.

Where necessary an interpreter should be present.[247]

The interrogation or questioning of a suspect is perhaps the most important phase of any investigation.

The ability to interrogate is a skill that must be practised in order to be developed. Interrogation is not an exact science. However, the fundamentals can be taught and the importance of following proven procedures in interrogation must be appreciated.

Proficiency comes with the study of competent investigating officers and experience.

Prior to conducting a 'Record of Interview' an investigating officer should have prepared his or her interview.

When questioning a suspect it is important to consider:

- what was the state of mind of the suspect at the time of the commission of the offence;

- what did the suspect do;

  and

- who was there at the time.

---

245 See *The State v Linus Rebo Dakoa* (2009) N3586, [2009] PGNC 8 and *The State v David Yakuye Daniel* (2005) N2869, [2005] PGNC 89.

See however: *The State v Anton Turik and Wickie Jack Peltam* [1986] PNGLR 138; *The State v Simon Tanuma* [1999] PNGLR 475; *The State v Michael Balana* [2007] PGNC 12; *The State v Mana Turi* [1986] PNGLR 221; *The State v Allan Honiem* (1983) N421(M) and *The State v John Julio and others* (1996) N1446.

246 See *The State v William Nanua Kapris and others* (2010) N4139.

247 See International Human Rights Instrument titled, '*Body of Principles for the Protection of All Persons under Any Form of Detention or Imprisonment*', Principle 14.

Questioning of a young person, under the age of 18 years, should be conducted in the presence of:

- a parent;

  or

- a person responsible for his or her well-being,

otherwise a Court may rule that any admission was not 'voluntary', and therefore, inadmissible.

Naturally, if a confession is obtained every effort should be made to obtain corroboration by virtue of other evidence, including obtaining:

- statements of witnesses;

  and

- physical evidence.

Errors made in a 'Record of Interview' or a 'Voluntary Statement' should be marked with a cross and initialed by all persons present, and not covered over.

However, it is not necessary to try to obtain confessional evidence in respect of every offence.

For example, it is not necessary in relation to the conduct of an investigation into a 'public order offence' that a police officer observes being committed.

If a suspect needs to go to the toilet during the course of a 'Record of Interview' or the taking of a 'Voluntary Statement' then permission should be given and the 'Record of Interview' or the taking of the 'Voluntary Statement' should be formally suspended in writing. It should be noted in the 'Record of Interview' or 'Voluntary Statement' as to the reason for the suspension and what time the suspect went to the toilet and returned.

[2.0] TIMING

An investigating officer must endeavour to interview the suspect as soon as practicable after the commission of an offence, thereby eliminating any risk of distortion or misinterpretation of facts.

However, if the suspect is under the age of 18 years, and there is the possibility of the suspect being tired at night then the questioning should not commence until the following morning.

The interrogation must:

- be based on proven procedures for establishing the truth of the offence under investigation;
- be developed systematically and according to a plan and after adequate preparation;

  and

- comply with the rule of law.

[3.0] PREPARATION AND PLANNING

[3.1] INTRODUCTION

Preparation and planning before an interview is vitally important.

An investigating officer must bear in mind that he or she must deal with suspects expediently, and the failure to do so may have an adverse effect on the outcome of the case.

There is little point in questioning a suspect if it is later excluded by a Court due to a legal technicality arising from non-compliance with the law.

On some occasions it may be possible to delay the interview until adequate preparation and planning has been completed, but on many occasions events will be more spontaneous and require an early interview.

In any event, there is always some time available for preparation and planning, and whatever time is available should be used productively.

An investigating officer should, whenever possible, follow the following rule:

'Investigate then Interview, rather than Interview then Investigate'.

[3.2] ESSENTIALS

The terms 'preparation' and 'planning' should not be considered individually, but as a collective process consisting of the following components:

- background information;
- planning the interview;
- legal considerations;

  and

- administrative arrangements.

Ideally, prior to interviewing a suspect an investigating officer should have:

- knowledge of the law relevant to the commission of the offence, including the law relating to:
    - the elements of the offence;

      and
    - any possible defences that may be raised;
- interviewed the witnesses or read their statements;
- read all other relevant documentation;

  and
- visited the crime scene, in appropriate circumstances.

[3.3] DISADVANTAGES

There are obvious disadvantages by interviewing a suspect prematurely without adequate preparation and planning.

Overlooking Evidence

While an interview is in progress, an investigating officer must assimilate what is being said whilst bearing in mind what is already known or believed.

An investigating officer who does not have a good grasp of the details of an investigation is unlikely to recognise some evidential facts as they emerge.

Important evidence that could have been gained from questions put to a suspect may be lost.

Failing To Identify Inconsistencies And Lies

An investigating officer who lacks knowledge of the wider aspects of the matter under investigation are unlikely to identify things said that are either:

- inconsistent with known facts;

  or
- deliberate lies.

Unnecessary Breaks In An Interview

An investigating officer who conducts a 'Record of Interview' prematurely is more likely to be forced to stop the interview part way through it in order to make further inquiries.

This is a waste of valuable investigative time.

Loss Of Control Of The Interview

An ill-prepared investigating officer may have difficulty in controlling the direction of an interview.

A suspect may quickly capitalise on such lack of knowledge and take control.

[4.0] INTERVIEW PLAN

An interview plan is a written list of issues to be covered during the course of conducting a 'Record of Interview', including:

- proving the elements of the charge;

  and

- negativing any possible defences that may be raised.

[5.0] SUSPECT'S ACCOUNT

An investigating officer should begin a 'Record of Interview' by allowing the suspect to give his or her own account of the facts surrounding the matter under investigation, remembering that the wording of the first question is of paramount importance.

An example of an opening question is as follows:

'What happened to John Rue at the Market last night?'

An interviewing officer should allow a suspect to give his or her account:

- in his or her own words;

  and

- at his or her own pace.

While a suspect is giving his or her account an investigating officer should not interrupt the flow of conversation, but rather allow the suspect to complete what he or she wishes to say.

A common fault is to interrupt a suspect before he or she has been able to give a full account. This often happens because the suspect appears to tell a lie or is inconsistent in some respect. It is very tempting for an investigating officer to immediately challenge a suspect who tells a blatant lie, particularly when there is evidence to contradict the version of the suspect. However, to challenge at an early stage may allow a dishonest suspect to re-adjust his or her account in accordance with the evidence.

To allow a suspect to:

- continue to tell lies;

  and

- compound earlier lies

can be a useful strategy.

It is however possible that the suspect is being truthful, but is mistaken.

Interruptions, whether intended to:

- correct an inconsistency;
- challenge a lie;

  or

- simply ask a question,

do not contribute to good interviewing as they inhibit the flow of information.

All issues raised during a 'Record of Interview' should be clarified.

For example, if the suspect states that he or she broke into a house at night, the next question could be:

'At what time did you break into the house?'.

Questions should be:

Simple	The questions should be easily understood. How, when, where, etc.
Short	Questions should be short as possible.
Logical	Questions should be asked in a logical sequence.
Singularly	One question should be asked at a time and not multiple questions in a single question.

Interview Questions

Open questions generally prompt broad answers and are used when it is necessary to elaborate on a particular issue.

Under no circumstances should a multiple question be asked.

For example:

'Where did you go next and who did you go with?'

[6.0] CHALLENGES

The term 'challenges' should not be misunderstood.

A challenge relates to the particulars of the account of the suspect that is inconsistent with the version of witnesses and/or forensic[248] or expert[249] evidence.

A challenge should be put to a suspect in the same manner as the questions earlier in the interview.

There is no need for:

- a raised voice;

  or

- offensive behaviour.

248 Refer also to the chapter titled 'Forensic Evidence'.

249 Refer also to the section titled 'Expert' in the chapter titled 'Opinion Evidence' in the text titled 'Injia on Criminal Practice and Procedure in Papua New Guinea and the Pacific'.

Such behaviour may result in the 'Record of Interview' being ruled inadmissible.

A challenge should be put calmly and in clear terms, allowing the suspect every opportunity to:

- understand what is being suggested;

  and

- account for it.

An example of a challenge is as follows:

- 'During the course of this interview you have consistently denied ever being inside the house occupied by Brett Kueng.

  But how do you account for the fact that your fingerprints were found inside that house?'

[7.0] EXHIBITS

It may be necessary to introduce an exhibit during the course of conducting a 'Record of Interview' by:

- showing the exhibit to the suspect;

  and

- asking the suspect for a comment.

For example:

'Do you agree that this is the knife that was located in your bedroom on 3rd September 2010?'

If an investigating officer wants comment with reference to a sketch plan of a crime scene, then the investigating officer should:

- prepare the sketch plan;

  and

- give the suspect the opportunity of commenting on it.

There is however no obligation on a suspect to assist police with their enquiries in relation to a sketch of a crime scene and no unfavourable comment or inference can be drawn by a Court by reason of their alleged failure to do so.[250]

[250] See *Fred Bukoya v The State* (2007) SC887.

[8.0] LISTEN ACTIVELY

There is little point in conducting a 'Record of Interview' if the investigating officer fails to listen to what the suspect is saying.

Total concentration is required, but often an investigating officer is:

- thinking about the next question;
- jumping to conclusions;

  or

- filtering out information that appears to be irrelevant.

All too often people say they are listening when they really are only hearing. Hearing is passive. A person does not have to do anything to hear.

Sometimes a person:

- is not even aware of;

  or

- does not take any notice of

some of the words or sounds that he or she is hearing.

But listening is active.

Listening is a:

- complex;

  and

- demanding

task that requires an investigating officer's:

- concentration;

  and

- analysis

throughout the whole of the 'Record of Interview'.

It is a valuable skill, as it:

- allows the investigating officer to interpret the information being provided;

  and

- contributes towards successful management of the conversation.

Listening actively enhances the evidential value of the interview, and, as important evidential facts emerge the investigating officer is more likely to identify their importance.

Listening actively requires:

- concentration on what is being said;
- understanding what is being said;
- remembering what has been said;

  and

- comparing what has been said.

An investigating officer:

- should listen intently to everything that is said and comparing it with what is already known;
- should use appropriate body language and facial expressions in order to show that he or she is interested and paying attention;
- must listen carefully and make notes, especially about issues that need to be clarified;

  and

- will not take a 'Record of Interview' competently if he or she fails to:
  - identify a significant remark;

    and

  - explore it.

[9.0] INTERROGATION PITFALLS

The common pitfalls in conducting a 'Record of Interview' are as follows:

Control

An investigating officer must at all times be in control of the 'Record of Interview'.

Anger

Anger is a forerunner for defeat.

An investigating officer should never get angry when conducting an investigation, and especially when questioning a suspect.

Threats

An investigating officer who resorts to threats has lost the control of the 'Record of Interview' and the admissibility of any subsequent admissions may be challenged.

Ill-prepared

An investigating officer should not conduct a 'Record of Interview', unless he or she is appropriately prepared.

Prejudices

An investigating officer must disregard personal feelings and be unbiased and completely objective, influenced only by the facts.

Degrading The Suspect

Regardless of the offence committed, the suspect is a human being and must be treated with dignity and respect.

Not Listening Actively

A investigating officer must throughout the course of a 'Record of Interview' be listening actively.

Multiple Questions

An investigating officer should not ask a question that is so worded that it contains two questions.

EXHIBITS

[1.0] INTRODUCTION

Special care should be taken of property likely to be an exhibit in court.

Exhibits play a critical role in the investigation and prosecution of criminal offences.

Exhibits have often been described as a 'silent witness'[251], and their value as evidence cannot be over-emphasised.

The correct handling of an exhibit will ensure that it is capable of being admissible as evidence, subject to:

- the question of relevance;

  and

- other legal issues relating to the issue of admissibility.

At times, something seized as an exhibit might prove not to have any 'probative value[252]'. In such circumstances, there is no need to tender it in court.

Precautions must be taken to ensure that an exhibit is preserved in the same condition in which it was found.

A magistrate has the authority to:

- summons a person as a witness;

  and

- compel that person to bring and produce for the purpose of evidence all documents and writings in that person's possession or power.[253]

At a pre-trial review hearing both the prosecution and defence are to inform the National Court in relation to:

- the exhibits that are to be sought to be admitted;

  and

- whether such exhibits are to be admitted by consent.[254]

---

[251] See *Williams v R* [2005] NZCA 315, per Gendall J.

[252] Refer also the section titled 'Weight' in the chapter titled 'Evidence' in the text titled 'Injia on Criminal Practice and Procedure in Papua New Guinea and the Pacific'.

[253] See section 71 of the *District Courts Act* (Ch. 40).

[254] See Order 2, Division 1, rule 6(f) of the *Criminal Practice Rules 1987.*

EXHIBITS

A statement of a witness, including a police officer, should state immediately after referring to an exhibit:

- 'I now seek to produce [identify the exhibit] to the Court.

  Tendered And Marked As Exhibit No. ……………'

Once an exhibit is admitted by the Court as evidence in a trial, the exhibit becomes the property of the Court and remains in the Court's custody. However, the Court may grant leave to the prosecution to remove the exhibit from the Court's custody for safe-keeping during the trial.

Upon completion of the trial, the Court may make orders as follows:

- return the exhibit to its owner;

  or

- forfeit the exhibit to the State to be retained or disposed off.[255]

[2.0] STATUTORY PROVISIONS

Section 12 of the *Search Act* (Ch. 341) states:

> 'Where any thing is seized by a policeman under this Act or is handed to a policeman, he shall enter in a permanent register of property[256] –
>
> (a) a full description of the thing including where appropriate, a note of any identification marks; and
>
> (b) the time and date the thing was seized or received by him and in the case of things received by him the name and address of the person who handed the thing to him; and
>
> (c) the place and the person from whom the thing was seized; and
>
> (d) other details as are prescribed'.

Section 13 states (in part):

> '(1) Where any thing is seized under this Act by a policeman or is handed to a policeman, the thing shall be deemed to be in the possession of the State.

---

[255] See section 628 of the *Criminal Code* (Ch. 262).

[256] 'A record of things seized by, or handed to, a policeman shall be kept in a register of property in Form 5', see section 3 of the *Search Regulation* (Ch. 341).

(4) Anything referred to in Subsection (1), (2) or (3) may be retained in possession in accordance with that subsection for the purpose of examination and investigation and in the event that a person is charged with an offence in relation to that thing or in relation to which that thing is evidence the thing may, subject to any order to the contrary of a court, be retained in that possession until the charge and any subsequent proceedings on that charge have been determined'.

[3.0] EXHIBIT MANAGEMENT

All exhibits are to be managed in strict accordance with current policy.

In some circumstances it may be necessary for an Exhibit Officer to be appointed in respect of an investigation.

An Exhibit Officer is responsible for:

- recording all exhibits taken possession of;

  and

- the security of such exhibits.

Upon taking possession of an exhibit, an officer should:

- register the exhibit in an Exhibit Register;
- attach an Exhibit Label to the exhibit;

  and

- arrange for the exhibit to be stored securely.

Each exhibit should be allocated a number or letter which is identified in an Exhibit List[257] in the Case File.

[4.0] EXHIBIT HANDLING PROCEDURE

[4.1] INTRODUCTION

The general rule in handling an article is:

- to do so as little as possible;

  and

- to do it in such a way as to leave the article in its original condition.

257 See Appendix 10.

[4.2] PRESERVATION

[4.2.1] INTRODUCTION

Exhibits must be preserved so that they remain, as far as possible, in their original state so that they may be produced in court in the condition in which they were found.[258]

An article may bear fingerprints, dust, hairs or fragments of matter, or may contain something, which will be upset or displaced by careless handling.

An article may bear hairs or dust that are of importance, but of no value if found elsewhere; a weapon or implement bearing fingerprints may have these obliterated by careless handling.

This not only applies to movable exhibits, but is just as important in the case of immovable articles, such as door-handles, padlocks, window-fastenings, etc.

A spider's web across a small opening may give information of great value, as also may an indentation in a piece of wood, if, for example, the amount and nature of the dust that has accumulated on it are observed.

It is, therefore, advisable to:

- carefully examine anything before handling it;

  and

- note whether any movement or handling is likely to disturb or obliterate any trace evidence that may subsequently prove to be of importance.

Whilst this practice is already generally recognised as regards fingerprints, it is just as important with regard to material traces.

After a preliminary examination has been made with the special points having been noted in writing and the officer conducting the examination being satisfied that it may safely be handled it should be handled in such a manner so as to preserve any fingerprints or other trace evidence.

The general rule is:

> to hold the article only by such parts as are unlikely to have been touched by the hands of the accused person, whose fingerprints may be on it.

Therefore:

> A tumbler should be lifted with one finger on the rim and the thumb under the base.

---

[258] Refer also to the section titled 'Securing And Preserving An Incident/Crime Scene' in the chapter titled 'Incident Management'.

- A piece of glass etc. should be held by the edges without touching the flat surface.
- A bottle should be lifted with one hand on the rim of the neck and the other hand under the base.
- A knife should be lifted with one finger (or a cork if too sharp) at the end of the blade and the other hand against the end of the handle.
- A firearm should be lifted by the outside of the trigger guard or knurled surface incapable of retaining a fingerprint.
- Papers should not be handled without gloves. They may be lifted with forceps or tongs.

Great care should be used in the handling of any sheets of paper, books, stamps, etc., since the trace evidence on these may be readily obliterated even by ordinary handling.

An article may bear fingerprints and hence should be:

- handled only with gloves or something on the hands;

  or

- lifted with some instrument (forceps, tongs, etc.).

An article should not be powdered for the development of fingerprints before being submitted to the expert, since such powdering may nullify other examinations. An article may show traces of erasures, by chemical processes or by rubbing. Hence, the state of the surface is of importance.

An article should be protected from further exposure.

There may be traces of dust, or other substances liquids that are easily dislodged or removed.

Their importance may depend upon:

- the way in which they have been folded.

  Hence they should be protected from further folding;

  and

- indentations on the surface, such as are produced on the second sheet of a pad after writing with a pen or hard pencil.

Single documents or pieces of paper should, therefore, be placed separately in envelopes or folded sheets of cellophane of suitable size, in the condition in which they are found, unless they show dust or fragments which can be readily dislodged, in which case these fragments should be collected and packed as suggested under 'packing'. Protection from light may be afforded by enclosing the inner cellophane envelope or sheet in a larger outer envelope of brown paper or similar material. No mark should be made on the document, but a label should be attached to the cellophane envelope.

When it is suspected or seen that there may be removable traces, other than fingerprints, special precautions must be taken as it is not possible to lay down any definite rules.

Each article must be treated according to its condition or the circumstances of the case.

Where knots are concerned, it is in many cases advisable to cut the string or cord, rather than to undo the knot, since the way in which it is made may be of some importance. When rope is found passing over a beam or other support in case of suicide or homicide, it may be of the greatest importance to know in which direction the surface fibres have been brushed.

When mud or other stains are found on an article (boot, tyre, etc) which has come in contact with the ground, the order in which the stains have been made may give valuable information. A piece of clothing may bear dust or other stains, whose value lies in the exact place in which they occur, whether on the surface or between the fibres of the threads. The edge of a tear in clothing may give information from the condition of the torn fibres forming the threads at the edges.

It may be noted that when sand or dry earth is thought to be stained (with blood, etc), the small amount bearing the stain should be collected, rather than a large amount which would only render the examination for the stain more difficult or even abortive, since the small stained portion may be lost amongst the larger unstained mass.

In some cases it is not possible to retain the exhibit intact.

For example, in many testing procedures, the exhibit may have to be altered or destroyed.

However, all precautions must be taken to ensure that exhibits are delivered to the laboratory in their original condition.

[4.2.2] LOSS PREVENTION

Small items (such as hair fibres and paint flakes) may be lost from packages which are not properly sealed.

Envelopes are unsuitable for small samples of this type since the contents may be lost from unsealed corners of the envelope.

Volatile liquids from arson cases may evaporate if the containers are not airtight.

[4.2.3] DETERIORATION OR DAMAGE

Biological specimens, i.e. wet blood, may deteriorate rapidly since it is not permissible to use preservatives.

Exhibits should therefore be delivered to the laboratory immediately.

The deleterious effects of weather must also be avoided as wind or rain may ruin an otherwise valuable shoe impression or rain may wash away a bloodstain.

If the blood cannot be delivered to the laboratory immediately it should be dried in the sun where possible and then delivered by whatever means possible.

[4.2.4] CONTAMINATION

Exhibits which are not properly packed may become contaminated by dust or grease from hands.

When several exhibits are bundled together in one parcel, one may contaminate the other, i.e. bloodstains and semen.

[4.3] PACKING

[4.3.1] INTRODUCTION

In deciding on the method of packing of any particular article or substance, an investigating officer should ask himself or herself whether the method chosen is adequate to prevent:

- loss during transit;
- contamination from packing or from outside sources;
- mechanical damage from jolting or crushing;

  and
- the risk of damage being done by leakage, escape, ignition or explosion of corrosive, noxious, explosive or dangerous articles.

Each exhibit should:

- be packed separately;

  and
- not be allowed to come into contact with the other exhibits.

However, there is no objection, of course, to a number of separate packages being made up into one parcel for transmission to an expert.

Special care should be taken to avoid the following mistakes:

- the use of wet or dirty containers;
- the use of containers with distinctive smells;
- the use of dirty or unsuitable stoppers;
- insufficient protection of glass bottles or fragile containers during transit;
- the use of thin cardboard boxes that cannot be securely closed and are liable to be crushed in transit;
- the use of ordinary envelopes for powders;
- the packing of several articles insecurely in one package;
- contamination of one article by contact with another;

  and

- the lavish use of sealing wax.

  If sealing wax is placed round a stopper, it is very difficult to remove the stopper without letting some of the wax fall into the bottle.

  It is better to tie the container with tape or string, sealing the ends.

[4.3.2] SMALL SAMPLES OF DRY MATERIAL

Transparent envelopes of cellophane or other such paper, such as are used by stamp collectors.

These have the advantage of being non-fibrous and thus will not contaminate the sample with foreign fibres.

Alternatively, small round flat tin boxes may be used, the lid being secured in position by a strip of adhesive plaster.

Plain glass tubes with rubber stoppers can be used for packing dust; they need careful protection during transit, which may be secured by enclosing the glass tubes in special wooden tubes, such as are used for sending glass phials containing bacteriological specimens.

[4.3.3] LARGE SAMPLES OF DRY MATERIAL

Clean, stout, wide mouthed bottles with substantial stoppers should be used.

[4.3.4] LIQUIDS

Clean, dry glass bottles with narrow necks and with glass stoppers should be used.

Corks should be avoided for acid or alkaline liquids.

Rubber bands should not be used for petrol, paraffin, acids or any active liquid.

[4.3.5] CLOTHING AND SUCH MATERIALS (WITH SEMEN, BLOOD, DUST, ETC.)

Clothing and such materials with semen, blood, dust, etc. must be handled as little as possible.

If moist they should be allowed to dry naturally, and not be dried using artificial heat, before they are packed.

Notes should be made as to their state when found; it may be of the greatest importance to know, for instance, whether blood was fluid or had clotted at a particular stage.

Garments, etc., should be folded so to place the stains as flat as possible, and then wrapped separately in clean paper and packed between sheets of fairly rigid material, such as cardboard or three-ply wood, or in a box so that they cannot be rubbed or crushed.

If dust or hairs or other matter is likely to be displaced in packing or transport this matter should be removed and packed separately.

But the rule is:

there should be as little interference as possible.

If anything is removed, the spot from which it is taken should be:

- marked;

  and

- noted on the exhibit label.

The expert should receive the article as nearly as possible in the original state in which it was found.

[4.3.6] MATERIALS FROM POISONING CASES

The organs should be packed and forwarded by the medical officer doing the postmortem, but it should be sent for analysis.

If arsenical poisoning is suspected cuttings from the nails and hair should also be forwarded.

In all cases where a body has been buried, samples:

- of the surrounding media (the substance surrounding the body, including shroud, sawdust, wood from coffin, earth above and below the body and coffin);

  and

- from the adjacent area where no body has been buried or laid (the latter being for comparison purposes)

should be collected.

From the crime scene, any stains on floors or fluid in open receptacles must be packed carefully.

[4.3.7] WET EXHIBITS

Wet exhibits, such as bloodstained clothing, may present some problems.

If these are sealed in plastic bags, bacterial decomposition may proceed to such a stage that no tests will succeed.

The article should be delivered to the laboratory immediately.

But where this is not possible, it should be hung out to dry and then packed in the normal way.

On no account should bloodstained clothing be subjected to heat to accelerate drying, instead it should be allowed to dry by natural means.

[4.3.8] POST-MORTEM EXHIBITS

Collection and submission of post-mortem exhibits and specimens from victims is the responsibility of police.

It is necessary for the investigating officer responsible for an investigation involving a post-mortem examination to ensure that:

- the proper control samples;

and

- any other specimens that may be of value

are taken from the body of the victim by the medical practitioner at the time of the post-mortem examination and submitted to the appropriate laboratory as early as practicable.

Specimens and control samples that may be considered relevant at the time may be lost for all time if not taken at the post-mortem.

Clothing from the body must be removed with care to:

- avoid loss of any material thereon;

  and

- prevent any contamination.

The clothing must not be cut off as this may ruin stab marks and bullet holes for later examination. It should be allowed to dry out in room temperature before it is packed away or parceled up.

Remember, blood and seminal stains will rapidly decompose if not dried out before the clothing is parceled up.

Fingerprints of all such victims must be taken.

If there is likely to be any difficulty in identifying the body and the features are not decomposed then photographs of the face of the deceased person should be taken at a number of angles, full-face, profile and 3/4 views, and then from a position similar to that from which photographs would be taken of a living person.

Distortion must be avoided, otherwise the photographs are useless, particularly for superimposing over existing photographs for comparison purposes. These photographs must be taken before the post-mortem is commenced, otherwise the removal of the top of the skull will distort the features.

Dentures must be retained if identification is proving difficult and a dental chart of the deceased person's natural teeth should be prepared by a qualified dentist.

Rope, or any other strangling device tied around the neck of a deceased person must be cut off without interfering with any knot. The cut edges must be made clearly identifiable by placing some colored tape or similar medium around the exhibit cord on either side of the cut.

Photographs of gunpowder residue around bullet holes and shotgun pellet patterns, taken with a size chart should be included to enable the diameter of the area of powder residue staining and shotgun pellet pattern to be accurately gauged.

This practice assists in determining the distance between the muzzle of the weapon and the deceased when the weapon discharged. Swabbing should then be taken of the gunpowder residue for analytical purposes.

Bullets, sections of bullets, shotgun pellets, wads (which may be either cardboard, cork or plastic) must be collected from the body and carefully preserved. The attention of the medical practitioner must be drawn to the necessity of exercising the utmost care in the removal of bullets from the body to avoid damage to them. Metal instruments must not be allowed to come into contact with the bullets.

Remember, an X-Ray can be used to advantage in locating bullets, shotgun pellets, etc.

[4.4] DISTINGUISHING MARKS

Each article or substance taken must have allotted to it a distinctive mark such as a letter or number in order to connect it with the crime scene.

Make it simple, i.e. use series such as PI, P2, P3, etc., which may be extended indefinitely and may be varied by using different letters for different rooms or areas.

This mark should never be made on the article itself, but on a label attached.

The exception in certain cases will be where an expert may place a small mark on an article in a suitable position to avoid confusion when several are being handled together for comparison.

[4.5] LABELLING

Each article or sample of material taken must be securely labelled so that it can be identified immediately.

This must be done in such a way that the label will not become detached in packing or handling and will be proof against unauthorised or accidental removal.

All labels must be affixed that they will not in any way damage the exhibit.

In all cases where the label cannot be affixed to the article, it must be attached to the container.

All exhibits must be clearly labelled so that they can be identified later in court as the items concerned in the case.

An Exhibit Label must have the following details:

- the date;
- the name and rank of the Investigating Officer;

- the name of the accused person;
- the details of the charge(s);
- who located the exhibit;

  and

- where was the exhibit located.

The object of labeling is:

- to ensure that an exhibit can be readily identifiable;

  and, where necessary

- to provide evidence of its history from the time it was taken possession of until it is produced in court.

When exhibits are taken to a laboratory, the investigating officer must prepare a label for each group of exhibits submitted.

[5.0] BEST EVIDENCE RULE[259]

A fair trial for an accused person necessarily extends to:

- the preservation of;

  and

- the retention of

material evidence of his or her guilt or innocence.[260]

Therefore, evidence relevant to the guilt or innocence of an accused person, including the preservation of articles which may give rise to the reasonable possibility of securing relevant evidence, must so far as necessary and practicable, be kept until the conclusion of a trial.[261]

---

[259] As regards the law in relation to the 'Best Evidence Rule', refer to the chapter titled 'Evidence' in the text titled 'Injia on Criminal Practice and Procedure in Papua New Guinea and the Pacific'.

[260] See *Dillon v O'Brien and Davies* (1887) 20 LRIR 300, per Palles CB and *R v Lushington; ex parte Otto* (1894) 1 QB 420.

[261] See *Braddish v Director of Public Prosecutions and another* [2002] 1 ILRM 151, [2001] IESC 45, [2001] 3 IR 127; *Robert Murphy v Director of Public Prosecutions* [1989] ILRM 71, per Lynch J at 76 and *Dunne v Director of Public Prosecutions* [2002] IESC 27, [2002] 2 IR 305, [2002] 2 ILRM 241.

EXHIBITS

Traditionally police have always attempted to present the actual exhibit relating to a crime to the Court.

The reason for this is that the actual item, viewed and considered by a Court is far more persuasive and informative than a description offered in a statement by a police officer, the victim or the owner.

This is true to a certain extent. However, it is quite obvious that large exhibits, or live exhibits have never been able to be presented to a court, and so the belief is really only partially true.

There are, however, sufficient means by which an exhibit can be:

- recorded;

  and

- presented to a Court,

without retention of the actual item.

Photographing, fingerprinting or analysis can be undertaken thereby allowing the return of the property to the owner or disposal.

Only items of a unique or controversial nature need necessarily be actually tendered, such as murder weapons, implements used in armed hold-ups or serious assaults, documents, defective vehicle parts, money or other articles with unique or distinctive characteristics.

According to the 'best evidence rule':

- an original exhibit should be produced, if possible[262]; and
- a copy of a document may be produced if there is evidence that the original is lost[263].

  A carbon copy is admissible as primary evidence.[264]

  In order to admit a photostat photocopy, the prosecution must prove:

  - that the original existed which would have been admissible in itself;
  - that the copy is a true and faithful copy of the original;
  - that the original is lost or destroyed;

---

[262] See *R v Kwaimanisi* [1995] SBHC 47.

[263] As regards the admissibility of a copy of a record of interview or voluntary statement, see *The State v Wangabin Tonieng and others* (1986) N542, [1986] PGNC 5.

[264] See *R v Collins* (1960) 44 Cr App R 170; *Durston v Mercuri* [1969] VR 507; *Buckley v Macken* (1961) 1 NZLR 46; *Hay v Mitchell* (1973) 2 NSWLR 736 and *The State v Matanigasau* [2003] FJHC 103.

- that a diligent search was made for it;

  and

- that there is evidence of how the original was kept before it was lost and of how the copy was made and tendered.[265]

Irrespective, if an exhibit has been lost there should be evidence given by the investigating officer and the officer who was responsible for the safe-keeping of the exhibit, that:

- the exhibit is lost;
- why it is lost;

  and

- what has been done in an attempt to locate it.[266]

  Those witnesses may then give secondary evidence in describing the missing exhibit.[267]

In order to determine whether the explanation of the prosecution was satisfactory, a Court will analyse the circumstances surrounding the loss of the evidence.[268]

Relevant considerations include:

- whether the evidence has been lost because of acts or omissions by the police involving bad faith[269];

  and

- whether it is probable that the evidence would have been of real assistance to the defence in the circumstances of the particular case because it would have contributed to creating a reasonable doubt.[270]

---

[265] See *R v Vincent Lobendahn* (1972) 17 FLR 1 and *The State v Matanigasau* [2003] FJHC 103.

[266] See *Birch v The State* [1979] PNGLR 75, [1979] PGSC 6.

See also: *Butera v Director of Public Prosecutions (Victoria)* (1987) 62 ALJR 7 and *R v La* (1997) 116 CCC (3d) 97.

[267] See *Butera v Director of Public Prosecutions (Victoria)* (1987) 62 ALJR 7 at 9.

[268] See *R v La* (1997) 116 CCC (3d) 97.

[269] In *Arizona v Youngblood* (1988) 488 US 51 Rehnquist CJ stated:
'We therefore hold that unless a criminal accused person can show bad faith on the part of the police, failure to preserve potentially useful evidence does not constitute denial of due process of law'.

[270] See *R v Harmer* [2003] NZCA 126.

On appeal, the issue is whether the unavailability of the evidence to the defence appears to have given rise to a miscarriage of justice.[271]

There will be no violation of an accused person's right to a fair trial, unless the accused person establishes that the non-disclosure has probably prejudiced, or had an adverse effect on his or her ability to make full answer and defence.[272]

[6.0] CONTINUITY OF POSSESSION

If any exhibit is to be admissible then the continuity of its possession must be proven.

The underlying purpose of testimony relating to the chain of custody or continuity of possession is:

> to prove that the evidence which is sought to be tendered has not been altered, compromised, contaminated, substituted or otherwise tampered with,

thus ensuring its integrity from collection to its production in court.[273]

Proof of continuity is not a legal requirement and gaps in continuity are not fatal to the prosecution's case, unless such gaps raise a reasonable doubt about the exhibit's integrity.[274]

However, not every person who had possession of an exhibit from the time of the commission of the offence until its production in court must be called to give evidence.[275]

The prosecution must prove that the exhibit:

- taken from a crime scene;
- transported to a police station and anywhere else for examination;

  and
- then produced in court

---

[271] See *R v Harmer* [2003] NZCA 126.

Refer also to the chapter titled 'Appeals' in the text titled 'Injia on Criminal Practice and Procedure in Papua New Guinea and the Pacific'.

[272] See *R v La* (1997) 116 CCC (3d) 97.

[273] See *R v Larsen* 2001 BCSC 597, per Romilly J.

[274] See *R v Larsen* 2001 BCSC 597, per Romilly J.

[275] See *R v Stafford* [2009] QCA 407; *R v Butler* [2009] QCA 111; *R v Larsen* 2001 BCSC 597, per Romilly J and *Barry v New Zealand Police* [2008] NZHC 438.

is the same exhibit and that it has not been contaminated.

Obviously, if a number of police officers had possession of an exhibit at the same time then only one of those officers would need to be called to give that evidence.

Proving continuity of possession is of particular importance if an exhibit needs to be analysed by an expert.

In order for:

- the opinion evidence of an expert[276];

  or

- a certificate issued under any statutory provision

to be admissible the prosecution must prove the continuity of possession from:

- the possession of the accused person,

  to

- the examination or analysis conducted by the expert.

[276] Refer also to the section titled 'Opinion Evidence' in the chapter titled 'Evidence' in the text titled 'Injia on Criminal Practice and Procedure in Papua New Guinea and the Pacific'.

FORENSIC EVIDENCE

[1.0] INTRODUCTION

In order to determine what has occurred it may be necessary to secure and preserve:

- the crime scene;

  and

- any secondary crime scene.

For the safety and security of the public and in order to establish a safe and effective operational environment, it is at times necessary to isolate and contain an incident.

Isolation and containment are necessary to:

- separate and protect the public from the incident;

  and

- preserve the continuity of any evidence at the scene.

As soon as possible after arriving at a crime scene it is the responsibility of the First Response Officer to ensure that the scene is protected and therefore, preserved.

Upon concluding that an offence has been committed the scene is to be treated as a crime scene.

The investigating officer will have to then determine whether there is the potential for forensic evidence to be collected:

- at the crime scene;

  and

- from the suspect[277].

Until that evidence is collected the crime scene must remain protected and preserved.

[2.0] ROLE OF THE SCENES-OF-CRIME OFFICER

A Scenes-of-Crime Officer is responsible at a crime scene for:

- the collection of physical and trace evidence;
- the collection of comparative samples, as required;

  and

277 See section 22 of the *Arrest Act* (Ch. 339).

- making an assessment as to whether particular forensic specialists should attend the crime scene.

However, a Scenes-of-Crime Officer will not necessarily be available and in such circumstances the evidence should still be collected.[278]

[3.0] TYPES OF EVIDENCE

[3.1] INTRODUCTION

An investigating officer needs to understand the types of evidence that may be present at a crime scene.

[3.2] PHYSICAL EVIDENCE

The term 'physical evidence' is used to describe:

> any item, large or small, in any state (solid, liquid or gas) and in any condition (living, dead or inanimate, for example, plants).

Therefore, physical evidence can take any form.

[3.3] TRACE EVIDENCE

The term 'trace evidence' is used to describe:

> physical evidence that is very small, such as hairs, fibres and paint particulars.

Such evidence is normally invisible to the naked eye.

In the case of a offender, it is very good evidence because the offender does not realise it is there and therefore, will not attempt to dispose of it.

Generally trace evidence can be obtained from the clothing of the offender.

[4.0] EVIDENTIARY VALUE

All forensic evidence is of evidentiary evidence.

The value of forensic evidence is however determined by how useful it is in:

- verifying that an offence has been committed;
- identifying the person responsible;

[278] Refer also to the chapter titled 'Exhibits'.

and

- exonerating any other person who may be under suspicion.

A Court must however be satisfied not only as to its relevancy, but also its reliability.[279]

[5.0] BIOLOGICAL EVIDENCE

[5.1] BLOOD

In most crimes of violence, such as a homicide offence, sexual offence and an offence involving a shooting or serious assault, blood will be either from the victim or the offender or both.

Blood can be used to:

- determine the sequence of events at a crime scene;

  and

- tie a suspect to a particular crime scene.

Sometimes the location of a bloodstain at a crime scene is obvious, while at other times a detailed search is required using chemical screening tests for blood.

These tests can be carried out by a crime scene examiner or a biologist from the National Forensic Science Centre.

With blood splatter, contact smears or pools of blood are present at a crime scene. An interpretation of the events that caused them should be attempted.

Blood splatter interpretation is conducted by staff at the National Forensic Science Centre.

The types of information that can be obtained from blood splatter are as follows:

- the origin of blood (whether from the victim or the offender);
- the distance between the impact area and its origin at the time of the commission of the offence;
- the type and direction of impact;
- the number of blows struck;
- the position of the victim during blows;

[279] See *Daubert v Merrell Dow Pharmaceuticals Inc* (1993) 509 US 579,[1993] USSC 99.

- the movement and direction of the offender and victim during the commission of the offence and after;

  and

- which hand the blows were struck with.

Blood typing or grouping is conducted by the forensic scientists at the National Forensic Science Centre.

To identify the origin of the blood, a comparison sample must be obtained from:

- the suspect[280];

  and

- the victim.

[5.2] HAIR

Hairs are found at any crime scene, from homicides to break and enters.

At the point of entry to a crime scene there may be a few strands of hair caught on the window or on a shrub outside.

Hairs most commonly found at a crime scene are those from the head and pubic region.

Forensic scientists at the National Forensic Science Centre are, to a limited degree, able to distinguish animal hair from human hair and, in most cases, determine from what part of the body the hair comes from.

[5.3] SALIVA

Saliva is an excellent source of DNA.

DNA stands for deoxyribonucleic acid and is found in most of the body's cells.

The probability of two people having the same DNA profile is statistically almost incomprehensible.

However, the extraction of DNA from blood, semen or other bodily tissue is a very complex process and can be very expensive.

---

280 See section 22 of the *Arrest Act* (Ch. 339).

DNA analysis is currently not yet available in Papua New Guinea. Any inquiries for such testing should be made through the National Forensic Science Centre.

[5.4] SEMINAL FLUID

Although blood is the most commonly encountered physiological fluid at a crime scene, seminal fluid is a close second largely due to its high incidence at offences of a sexual nature.

Seminal fluid consists of a highly proteinaceous serum that contains a large number of spermatozoa.

Seminal stains will occur on the clothing of a victim and offender, especially the underclothing and on the bedding or surface where the sexual act occurred.

There may be sample on the victim that may be taken by a medical practitioner.

In all cases, where possible, the entire exhibit should be collected and transported to the National Forensic Science Centre.

The identification of seminal fluid is only a reliable indication of recent sexual activity.

[5.5] OTHER BIOLOGICAL EVIDENCE

Other biological evidence that may be useful as evidence includes skin, muscle, fat, organs, intestines and bones.

Limited tests can be carried out at the National Forensic Science Centre and tests on stomach contents, liver, kidneys, etc will have to be carried out overseas.

[6.0] CHEMICAL EVIDENCE

[6.1] ACCELERANTS

Accelerants are flammable liquids used by arsonists to accelerate the spread of a fire.

The examination of a fire scene by a forensic officer is to determine:

- the origin of the fire;

  and

- the cause of the fire.

Once the forensic officer has determined the origin of the fire, samples of debris are collected from that area.

These samples are subjected to laboratory tests at the National Forensic Science Centre.

The presence of flammable liquids in fire debris as well as other indicators present at a crime scene may be evidence to support the offence.

[6.2] EXPLOSIVES

Determining the size of an explosion scene can be quite difficult because the radius of interest is not always obvious.

During an explosion the explosive substance generates a fireball of expanding burning gas.

The blast can carry with it small particles of unexploded matter.

Depending on the explosive used, this unexploded matter has often been located on lightweight materials, such as fibres.

Blank and background samples and swabs need to be collected for analysis at the National Forensic Science Centre.

[6.3] GLASS

Glass comparisons are commonly used in cases of break and enter and wilful damage.

When a person breaks a glass window, either:

- with their body;

  or

- with an instrument,

glass is transferred to their clothing and shoes.

A comparison glass sample must be collected from the broken window or object.

If more than one window or item is broken, separate samples of glass must be collected from all possible sources.

Glass can be analysed by scientific officers using a GRIM (glass refractive index management machine) that measures the refractive index and a SEM (scanning electron microscope) that measures elemental composition.

However, such examinations are currently not yet available in Papua New Guinea.

[6.4] GREASE AND OIL

Grease and oil can be associated with a stolen vehicle and arson.

It is possible to give evidence, with absolute confidence, that two oils are different and of different origins.

The extent to which two oils can be said to different depends on a large number of variables.

The presence of unburnt oil can be of real use depending on sample preservation and sampling.

Limited examination facilities are available at the National Forensic Science Centre.

[6.5] GUNSHOT RESIDUE

In cases of shootings it is important to establish who fired the weapon.

When a firearm is discharged there are vaporized constituents of the priming composition, referred to as 'gunshot residue', that may be on the hands or clothing of the offender.

However, gunshot residue tests are currently not yet available in Papua New Guinea.

[6.6] PAINT

Paint comparison is useful in the investigation of cases of break and enter and wilful damage.

Paint transfer can occur from a door to a wrench (break and enter) or from a paint can to a wall (wilful damage).

Paint samples transfer can occur as a consequence of a smear, gaze, chip or spray.

A comparison (control) sample must be collected from the suspected source.

Paint samples are compared by staff at the National Forensic Science Centre microscopically.

Whilst such an examination is unable to prove that the paint chip on a wrench came from a particular door it can confirm whether paint of the same elemental composition as that on the door was found on the wrench.

Laboratory examination consists of microscopic examination, and in the case of a paint chip, layer number and type.

Whilst such an examination cannot be conducted at the National Forensic Science Centre it can be conducted at the UPNG Chemistry Department.

[6.7] SEXUAL LUBRICANT

Lubricants used in conjunction with an offence of a sexual nature, takes many forms and can be located in various places.

Some common lubricants include baby oil and vaseline.

In order to link people with this evidence there is the need for a comparative analysis. Preserving a crime scene, includes the victim and suspect.

Their clothing is required for such an analysis.

Whilst such a comparative analysis is currently not yet available in Papua New Guinea, evidentiary material should always be taken possession of.

[7.0] IMPRESSION EVIDENCE

[7.1] IMPERFECTIONS

Minute imperfections can be seen on a variety of objects, such as shoes or tools.

These imperfections will produce markings on other surfaces during normal use.

These markings are often characterised by the type of object used and, in many cases, are unique to that object.

Microscopic imperfections are the result either of manufacture, or random or accidental damage during use.

In order to leave a mark, the object must be harder than the surface on which it is applied.

[7.2] TYPES OF MARKS

[7.2.1] INTRODUCTION

There are two types of marks:

- compression;

  and

- scraping.

[7.2.2] COMPRESSION MARKS

Compression marks are left when an object is simply pressed into a surface capable of showing up the impression.

Examples of compression marks, include:

- footwear impressions;
- toolmarks;
- toothmarks;
- tyremarks;

  and
- impressions on a typed document.

[7.2.3] SCRAPING MARKS

Scraping marks are made by pressure combined with movement of the object across a surface.

The resulting mark possesses microscopic striations from the object.

Examples of scraping marks include:

- toolmarks with movement, such as tyre lever scratch marks on a safe;

  and
- ballistics, ie., marks on projectile fired from a firearm.

[7.3] FOOTWEAR IMPRESSIONS

Impressions of footwear at a crime scene may or may not be visible to the naked eye.

In some situations strong oblique light can help to see footwear impressions more clearly.

Shoe impressions can be found on counters, tables, chairs or papers.

A shoe impression in soil or fine powder on a smooth surface can be lifted with an electrostatic dust lifter, preserving the entire impression.

Such an examination can be carried out at the National Forensic Science Centre.

[7.4] TOOL MARKS

A tool can be identified as an individual tool by surface features, the result of the manufacturing process, wear and damage.

When a tool is applied to a surface it may leave a mark that has its own distinct features.

For example, during a break and enter, a screwdriver is used to jimmy open an aluminum window leaving a scratch or score mark on the metal frame. A cast of this mark, made using impression material suitable for forensic applications, can be taken and held for later comparison. If the screwdriver is found in the possession of a suspect, it can be used to produce test marks. Casts of these test marks can then be compared to the exhibit cast by means of a comparison microscope. This can identify the screwdriver as the tool used in the break and enter.

These same principles can be applied by the toolmark examiner to the identification of a wide variety of tools, including pliers, bolt cutters and knives.

Such examinations can be conducted at the National Forensic Science Centre.

[7.5] TOOTH MARKS

Tooth marks are mainly compression marks (although striation marks can occur) that occur in foodstuffs, such as applies, cheese, chewing gum or bread, or on the skin of a victim or offender.

The relative position of teeth, their width, the distance between teeth, the ridges on the edge of the teeth and any unusual characteristics can show in a bite mark.

It is sometimes possible to positively identify an offender from a bite mark.

Such an examination may be arranged with the assistance of the National Forensic Science Centre.

[7.6] TYRE MARKS

Tyre impressions left at a crime scene can provide information similar to that provided by footwear comparisons.

In most cases the characteristics of the tyre can be determined.

Such examinations can be carried out at the National Forensic Science Centre.

[7.7] TYPED-DOCUMENT IMPRESSIONS

An examination of a typed document is done at the Document Examination Centre of the National Forensic Science Centre.

The individual marks made by a typewriter may be unique to that particular typewriter.

These marks can show up on a typed document.

In some cases, the make and model of the typewriter can be determined from the typed document.

The document examiner will, in most cases, need the suspect typewriter for comparison.

Fingerprint examination can also be conducted on the typed document.

Usually this is done after the examination by the document examiner because the fingerprinting process may obscure the document to some extent.

[7.8] BALLISTICS[281]

[7.8.1] MARKS

The manufacturing process of firearm components, such as the barrel, firing pin, extractor and ejector, leave microscopic surface markings.

These markings have been found to be unique to each weapon, showing significant variation even between weapons manufactured consecutively.

When a round of ammunition is fired, marks corresponding to the microscopic marks on the weapon, may be left on the carriage case or projectile.

Accidental damage and wear may add to or alter the weapon's fingerprint over time.

When it is necessary to establish whether or not a particular weapon has been used in a shooting, the firearm examiner will compare the exhibit cartridge case or projectile to those test fired from the suspect weapon. These comparisons are carried out using a comparison microscope. This instrument allows two objects to be viewed simultaneously so that microscopic marks caused by firing can be compared and assessed. By this means a suspect weapon can be positively identified or excluded from an investigation.

The ballistics experts at the National Forensic Science Centre perform many other functions, not just the identification of a firearm. A ballistics expert may be involved in crime scene interpretation and determining the sequence of events at a crime scene.

---

[281] See also: section 6.5 'Gunshot Residue'.

This is done through:

- the use of chemical screening tests for lead or copper projectiles;
- calculating trajectories by means of the relative locations of areas of gunshot damage and/or the appearance of areas of gunshot damage;
- calculating the relative position of offenders and victims, by blood splatter interpretation, including blood splatter on the clothing of an offender and location of cartridge cases;

  and

- determining the type of weapon used by identifying cartridge cases or projectiles from the appearance of wounds or property damage.

[7.8.2] FUNCTION TESTING OF A FIREARM

Allegations are frequently made about the functioning or safety aspects of a firearm involved in a shooting offence.

It may be suggested that:

- the firearm discharged when dropped or struck;

  or

- the components of the firearm may have malfunctioned.

A firearms examiner can perform tests on the firearm in order to determine whether it is prone to fire without operating the trigger.

Extensive test firing may be conducted to establish the frequency and nature of any malfunction.

[7.8.3] RANGE DETERMINATION

When a firearm is discharged, unburnt propellant powder, primer particles and soot emerge from the barrel along with the projectile.

Due to the small size of the individual particles they have a relatively short range (between 30 centimetres and 3 metres).

As a result, their presence in the vicinity of a wound or other gunshot damage may be used to determine the range from which the shot was fired.

In making this determination a firearms examiner will fire the suspect firearm against targets from varying ranges.

These range determinations are essential in cases where the range is a critical factor, such as when a shot is alleged to have been fired in the course of a struggle.

[8.0] FINGERPRINTS[282]

[8.1] INTRODUCTION

Fingerprint evidence can be of prime importance to an investigating officer.

Its ability to positively identify people who have come into contact with:

- surfaces at a crime scene;

  or

- objects connected to the crime scene

is widely acknowledged.

Fingerprints should be taken for comparison purposes.

[8.2] STATUTORY PROVISION

Section 21 of the *Arrest Act* (Ch. 339) enables a police officer to take the fingerprints and palm prints of any person on a charge of committing an offence.

[8.3] GENERAL PRINCIPLES

The evidence of fingerprints or palm prints alone is sufficient evidence of identity to support a conviction, subject to:

- their location;

  and

- the circumstances of the case.[283]

---

[282] As regards the law in relation to 'Fingerprint Evidence', refer also to the chapter titled 'Evidence' in the text titled 'Injia on Criminal Practice and Procedure in Papua New Guinea and the Pacific'.

[283] See *R v Koito-Gaocatal* [1967–1968] PNGLR 217, [1967] PGSC 26; *The State v Jack Kumul Ure Kore* (1999) N1856 and *The State v Jupui Kapera* (1986) N567.

See also: *Blacker v R* (1910) 10 CLR 604; *R v Castleton* (1910) 3 Cr App R 74 and *R v Court* (1960) 44 Cr App R 242.

The fact of the individuality of the corrugations of the skin on the fingers of the human hand is recognised as to require very little, if any, evidence of it.[284]

A fingerprint is, therefore, in reality an unforgeable signature.[285]

A Court may take 'judicial notice[286]' that no two people have identical fingerprints.[287]

If there are fewer than eight similar ridge characteristics, it is highly unlikely that a Court will exercise its discretion to admit such evidence and, save in wholly exceptional circumstances, the prosecution should not seek to adduce such evidence.

If there are eight or more similar ridge characteristics, a Court may exercise its discretion in favour of admitting the evidence.

How the discretion is exercised will depend on all the circumstances of the case, including in particular:

- the expertise of the fingerprint expert;
- the experience of the fingerprint expert;
- the number of similar ridge characteristics;
- whether there are dissimilar characteristics;
- the size of the print relied on, in that the same number of similar ridge characteristics may be more compelling in a fingerprint of print than in an entire print;

  and

- the quality and clarity of the print on the item relied on, which may involve, for example, consideration of possible injury to the person who left the print, as well as factors such as smearing or contamination.[288]

---

284 See *Parker v R* (1912) 14 CLR 681.

285 See *Parker v R* (1912) 14 CLR 681.

286 Refer also the section titled 'Judicial Notice' in the chapter titled 'Court Procedure' in the text titled 'Injia on Criminal Practice and Procedure in Papua New Guinea and the Pacific'.

287 See *The State v Jupui Kapera* (1986) N567.

288 See *R v Koito-Gaocatal* [1967–1968] PNGLR 217, [1967] PGSC 26.

See also: *R v Buckley* (1999) 163 JP 561.

[9.0] MECHANICAL EXAMINATION

In cases of 'Dangerous Driving' and 'Driving Without Due Care And Attention' arrangements should be made to have the vehicle driven by the offender mechanically examined for defects.[289]

[10.0] PHOTOGRAPHIC EVIDENCE[290]

Photographs are the best means of providing a description of a crime scene to a Court.

It does not matter who takes a photograph.

The issue of admissibility is:

> whether the witness who is seeking to tender the photograph as an exhibit is able to give evidence as to what the photograph depicts.

[11.0] HANDWRITING EVIDENCE[291]

[11.1] STATUTORY PROVISION

Section 31 of the *Evidence Act* (Ch. 48) states:

> 'A comparison of a disputed hand-writing with a sample of hand-writng proved, to the satisfaction of the court, to be genuine may be made by witnesses, and the hand-writings and the testimony of the witnesses respecting them may be submitted to the court as evidence of the genuineness or otherwise of the hand-writing in dispute'.

---

[289] As regards the law in relation to the offences of 'Dangerous Driving' and 'Driving Without Due Care And Attention', refer to the chapter titled 'Traffic Offences' in the text titled 'Injia on Criminal Offences in Papua New Guinea and the Pacific'.

[290] As regards the law in relation to 'Photographic Evidence', refer also to the chapter titled 'Evidence' in the text titled 'Injia on Criminal Practice and Procedure in Papua New Guinea and the Pacific'.

[291] As regards the law in relation to 'Handwriting Evidence', refer also to the chapter titled 'Evidence' in the text titled 'Injia on Criminal Practice and Procedure in Papua New Guinea and the Pacific'.

[11.2] GENERAL PRINCIPLES[292]

The issue whether an accused person is the author of a particular document can be proved by:

- an admission by the accused person;
- a witness who observed the accused person write the document[293];
- the evidence of a witness who had regularly corresponded with the accused person and who is able to recognise the handwriting of the accused person to the satisfaction of the Court[294];

  or

- the opinion evidence of a handwriting expert[295].

The Court must be satisfied 'beyond reasonable doubt[296]' that the disputed writing is genuine.[297]

A document examiner at the National Forensic Science Centre is competent to:

- make a determination as to whether a document is forged;

  and

- make a determination as to who is the author of a particular document, provided a suitable comparative document is provided.

---

[292] See also: *R v Smith (Hereford) (a)* (1909) 3 Cr App R 87 at 90.

[293] See *R v O'Brien* (1912) 7 Cr App R 29 and *R v McCartney and Hansen* (1928) 20 Cr App R 179.

[294] See *R v O'Brien* (1912) 7 Cr App R 29.

[295] See *R v Rickard* (1918) 13 Cr App R 140; *R v Tilley and Tilley* (1961) 45 Cr App R 360 at 364 and *R v Smith* (1968) 52 Cr App R 648, [1968] Crim LR 674.

As regards the law in relation to 'Opinion Evidence', refer also to the chapter titled 'Evidence' in the text titled 'Injia on Criminal Practice and Procedure in Papua New Guinea and the Pacific'.

[296] Refer also to the chapter titled 'Proof Of Issues' in the text titled 'Injia on Criminal Practice and Procedure in Papua New Guinea and the Pacific'.

[297] See *R v Ewing* [1983] QB 1039, (1983) 77 Cr App R 47.

Although expert evidence is not essential for a Court to come to a conclusion on a comparison of disputed handwriting, a Court must warn itself of the dangers involved in proceeding without expert testimony.[298]

A photocopy of a disputed writing may be used for the purpose of comparison, if there is evidence that the original has been lost.[299]

[12.0] CANNABIS IDENTIFICATION

[12.1] INTRODUCTION[300]

In general cannabis and marijuana refer to the same thing.[301] The substance taken out of a cannabis plant is a drug and a part of a cannabis plant in its natural state is also a dangerous drug. Marijuana is just another name for cannabis.[302]

A marijuana plant is in fact a plant of the genus cannabis from the flowers and leaves of which is derived the hallucinogenic drug variously known as Indian Hemp, hashish, bhang, ganga, charas, churrus, marijuana or pot. It is usually prepared in the form of cigarettes, known as 'reefers'. This narcotic is a dangerous drug.[303]

[12.2] PROOF

[12.2.1] INTRODUCTION

There is no provision in the *Dangerous Drugs Act* (Ch. 228) that permits the tendering of a certificate.

---

298 See *The State v Baine* [1990] 1 PNGLR 1 and *R v Magalu* [1974] PNGLR 188, [1974] PGSC 21.

See also: *R v Derrick* (1910) 5 Cr App R 162.

See however: *R v O'Sullivan* (1969) 53 Cr App R 274 and *R v Tilley and Tilley* (1961) 45 Cr App R 360.

299 See *Lockheed Arabia v Owen* [1993] 3 WLR 468, (1993) 3 All ER 641, [1993] QB 806.

300 As regards the law in relation to 'Drug Offences', refer also to the chapter titled 'Drug Offences' in the text titled 'Injia on Criminal Offences in Papua New Guinea and the Pacific'.

301 See *Mickey Wassey v The Police* (2005) N2922, [2005] PGNC 70.

302 See *Angel Anis v Jayjay Waiyo* (1990) N18.

303 See *Richard Cheong v Vincent Nemil* [1981] PNGLR 472 at 473.

The prosecution may either:

- rely on an admission by the accused person;
- rely on a Formal Admission[304];
- call the analyst to give evidence[305];
- rely on the tendering of an affidavit[306] subject to the provisions of sections 34 and 35 of the *Evidence Act* (Ch. 48) with the consent of the accused person and the Court;

  or

- rely on the opinion evidence of a suitably qualified police officer by virtue of his or her personal and professional experience in dealing with the alleged dangerous drug.

[12.2.2] AFFIDAVIT

An affidavit from an analyst must state:

- his or her qualifications for identifying cannabis and its derivatives;
- the recognised method or methods used for such identification;
- the steps taken on the particular occasion;

  and

- the results, some conclusion as to what it was in the material subjected to analysis which constituted the cannabis and in particular the quantity of cannabis identified should have been clearly stated.[307]

---

304 Refer also to the section titled 'Formal Admission' in the chapter titled 'Court Procedure' in the text titled 'Injia on Criminal Practice and Procedure in Papua New Guinea and the Pacific'.

305 In that regard contact the Forensic Biology Section, National Forensic Science Centre at Port Moresby or the Papua New Guinea Forest Research Institute at Lae.

306 See Appendix 11.

307 See *Maxwell Arthur Schliebs v H Singh* [1981] PNGLR 264 at 371.

However, for an affidavit from an analyst to be admissible the prosecution must prove continuity of the dangerous drug from:

- the position where it was located;

  to

- when it was analysed.

The prosecution must therefore be able to prove which person/s had possession of the dangerous drug between those locations.

[12.2.3] OPINION EVIDENCE

In order for the prosecution to rely on the opinion evidence[308] of a police officer as to the identification of cannabis the following questions need to be addressed in their statement:

- What do you believe it is?

Professional Experience

- How long have you been a police officer?
- Have you previously arrested accused persons in relation to cases involving marijuana under section 3 of the *Dangerous Drugs Act* (Ch. 228) in which the accused persons were convicted?
- How many cases were there approximately?
- Is what that is alleged to be in the possession of the accused person the same leafy material as those cases involving marijuana which those accused persons were convicted?
- Are there any similar characteristics between the marijuana in those cases and the case involving this accused person?
- What are those characteristics?

Personal Experience

- Have you observed any person consume marijuana in your presence in your personal life?
- Why do you believe that it was marijuana?

---

[308] Refer also to the section titled 'Lay Person' in the chapter titled 'Evidence' in the text titled 'Injia on Criminal Practice and Procedure in Papua New Guinea and the Pacific'.

- How was it consumed?
- Were you able to observe what was being consumed?
- Are there any similar characteristics between the marijuana consumed in those circumstances and the case involving this accused person?
- What are those characteristics?

[1.0] CONSTITUTIONAL PROVISIONS[309]

Section 35 of the *Constitution of the Independent State of Papua New Guinea* states:

'(1) No person shall be deprived of his life intentionally except–

(a) in execution of a sentence of a court following his conviction of an offence for which the penalty of death is prescribed by law; or

(b) as the result of the use of force to such an extent as is reasonable in the circumstances of the case and is permitted by any other law–

(i) for the defence of any person from violence[310]; or

(ii) in order to effect a lawful arrest[311] or to prevent the escape of a person lawfully detained[312]; or

(iii) for the purpose of suppressing a riot, an insurrection or a mutiny[313]; or

---

309 See also: section 178 of the *Constitution of the Autonomous Region of Bougainville*.

310 The force used must be reasonable in the circumstances of the case *and* permitted by any other law.

In relation to the use of force the provisions of sections 269, 270 and 271 of the *Criminal Code* (Ch. 262) must be considered.

Refer to the subsection titled 'Defences' in the chapter titled 'Offences Against The Person' in the text titled 'Injia on Criminal Offences in Papua New Guinea and the Pacific'.

See also: International Human Rights Instruments titled 'Basic Principles on the Use of Force and Firearms by Law Enforcement Officials' and 'Basic Principles on the Use of Force and Firearms by Law Enforcement Officials'.

311 The force used must be reasonable in the circumstances of the case *and* permitted by any other law.

In relation to the use of force the provisions of section 14(1)(c) and (2) of the *Arrest Act* (Ch. 339) must be considered.

312 The force used must be reasonable in the circumstances of the case *and* permitted by any other law.

In relation to the use of force the provisions of section 14(1)(c) and (2) of the *Arrest Act* (Ch. 262) must be considered.

313 The force used must be reasonable in the circumstances of the case *and* permitted by any other law.

In relation to the use of force the provisions of sections 259 and 260 of the *Criminal Code* (Ch. 262) must be considered.

Those statutory provisions however do not relate to the suppression of an insurrection or a mutiny.

(iv) in order to prevent him from committing an offence[314]; or

(v) for the purpose of suppressing piracy or terrorism or similar acts[315]; or

(c) as the result of a lawful act of war.

(2) Nothing in Subsection (1)(b) relieves any person from any liability at law in respect of the killing of another[316]'.

Section 41 states:

'(1) Notwithstanding anything to the contrary in any other provision of any law, any act that is done under a valid law but in the particular case–

(a) is harsh or oppressive; or

(b) is not warranted by, or is disproportionate to, the requirements of the particular circumstances or of the particular case; or

(c) is otherwise not, in the particular circumstances, reasonably justifiable in a democratic society having a proper regard for the rights and dignity of mankind,
is an unlawful act.

(2) The burden of showing that Subsection (1)(a), (b) or (c) applies in respect of an act is on the party alleging it, and may be discharged on the balance of probabilities.

(3) Nothing in this section affects the operation of any other law under which an act may be held to be unlawful or invalid'.

---

[314] The force used must be reasonable in the circumstances of the case *and* permitted by any other law.

In relation to the use of force the provisions of section 264 of the *Criminal Code* (Ch. 262) must be considered.

An officer who intentionally shoots a person in order to prevent him or her from escaping and in doing so causes that person's death is guilty of the offence of 'Murder', see *The State v John Kule* (2009) N3619.

[315] There is no statutory provision that relates specifically to the suppression of piracy, terrorism or similar acts.

See Division 1 of Part V of the *Criminal Code* (Ch. 262).

[316] As regards the law in relation to 'Homicide Offences', refer to the chapter titled 'Offences Against The Person' in the text titled 'Injia on Criminal Offences in Papua New Guinea and the Pacific'.

Section 42 states (in part):

(1) No person shall be deprived of his personal liberty except –

(c) by reason of his failure to comply with the order of a court made to secure the fulfilment of an obligation (other than a contractual obligation) imposed upon him by law; or

(d) upon reasonable suspicion of his having committed, or being about to commit, an offence; or

(e) for the purpose of bringing him before a court in execution of the order of a court; [...]

(2) A person who is arrested or detained –

(a) shall be informed promptly, in a language that he understands, of the reasons for his arrest or detention and of any charge against him[317]; and

(b) shall be permitted whenever practicable to communicate without delay and in private with a member of his family or a personal friend, and with a lawyer of his choice (including the Public Solicitor if he is entitled to legal aid)[318]; and

(c) shall be given adequate opportunity to give instructions to a lawyer of his choice in the place in which he is detained,

and shall be informed immediately on his arrest or detention of his rights under this subsection.

(3) A person who is arrested or detained –

(a) for the purpose of being brought before a court in the execution of an order of a court; or

(b) upon reasonable suspicion of his having committed, or being about to commit, an offence,

---

[317] See section 14 of the *Arrest Act* (Ch. 339).

[318] Refer also to the section titled 'Right To Representation' in the chapter titled 'Rights Of An Accused Person' in the text titled 'Injia on Criminal Practice and Procedure in Papua New Guinea and the Pacific'.

shall, unless he is released, be brought without delay before a court or a judicial officer and, in a case referred to in paragraph (b), shall not be further held in custody in connection with the offence except by order of a court or judicial officer.[319]

(4) The necessity or desirability of interrogating the person concerned or other persons, or any administrative requirement or convenience, is not a good ground for failing to comply with Subsection (3), but exigencies of travel which in the circumstances are reasonable may, without derogating any other protection available to the person concerned, be such a ground.

(5) Where complaint is made to the National Court or a Judge that a person is unlawfully or unreasonably detained –

(a) the National Court or a Judge shall inquire into the complaint and order the person concerned to be brought before it or him; and

(b) unless the Court or Judge is satisfied that the detention is lawful, and in the case of a person being detained on remand pending his trial does not constitute an unreasonable detention having regard, in particular, to its length, the Court or a Judge shall order his release either unconditionally or subject to such conditions as the Court or Judge thinks fit.

(6) A person arrested or detained for an offence (other than treason or wilful murder as defined by an Act of the Parliament) is entitled to bail at all times from arrest or detention to acquittal or conviction unless the interests of justice otherwise require.[320]

(7) Where a person to whom Subsection (6) applies is refused bail –

(a) the court or person refusing bail shall, on request by the person concerned or his representative, state in writing the reason for the refusal; and

(b) the person or his representative may apply to the Supreme Court or the National Court in a summary manner for his release'.

---

[319] Refer also to:

- the section titled 'Bail' in the chapter titled 'Case File'; and
- the section titled 'Right To Bail' in the chapter titled 'Rights Of An Accused Person' in the text titled 'Injia on Criminal Practice and Procedure in Papua New Guinea and the Pacific'.

[320] Refer also to:

- the section titled 'Bail' in the chapter titled 'Case File'; and
- the section titled 'Right To Bail' in the chapter titled 'Rights Of An Accused Person' in the text titled 'Injia on Criminal Practice and Procedure in Papua New Guinea and the Pacific'.

Section 44 states (in part):

> 'No person shall be subjected to the search of his person or property or to entry of his premises, except to the extent that the exercise of that right is regulated or restricted by a law–
>
> (a) that makes reasonable provision for a search or entry –
>
> (i) under an order made by a court; or
>
> (ii) under a warrant for a search issued by a court or judicial officer on reasonable grounds, supported by oath or affirmation, particularly describing the purpose of the search'.

Section 49 states:

> 'Every person has the right to reasonable privacy in respect of his private and family life, his communications with other persons and his personal papers and effects, except to the extent that the exercise of that right is regulated or restricted by a law that complies with Section 38 (*general qualifications on qualified rights*)'.

[2.0] GENERAL PRINCIPLES

Whilst under the underlying law the obligations and duties of all police officers, include taking all necessary steps to:

- protect life;
- prevent offences from being committed[321];
- detect offences[322] and bring offenders to justice[323];
- keep the peace[324];

  and
- protect property[325]

a police officer must at all times act in compliance with the law.

---

[321] See *Nogo Suzuke and another v The State*, WS No. 951/94(H).

[322] See *Nogo Suzuke and another v The State*, WS No. 951/94(H).

[323] See *Nogo Suzuke and another v The State*, WS No. 951/94(H).

[324] See *Nogo Suzuke and another v The State*, WS No. 951/94(H).

[325] See *The State v Smith William* (1995) N1380.

A person may not be deprived of his or her personal liberty, except as authorised by the law, including:

- to prevent the continuance or renewal of a breach of the peace[326], provided that the force used is:

    - reasonably necessary for its prevention;

      and

    - reasonably proportioned to the danger to be apprehended from its continuance or renewal.[327]

  Therefore, in relation to a breach of the peace a person may be detained without the need to be arrested;

- upon reasonable suspicion that a person has committed or being about to commit an offence[328];

  When the situation calls for the use of force to prevent the commission of an offence, the force used must be:

    - justifiable;

    - reasonable;

      and

---

[326] A breach of the peace arises where:

- there is an actual assault;

  or

- public alarm and excitement are caused by a wrongful act, see *Siwi Kurondo v Lindsay Dabiri* (1980) N258 and *Utala Samana v Demas Waki* [1984] PNGLR 8 at 14-15, [1984] PGSC 11. See also: *R v Howell* [1982] 1 QB 416, [1981] 3 All ER 383, [1981] 3 WLR 501, [1981] Crim LR 697, (1981) 73 Cr App R 31 at 37.

Mere annoyance, and disturbance or insult to a person or abusive language of great heat and fury without personal violence, are not generally sufficient, see *Siwi Kurondo v Lindsay Dabiri* (1980) N258 and *Utala Samana v Demas Waki* [1984] PNGLR 8 at 14-15, [1984] PGSC 11. See also: *R v Howell* [1982] 1 QB 416, [1981] 3 All ER 383, [1981] 3 WLR 501, [1981] Crim LR 697, (1981) 73 Cr App R 31 at 37.

[327] See section 41 of the *Constitution of the Independent State of Papua New Guinea* and section 258 of the *Criminal Code* (Ch. 262).

[328] See section 42(1)(d) of the *Constitution of the Independent State of Papua New Guinea*.

  - not excessive.[329]

- for the purpose of bringing a person before a Court in execution of an order of a Court[330];

  and

- for the purpose of a search as is regulated or restricted by a law331.

All persons deprived of their liberty shall be treated with humanity and with respect for the inherent dignity of the human person.[332]

Therefore, even when applying force in the apprehension of any person a police officer is not to apply as much force as he or she may choose.[333]

Excessive force is force beyond that reasonably necessary in the circumstances of any particular case, including:

- any force when no force was necessary;
- more force than was reasonably necessary;

  and

- any force when the necessity of using force was no longer necessary.

An officer must, at all times, only use the minimum amount of force necessary in the performance of his or her duty.

Section 281 of the *Criminal Code* (Ch. 262) states:

> 'Even where the use of force by one person to another is lawful, the use of more force than is justified by law under the circumstances is unlawful'.

A police officer who uses force that is unreasonable, and therefore:

- unjustified;

  and

- unlawful

329 See *The State v Smith William* (1995) N1380.

330 See section 42(1)(e) of the *Constitution of the Independent State of Papua New Guinea*.

331 See section 44 of the *Constitution of the Independent State of Papua New Guinea*.

332 See section 37(17) of the *Constitution of the Independent State of Papua New Guinea*.

333 See sections 244 and 281 of the *Criminal Code* (Ch. 262).

in the circumstances

- should be charged with the relevant criminal offence;
- should be charged with the relevant disciplinary offence;

  and

- depending on the circumstances, should be dismissed.

A non-violent method of apprehending an offender is to be attempted first[334], depending on the circumstances.

Force is to be used only when strictly necessary.[335]

No exceptions or excuses shall be allowed for unlawful use of force.[336]

Use of force is to be always proportional to lawful objectives.[337]

Restraint is to be exercised in the use of force.[338]

---

[334] See section 41 of the *Constitution of the Independent State of Papua New Guinea.*

See also: International Human Rights Instruments titled, 'Universal Declaration of Human Rights', Article 26 and 'International Convention on the Elimination of All Forms of Racial Discrimination', Articles 2 and 5.

[335] See section 41 of the *Constitution of the Independent State of Papua New Guinea.*

See also: International Human Rights Instruments titled, 'Universal Declaration of Human Rights', Articles 2 and 3; 'International Convention on the Elimination of All Forms of Racial Discrimination', Articles 2 and 5 and 'Code of Conduct for Law Enforcement Officials', Articles 1 and 2.

[336] See section 41 of the *Constitution of the Independent State of Papua New Guinea.*

See also: International Human Rights Instruments titled, 'International Covenant on Civil and Political Rights', Articles 2, 3 and 26; 'Convention on the Elimination of All Forms of Discrimination Against Women', Preambular paragraphs 5, 8, 9 and 10 and Articles 2(1)(e), 2(2) and 5(e); 'Convention on the Elimination of All Forms of Discrimination Against Women', Preambular paragraphs 3, 9 and 14 and Articles 2(d)-(f), 3, 5(a) and 7(b) and 'Code of Conduct for Law Enforcement Officials', Preambular paragraph 8(a).

[337] See section 41 of the *Constitution of the Independent State of Papua New Guinea.*

See also: International Human Rights Instruments titled, 'Universal Declaration of Human Rights', Article 3 and 'International Covenant on Civil and Political Rights', Article 9(1).

[338] See section 41 of the *Constitution of the Independent State of Papua New Guinea.*

See also: International Human Rights Instruments titled, 'Universal Declaration of Human Rights', Article 10 and 'International Covenant on Civil and Political Rights', Article 14.

Damage and injury are to be minimised whenever force has to be used.[339]

An officer must not abuse his or her powers or act arbitrarily.[340]

[3.0] ARREST AND DETAIN

[3.1] INTRODUCTION[341]

A police officer has the same powers as a Constable under the underlying law[342], except as those powers are modified by or under an Act.[343]

The following have been abolished:

- all powers at common law to arrest a person;

  and

[339] See International Human Rights Instruments titled, 'Universal Declaration of Human Rights', Article 11(1) and 'International Covenant on Civil and Political Rights', Article 14(2).

[340] See *The State v Smith William* (1995) N1380.

[341] **Citizen's Power To Arrest**

A civilian may arrest an offender without warrant for committing an offence the penalty for which is imprisonment, subject to section 5 of the *Arrest Act* (Ch. 339) and may aid a police officer in effecting an arrest.

See also: section 6 of that Act.

Any person who is a witness to a crime may affect citizen's arrest and detain the person, but must use reasonable force and must convey the person arrested to a police station as soon as possible, see *Fama Sogio v Johon Negrefa and The State* (1996) N1482.

A citizen witnessing a crime being committed has no legal obligation to stop or prevent it, but he or she does have the standing to effect a citizen's arrest, see *Steamships Trading Company Ltd v Garamut Enterprises Ltd* (2000) N1959 and *McKenzie v The State* (1998) SC596.

See also: L. Kalinoe, Citizen's Arrests and the Lawfulness of Routine Searches by Security Guards: *McKenzie v The State* (1998) SC596, [1998] MLJ 8, [1998-99] 26 MLJ 178.

Juvenile Courts Act

In relation to:

- the detention of an infant (under the age of seven years);

  and

- the arrest of a juvenile (under the age of 18 years),

refer to the section titled 'Arrest and Detention' in the chapter titled 'Juvenile Offenders'.

[342] Refer also to the chapter titled 'Sources Of Law' in the text titled 'Injia on Criminal Practice and Procedure in Papua New Guinea and the Pacific'.

[343] See section 140 of the *Police Act 1998*.

- all duties and responsibilities imposed by the common law in relation to the arrest of a person.[344]

There are civil remedies if a police officer wrongfully exercises his or her power to arrest and detain.[345]

An accused person who is arrested, held in custody but is not charged, is thereby falsely imprisoned and may seek damages from the arresting officer and the State pursuant to section 57 of the *Constitution of the Independent State of Papua New Guinea*.[346]

A police officer may arrest an accused person, with or without a warrant, subject to:

- the provisions of sections 35 and 42 of the *Constitution of the Independent State of Papua New Guinea*;

- the provisions of the *Arrest Act* (Ch. 339).[347]

  All statutory provisions that provided the power to arrest passed prior to the commencement date of the *Arrest Act* (Ch. 339) in 1977 were impliedly repealed by that Act upon its commencement.[348]

  Therefore, for example section 40 of the *Motor Traffic Act* (Ch. 243) was impliedly repealed in 1977;

  and

---

[344] See section 30 of the *Arrest Act* (Ch. 339), subject to section 24 'Contempt of Parliament' of that Act.

[345] See *The State v Andrew Maurup* (1991) N1033.

See also: section 26 of the *Arrest Act* (Ch. 339), section 22 of the *Juvenile Courts Act 1991* and the provisions of the *Claims By and Against the State Act 1996*.

[346] See for example, *Kawi Yawi v Torepa Nenga; Anton Sinawai and The State* (2002) N2209.

See also: section 26 of the *Arrest Act* (Ch. 339).

[347] The *Arrest Act* (Ch. 339) applies to and is in addition to an arrest for any offence whether made by or under that Act or by any other law, other than in relation to the *Civil Aviation Act 2000* or the offence referred to as Contempt of Parliament, see section 2 of that Act.

The provisions of the *Arrest Act* (Ch. 339) that specify the circumstances in which a person may be arrested are in addition to and not in derogation of a provision of any other Act or subordinate enactment which confers a power of arrest, see section 23 of that Act.

[348] See *State v Kiap Bonga* [1988-89] PNGLR 360.

Refer also to the chapter titled 'Repeals' in the text titled 'Injia on Statutory Interpretation in Papua New Guinea and the Pacific'.

- specific provisions of statutes that provide the power to arrest that commenced after the commencement date of the *Arrest Act* (Ch. 339)[349].

Furthermore section 133 of the *Criminal Code* (Ch. 262) states:

> 'A person who, having arrested another person on a charge of an offence, wilfully delays taking him before a magistrate to be dealt with according to law is guilty of a misdemeanour.
>
> Penalty[350]: Imprisonment for a term not exceeding two years'.

As regards a breach of the peace[351], section 258 of the *Criminal Code* (Ch. 262) states:

> 'It is lawful for a person who witnesses a breach of the peace to interfere to prevent the continuance or renewal of it, and to use such force as is –
>
> (a) reasonably necessary for its prevention; and
>
> (b) reasonably proportioned to the danger to be apprehended from its continuance or renewal'.

Therefore, in relation to a breach of the peace a person may be detained without the need to be arrested.

---

[349] See *The State v Sedeka Biyama* (2008) N3532, [2008] PGNC 175 and *The State v Natpalau Tulong* (1994) N1297.

[350] This is an indictable offence [see section 3(2) of the *Criminal Code* (Ch. 262)] that cannot be dealt with summarily [see section 420(1) of the *Criminal Code* (Ch. 262)].

Refer also to the chapter titled 'Classification Of Offences' in the text titled 'Injia on Criminal Practice and Procedure in Papua New Guinea and the Pacific'.

[351] A breach of the peace arises where:

- there is an actual assault;

  or

- public alarm and excitement are caused by a wrongful act, see *Siwi Kurondo v Lindsay Dabiri* (1980) N258 and *Utala Samana v Demas Waki* [1984] PNGLR 8 at 14-15, [1984] PGSC 11. See also: *R v Howell* [1982] 1 QB 416, [1981] 3 All ER 383, [1981] 3 WLR 501, [1981] Crim LR 697, (1981) 73 Cr App R 31 at 37.

Mere annoyance, and disturbance or insult to a person or abusive language of great heat and fury without personal violence, are not generally sufficient, see *Siwi Kurondo v Lindsay Dabiri* (1980) N258 and *Utala Samana v Demas Waki* [1984] PNGLR 8 at 14-15, [1984] PGSC 11. See also: *R v Howell* [1982] 1 QB 416, [1981] 3 All ER 383, [1981] 3 WLR 501, [1981] Crim LR 697, (1981) 73 Cr App R 31 at 37.

[3.2] ARREST WITHOUT WARRANT[352]

Section 3 of the *Arrest Act* (Ch. 339) states:

'A policeman may, without warrant, arrest a person whom he believes on reasonable grounds[353] –

(a) is about to commit; or

(b) is committing; or

(c) has committed,

an offence[354]'.

Section 6 states:

'Notwithstanding Sections 3 and 5, where –

(a) a person is committing, is about to commit or has committed an offence relating to or affecting the use of a craft[355]; or

---

[352] As regards arresting an accused person for failing to comply with or contravening a bail condition, see section 4 of the *Arrest Act* (Ch. 339).

Refer also to:

- the section titled 'Bail' in the chapter titled 'Case File'; and
- the section titled 'Right to Bail' in the chapter titled 'Rights Of An Accused Person' in the text titled 'Injia on Criminal Practice and Procedure in Papua New Guinea and the Pacific'.

Citizen's Power To Arrest

Section 5 of the *Arrest Act* (Ch. 339) states:
'Subject to any requirements imposed by the law creating the offence, a person, other than a policeman, may, without warrant, arrest a person whom he believes on reasonable grounds–
(a) is committing; or
(b) has committed,
an offence for which the penalty is imprisonment'.

[353] 'For the purposes of this Act a person believes something on reasonable grounds if–
(a) he personally has that belief; and
(b) there are reasonable grounds for that belief', see section 1(3) of the *Arrest Act* (Ch. 339).

[354] Section 3(1) of the *Interpretation Act* (Ch. 2) defines the term 'offence' 'in relation to a law, as including:
'a breach or contravention of, or a failure to comply with, the law'.

[355] Section 1(1) of the *Arrest Act* (Ch. 339) defines the term 'craft' as meaning:
'an aircraft or vessel'.

(b) the person in command of a craft suspects on reasonable grounds that a person is committing, is about to commit or has committed an offence relating to or affecting the use of that craft,

the person in command of the craft or a person authorised by him may arrest that person without warrant'.

[3.3] WARRANT OF ARREST

[3.3.1] DUTY OF MEMBERS OF POLICE FORCE

Section 274 of the *District Courts Act* (Ch. 40) states:

'All members of the Police Force shall obey the warrants, orders and directions of Magistrates granted, given or done, and shall perform their several offices and duties in respect of those offices under the pains and penalties to which a member of the Police Force is liable for neglect of duty'.

[3.3.2] ISSUANCE

[A] CRIMINAL PRACTICE RULES

Order 3, Division 3 of the *Criminal Practice Rules 1987* states (in part):

'10. An application for a warrant to arrest a person may be made –

(a) Where an indictment has been presented against such person who has failed to appear for his trial, by production to the judge of the original indictment or a copy thereof, without other evidence; or

(b) Where an information has been presented by leave by order of the Court, at the time of granting leave or by evidence on Oath[356] showing –

(1) that the accused is likely to abscond; or

(2) that his arrest is necessary in the interests of justice; or

11. A warrant issued under Rule 10 shall be in Form 3'.

Order 3, Division 5 states (in part):

'17. Upon proof by affidavit or otherwise that a convicted person who entered into a recognizance as ordered by the Court is in breach of the conditions of the recognizance, the Court may issue a warrant for his arrest.

---

[356] Section 3(1) of the *Interpretation Act* (Ch. 2) defines the term 'oath' as including the making of a solemn declaration or affirmation.

18. A person arrested upon warrant issued under Rule 17 shall –

(a) be brought before the Court or a Judge as soon as possible; or

(b) if compliance with sub-rule (*a*) is not possible, then the person arrested shall be brought before a Magistrate to be dealt with according to law.

19. A warrant under Rule 17 shall be in accordance with Form 8'.

[B] DISTRICT COURTS ACT

Section 49 of the *District Courts Act* (Ch. 40) states:

'(1) Where an information is laid before a Magistrate –

(a) that a person is suspected of having committed an indictable offence[357] in the country; or

(b) that a person charged with having committed an indictable offence of which cognizance may be taken by the courts of Papua New Guinea is suspected of being in the country,

the Magistrate may, subject to Subsection (2), issue his warrant for the arrest of that person and cause him to be brought before a Court to answer to the information and to be further dealt with according to law.

(2) In a case referred to in Subsection (1), the Magistrate, if he thinks fit, instead of issuing his warrant in the first instance for the arrest of the person charged, may proceed by summons and issue a summons against the person charged.

(3) Notwithstanding the issue of a summons, a Magistrate may issue his warrant at any time before or after the time specified in the summons for the appearance of the accused person'.

[357] Refer also to the chapter titled 'Classification Of Offences' in the text titled 'Injia on Criminal Practice and Procedure in Papua New Guinea and the Pacific'.

Section 50 states:

'Where an information is laid before a Magistrate that a person is guilty of, or is suspected of having committed, a simple offence[358] in the country, the Magistrate may, on oath[359] being made before him substantiating the matter of the information to his satisfaction, instead of issuing a summons, issue in the first instance his warrant to apprehend the accused person and cause him to be brought before a Court to answer to the information and to be further dealt with according to law'.

Section 93 states:

'Where a person –

(a) is charged with –

(i) an indictable offence that shall not be tried summarily; or

(ii) an offence against Section 420 of the *Criminal Code 1974* where the offence is not to be tried summarily; and

(b) fails to appear in answer to a summons issued against him before the Court at the time and place specified in the summons, and it is made to appear to the Court on oath that the summons was duly served on him a reasonable time before the time appointed for appearing to it,

the Court may, on oath being made before it, substantiating the matter of the information to its satisfaction, issue its warrant for the arrest of the accused person to bring him before a Court to answer to the information and to be further dealt with according to the law'.

Section 125 states (in part):

'If, at the time and place appointed by a summons for hearing and determining an information of a simple offence, or an indictable offence triable summarily the accused person does not appear when called, and proof is made to the Court on oath[360], or in accordance with Section 47, of due service of the summons on the accused person a reasonable time before the time appointed for his appearance, the Court may –

---

[358] An offence that is not an indictable offence is punishable on summary conviction, see section 22 of the *Interpretation Act* (Ch. 2).

Refer also to the chapter titled 'Classification Of Offences' in the text titled 'Injia on Criminal Practice and Procedure in Papua New Guinea and the Pacific'.

[359] Section 3(1) of the *Interpretation Act* (Ch. 2) defines the term 'oath' as including:
'the making of a solemn declaration or affirmation'.

[360] Section 3(1) of the *Interpretation Act* (Ch. 2) defines the term 'oath' as including:
'the making of a solemn declaration or affirmation'.

(b) in the case of an information of a simple offence or an indictable offence triable summarily – on oath being made before it, substantiating the matter of the information to its satisfaction, issue its warrant for the arrest of the accused person to bring him before a Court to answer to the information and to be further dealt with according to law'.

A warrant may be issued on a Sunday as on any other day.[361]

A warrant issued by a magistrate is not avoided by reason of the magistrate dying or ceasing to hold office.[362]

Section 53 of the *District Courts Act* (Ch. 40) states:

'A warrant shall –

(a) state shortly the offence or matter of the information on which it is founded; and

(b) name or otherwise describe the person against whom it is issued; and

(c) order the police officer to whom it is directed to apprehend the accused person and to bring him before a Court to answer to the information and to be further dealt with according to law'.

Section 54 states:

'(1) A Magistrate, on issuing a warrant for the arrest of a person, may, by endorsement on the warrant, direct that the person named in the warrant, on arrest, be released on bail on his entering into a recognizance, oral or in writing, with or without sureties, for his appearance in accordance with the endorsement, and the endorsement shall fix the amount in which the principal and sureties (if any) are to be bound.

(2) Where an endorsement is made under Subsection (1), the recognizance in accordance with the endorsement may be taken in accordance with Section 84 and the accused person shall be discharged'.[363]

---

[361] See section 8 of the *District Courts Act* (Ch. 40).

[362] See section 12 of the *District Courts Act* (Ch. 40).

[363] Refer also to:

- the section titled 'Bail' in the chapter titled 'Case File'; and
- the section titled 'Right To Bail' in the chapter titled 'Rights Of An Accused Person' in the text titled 'Injia on Criminal Practice and Procedure in Papua New Guinea and the Pacific'.

[C] ARREST ACT

Section 8 of the *Arrest Act* (Ch. 339)[364] states:

> 'Where an information is laid before a court[365], other than a Local Court[366], that there are reasonable grounds for believing[367] –
>
> (a) that a person has committed an offence within the country; and
>
> (b) that it would not be practicable or desirable to proceed against the person by summons in that his arrest is necessary –
>
> (i) to ensure his appearance in court to answer a charge for the offence; or
>
> (ii) to prevent –
>
> (A) the continuation or repetition of the offence; or
>
> (B) the commission of a further offence; or
>
> (iii) to preserve the safety or welfare of a member of the public or of the person,
>
> the court may issue a warrant for the arrest of the person'.

---

[364] A warrant may be directed to all or any of the following:

- a named person;
- the officer for the time being in charge of police in a particular province or place; and
- all members of the Police Force, see section 11 of the *Arrest Act* (Ch. 339).

If a warrant of arrest has been lost or destroyed, a duplicate warrant may be issued, see *R v Leish Justices; ex parte Kara* [1981] Crim LR 628.

As regards arresting an accused person for failing to comply with or contravening a bail condition, refer to the section titled 'Right To Bail' in the chapter titled 'Rights Of An Accused Person' in the text titled 'Injia on Criminal Practice and Procedure in Papua New Guinea and the Pacific'.

Sections 6(3) and 7(3) of the *Criminal Law (Compensation) Act 1991* provide for the issuance of a warrant of arrest.

[365] Section 1(1) of the *Arrest Act* (Ch. 339) defines the term 'court' as meaning:

> 'any court, other than a Village Court, and includes a judge or magistrate of any court, other than a Village Court'.

[366] The *Local Courts Act* (Ch. 41) has been repealed.

[367] 'For the purposes of this Act a person believes something on reasonable grounds if –
(a) he personally has that belief; and
(b) there are reasonable grounds for that belief', see section 1(3) of the *Arrest Act* (Ch. 339).

Section 9 states:

> 'Where a complaint for an offence has been issued in a Local Court[368] the Court, if it considers it necessary, may issue a warrant for the arrest of the accused person'.

[3.3.3] EXECUTION

[A] ARREST ACT

Section 15 of the *Arrest Act* (Ch. 339) states:

> 'Where a warrant issued under Section 8, 9 or 10[369] is directed to a person –
>
> (a) in accordance with Section 11(a)[370] or (b)[371] – he shall, when executing the warrant, carry it with him and produce it on request; or
>
> (b) by virtue of Section 11(c)[372] only – he shall, on request of the arrested person, produce it as soon as practicable'.

[B] DISTRICT COURTS ACT

Section 51 of the *District Courts Act* (Ch. 40) states:

> 'A warrant to apprehend a defendant so that he may answer to an information may be directed to a police officer by name or generally to all police officers in the country without naming them, or to both'.

Section 52 states:

> 'Where a warrant is directed to all police officers, any police officer may execute the warrant as if it were directed specially to him by name'.

---

[368] The *Local Courts Act* (Ch. 41) has been repealed.

[369] The Heading is 'Issue Of Warrant For Breach Of Bail Condition'.

[370] A warrant may be directed to all or any of the following:–
(a) a named person.

[371] A warrant may be directed to all or any of the following:–
(b) the officer for the time being in charge of police in a particular province or place.

[372] A warrant may be directed to all or any of the following:–
(c) all members of the Police Force.

Section 10(3) of the *District Courts Act* (Ch. 40) states (in part):

> 'A warrant need not be returnable at a particular date but may remain in force until executed [...]'.[373]

Upon the execution of a warrant the police officer who executed the warrant shall immediately return the original warrant to the Clerk of a District Court.[374]

A warrant may be executed in any part of the country and may be executed on a Sunday.[375]

[C] CRIMINAL CODE

Section 246 of the *Criminal Code* (Ch. 262) states:

> 'It is lawful for a person who is –
>
> (a) charged by law with the duty of executing the lawful process of a court; and
>
> (b) required to arrest or detain another person under such process,
>
> and for every person lawfully assisting a person so charged, to arrest or detain the other person according to the terms of the process'.

Section 248 states (in part):

> 'Where –
>
> (b) a warrant was issued by a court, or person having authority under any circumstances to issue the warrant,
>
> it is immaterial whether or not the court or person had authority to pass the sentence or issue the process or warrant in the particular case, unless the person executing it knows that the sentence, process or warrant was in fact passed or issued without authority'.

Section 252 states:

> 'It is lawful for a person who is engaged in the lawful execution of any sentence, process or warrant, and for any person lawfully assisting him, to use such force as is reasonably necessary to overcome any force used in resisting the execution'.

---

373 See also: section 126 of the *District Courts Act* (Ch. 40).

374 See section 3 of the *District Courts Regulation* (Ch. 40).

375 See section 10(1) of the *District Courts Act* (Ch. 40).

[3.3.4] WARRANT OF COMMITMENT[376]

Section 7 of the *Arrest Act* (Ch. 339) states:

> 'Where a person, the subject of a warrant of commitment, is not in custody at the time the warrant is to be executed, the person authorised to execute the warrant may arrest that person without a warrant'.

Section 19 states:

> '(1) Notwithstanding Sections 16, 17 and 18 but subject to Subsection (2), where a warrant of commitment has been issued in respect of a person who is not in custody at the time and he is later arrested by the person or one of the persons to whom the warrant is directed, the person effecting the arrest shall convey the person arrested to a place of confinement in accordance with the warrant.
>
> (2) Where a person making an arrest referred to in Subsection (1) believes on reasonable grounds that the person arrested has committed an offence for which he has not been tried, the person making the arrest shall deal with the person arrested in accordance with Section 16 or 17, as the case may be'.

Section 20 states:

> '(1) Notwithstanding Section 17 but subject to Subsection (2), where a person has been arrested and taken to a police station and a warrant of commitment has been issued in respect of that person, the officer-in-charge of the police station shall take or cause the person to be taken to a place of confinement in accordance with the warrant.
>
> (2) Where the officer-in-charge believes that the person arrested committed an offence for which he has not been tried, the officer shall deal with the arrested person in accordance with Section 18'.

---

[376] Refer also to:

- the section titled 'Costs' in the chapter titled 'Court Procedure' in the text titled 'Injia on Criminal Practice and Procedure in Papua New Guinea and the Pacific'; and
- the section titled 'Fine' in the chapter titled 'Sentencing Options' in the text titled 'Injia on Sentencing in Papua New Guinea and the Pacific'.

[3.4] GENERAL REQUIREMENTS UPON ARREST

[3.4.1] ARREST ACT

Section 14 of the *Arrest Act* (Ch. 339) states:

'(1) Where an authorised person[377] intends to make an arrest and the person to be arrested –

(a) does not resist the arrest and the authorised person is aware that they speak a common language, the authorised person shall at the time of arrest –

(i) advise the person he is under arrest; and

(ii) advise the person arrested of the reason for his arrest; and

(iii) request the person arrested to accompany him to a police station, to a court or place of confinement, as the case may be; or

(b) does not resist the arrest and the authorised person is aware or ascertains –

(i) that they do not speak a common language; or

(ii) that he is unable to speak to the person arrested because the person arrested suffers from some mental or physical defect,

the authorised person shall indicate by reasonable means to the person arrested that –

(iii) he is under arrest, and

(iv) he is to accompany the authorised person; or

(c) resists the arrest, whether by force or by refusing to move, or seeks to evade arrest, whether by running away or by other means, the authorised person may, subject to Subsection (2), use all reasonable means to make the arrest.

(2) Subsection (1)(c) does not justify the use of greater force than is reasonable in the circumstances'.

---

[377] **Citizen's Power To Arrest**

Section 1(1) of the *Arrest Act* (Ch. 339) defines the term 'authorised person' as meaning:

'a person empowered to make an arrest under this Act or any other law or by a warrant and includes both police officers and civilians'.

Section 17 states:

'(1) Where a policeman makes an arrest he shall –

(a) take the arrested person without delay to a police station to be dealt with under Section 18 or before a court; and

(b) subject to Subsection (2), use all reasonable means to prevent the arrested person from escaping.

(2) Subsection (1)(b) does not justify the use of greater force than is reasonable in the circumstances'.[378]

Section 18 states:

'(1) Where a person has been arrested and taken to a police station, the officer-in-charge of the police station[379] shall –

(a) immediately release the person if he considers that –

(i) the person arrested did not commit the offence for which he was arrested or any other offence and there is no other reason to justify his detention under this Act or any other law; or

(ii) there are good reasons why the arrested person should not be proceeded against for an offence; or

(iii) proceedings can be effectively taken by way of summons against the arrested person; and

(b) if he does not release the person under Paragraph (a) – take the person into custody and enter in a permanent register of arrests the name of the person and if it appears that the person arrested –

---

[378] **Citizen's Power To Arrest**

Section 16 of the Arrest Act (Ch. 339) states:

'(1) Where a person, not being a policeman, makes an arrest, he shall –
(a) as soon as practicable but subject to Subsection (2), hand the arrested person over to a policeman or take the arrested person or cause him to be taken to a police station; and
(b) subject to Subsection (2), use all reasonable means to prevent the arrested person escaping.
(2) Subsection (1) does not justify the use of greater force than is reasonable in the circumstances'.

Any person who is a witness to a crime may affect citizen's arrest and detain the person, but must use reasonable force and must convey the person arrested to a police station as soon as possible, see *Fama Sogio v Johon Negrefa and The State* (1996) N1482.

[379] Section 1(1) of the *Arrest Act* (Ch. 339) defines the term 'officer-in-charge' in relation to a police station at a particular time, as meaning:

'the police officer who is in charge of the police station at that time'.

(i) has committed an offence – the nature of that offence; or

(ii) has been arrested for some other reason – that reason; and

(c) promptly inform the person arrested or cause him to be informed in language he understands of –

(i) the reason for his arrest; and

(ii) details of the charges against him; and

(iii) his right, immediately and in private –

(A) to communicate with a member of his family or a personal friend; and

(B) to give instructions to a lawyer of his choice, including the Public Solicitor if he is entitled to legal aid[380]; and

(d) as soon as practicable consider and accordingly grant or refuse bail in accordance with the *Bail Act 1977*[381]; and

(e) if bail is not granted under Paragraph (d) or if for any other reason the person arrested remains in custody at the station – take the person, or cause him to be taken, before a court without delay; and

(f) if bail is granted to the person by a court but for any reason the person remains in custody at the station after bail is granted – take the person or cause him to be taken before a court as soon as practicable after the expiration of 14 days after the bail is granted; and

(g) if bail is granted to the person but he remains in custody after being brought before a court on one or more occasions – take the person or cause him to be taken from time to time before a court as soon as practicable after the expiration of 14 days after the time he last appeared before a court.

(2) The officer-in-charge of a police station shall at all times permit persons arrested or detained at the police station –

---

380 Refer also to the section titled 'Right To Representation' in the chapter titled 'Rights Of An Accused Person' in the text titled 'Injia on Criminal Practice and Procedure in Papua New Guinea and the Pacific'.

381 Refer also to:

- the section titled 'Bail' in the chapter titled 'Case File' and
- the section titled 'Right To Bail' in the chapter titled 'Rights Of An Accused Person' in the text titled 'Injia on Criminal Practice and Procedure in Papua New Guinea and the Pacific'.

(a) whenever practicable, without delay and in private to communicate with –

(i) a member of his family or a personal friend; and

(ii) a lawyer of his choice, including the Public Solicitor if he is entitled to legal aid; and

(b) to give instructions to a lawyer of his choice, including the Public Solicitor if he is entitled to legal aid[382]'.

[3.4.2] DISTRICT COURTS ACT

Section 275 of the *District Courts Act* (Ch. 40) states:

> 'A member of the Police Force acting in accordance with Section 274, or any other person who arrests a person offending against law, and whom he may lawfully arrest by virtue of his office or otherwise, may lawfully take and convey the person so arrested to and before a Magistrate'.

[3.4.3] JUVENILE COURTS ACT

Section 20 of the *Juvenile Courts Act 1991* states:

'(1) Where an infant[383] is detained by a member of the Police Force, or in accordance with Subsection (2), the officer in charge[384] of the police station to which the infant is brought shall immediately –

(a) notify[385] a parent or a responsible person[386], and a Juvenile Court Officer, of the whereabouts and the reasons of the detention of the infant; and

(b) allow access to the infant by all or any of the persons referred to in Paragraph (a),

---

[382] Refer also to the section titled 'Right To Representation' in the chapter titled 'Rights Of An Accused Person' in the text titled 'Injia on Criminal Practice and Procedure in Papua New Guinea and the Pacific'.

[383] Means a person aged less than seven years, see section 2 of the *Juvenile Courts Act 1991*.

[384] Means the member of the Police Force in charge of the police station at the time of the detention or arrest, as the case may be, see section 19(1) of the *Juvenile Courts Act 1991*.

[385] Where notification etc., of a parent or responsible person is required under this Part, and such a parent or person cannot, with reasonable diligence, be found, it is sufficient to notify a Juvenile Court Officer only, see 19(2) of the *Juvenile Courts Act 1991*.

[386] Means a person other than a parent who agrees to accept control or care of the infant and includes a guardian of the infant, see the definition of the term 'responsible person' in relation to a juvenile as defined in section 2 of the *Juvenile Courts Act 1991*.

and shall, as soon as practicable –

(c) release the infant into the care of a parent or responsible person or Juvenile Court Officer; or

(d) where compliance with Paragraph (c) is not practicable – place the infant in a remand centre or in such other place as is approved by the Director for that purpose.

(2) Where an infant is detained by a person other than a member of the Police Force, the person shall immediately notify a Police Officer, who shall proceed in accordance with Subsection (1).

(3) Where an infant has been placed in a remand centre under Subsection (1)(d), the infant shall, as soon as practicable, be brought before a Magistrate, who shall order the release of the infant to a Juvenile Court Officer, a parent or a responsible person'.

Section 21 states:

'(1) In this Section –

"bail authority" means an authority empowered to grant bail in accordance with the *Bail Act 1977*[387].

(2) Where a juvenile[388] is arrested by a member of the Police Force, or in accordance with Subsection (3), the officer in charge[389] of the police station shall –

(a) immediately notify[390] a parent or a responsible person[391], and a Juvenile Court Officer, and shall allow access by all or any of them to the juvenile; and

---

387 Refer also to:

- the section titled 'Bail' in the chapter titled 'Case File'; and
- the section titled 'Right To Bail' in the chapter titled 'Rights Of An Accused Person' in the text titled 'Injia on Criminal Practice and Procedure in Papua New Guinea and the Pacific'.

388 Section 2 of the *Juvenile Courts Act 1991* defines the term 'juvenile' as meaning:
'a person aged not less than seven years and less than 18 years'.

389 Means the member of the Police Force in charge of the police station at the time of the detention or arrest, as the case may be, see section 19(1) of the *Juvenile Courts Act 1991*.

390 Where notification etc., of a parent or responsible person is required under this Part, and such a parent or person cannot, with reasonable diligence, be found, it is sufficient to notify a Juvenile Court Officer only, see 19(2) of the *Juvenile Courts Act 1991*.

391 Section 2 of the *Juvenile Courts Act 1991* defines the term 'responsible person' as meaning:
'a person other than a parent of a juvenile, who agrees to accept control or care of the juvenile, and includes a guardian of the juvenile'.

(b) place the juvenile in a remand centre or in such other place as is approved by the Director for that purpose; and

(c) notify a Juvenile Court Officer of the arrest, the reasons for the arrest and the place of detention.

(3) Where a juvenile is arrested by a person other than a member of the Police Force, the person shall immediately notify the police, who shall proceed in accordance with Subsection (2).

(4) Where a juvenile has been charged and placed on remand under Subsection (2), the Juvenile Court Officer notified shall –

(a) where the parent or responsible person has not yet been notified – notify a parent of the juvenile or a responsible person; and

(b) where the juvenile is on probation–notify a probation officer,

of the arrest of the juvenile.

(5) Where a juvenile is granted bail, the bail authority may require, as a condition of bail, that the juvenile be placed in the care of a parent or responsible person who agrees to accept him'.

[3.5] POWER TO DETAIN

In *SCR No. 5 of 1987; The State v Songke Mai and Gai Avi*[392] Kidu CJ stated[393]:

> 'It is apparent, in my view that section 42(2) [of the *Constitution of the Independent State of Papua New Guinea*] allows the police to detain a person without arresting him if the police suspect that he has committed an offence or is about to do so. The condition of this right to detain without arrest is that an Act of Parliament (as in cases of health, quarantine, immigration, etc) must provide for it. If such an Act is promulgated it would be sanctioned by section 42(1)(d) of the Constitution. At present I am not aware of any statute which permits police to detain a person suspected of having committed an offence or of being about to commit an offence without arresting him'. [words in brackets added]

A person is lawfully detained when he or she is deprived of his or her personal liberty by an act of Parliament and that deprivation of his or her personal liberty is sanctioned by section 42(1)(a) – (h) of the *Constitution of the Independent State of Papua New Guinea.*[394]

---

392 [1988-89] PNGLR 56, [1988] PGSC 22.

393 at 61.

394 See *SCR No. 5 of 1987; The State v Songke Mai and Gai Avi* [1988-89] PNGLR 56, [1988] PGSC 22.

See also: *The State v Wic Kor* [1983] PNGLR 24.

A person may be lawfully detained:

- for the purpose of an arrest and as a consequence of that arrest;

  and

- under the provisions of the *Search Act* (Ch. 341) for the purpose of a search[395].

[3.6] GENERAL PRINCIPLES

Both:

- the 'arrest' of a person;

  and

- the 'detaining' of a person

involve deprivation of liberty as distinguished from a restriction of his or her freedom of movement.[396]

An arrest is a serious interference with personal liberty.[397]

It is not something to be taken lightly.[398]

Police should never abuse their power to arrest.[399]

The process of 'arrest' under the *Arrest Act* (Ch. 339) or any other statute ordinarily involves:

- the deprivation of liberty of the person arrested;

  and

---

395 Refer also to the section titled 'Search And Seize' in this chapter.

396 See *SCR No. 5 of 1987; The State v Songke Mai and Gai Avi* [1988-89] PNGLR 56, [1988] PGSC 22.

397 See *Peter Hou v The Attorney-General* [1990] SILR 88, per Ward CJ at 90.

398 See *Peter Hou v The Attorney-General* [1990] SILR 88, per Ward CJ at 90.

399 See *R v McDermott* (1948) 76 CLR 501, per Dixon J at 513 and *R v Williams* (1986) 161 CLR 278.

- some form of physical or non-physical 'detention'.[400]

A defacto arrest by seizure of his or her person or by words in circumstances calculated to bring and which did bring to that person notice that he or she is under compulsion in respect of some criminal matter – may, in a particular case, amount to the requisite deprivation of liberty.[401]

A person should only be arrested if it is the arresting officer's intention to prosecute him or her for an offence.[402]

There is still currently no such statute that permits police to detain any person for questioning.

Therefore, a person should not be arrested or detained without consent merely for the purpose of asking questions.[403]

Section 42(3) of the *Constitution of the Independent State of Papua New Guinea* confers the following rights on a person who is arrested and detained:

- the accused person must be brought before a court 'without delay';

  and

- the accused person is not to be detained in custody any longer except by a court order.[404]

It is important that police officers should bear in mind that it is both:

- stupid;

  and

- unlawful,

[400] See *Ronald Alexander McKenzie v The State* [1999] PNGLR 526, (1998) SC596, [1998] MLJ 8, [1998-99] 26 MLJ 178.

[401] See *SCR No. 5 of 1987; The State v Songke Mai and Gai Avi* [1988-89] PNGLR 56, [1988] PGSC 22.

[402] See *R v Chalkley and Jeffries* [1998] 2 All ER 155, [1998] 2 Cr App R 79, [1999] Crim LR 215 and *Hallam v Karger* (1985) 18 A Crim R 221.

[403] See *Mackenzie v R* [2004] WASCA 146; *Williams v R* (1986) 161 CLR 278 at 284-285; *Salihos v R* (1987) 78 ALR 509, per Burt CJ at 513 and Kennedy J at 521 and *Norton v R* (2001) 24 WAR 488.

[404] See *The State v Dakoa* (2009) N3586, [2009] PGNC 8 and *Re Conditions of Detention at Bialla Police Lock-Up, West New Britain Province* (2006) N3022.

to keep an accused person in custody for a minute longer than they should.[405]

There are civil remedies if a police officer wrongfully exercises his or her power to arrest and detain.[406]

An accused person who is arrested, held in custody but is not charged, is thereby falsely imprisoned and may seek damages from the arresting officer and the State pursuant to section 57 of the *Constitution of the Independent State of Papua New Guinea.*[407]

At the time of the arrest or detention, a police officer:

- should:
  - advise the accused person verbally that he or she is under arrest[408] or detention;

    or

  - indicate by reasonable means to the accused person that he or she is under arrest[409] or detention, if unable to do so verbally.

  A person is 'arrested' when:

  - he or she is deprived of his or her personal liberty;

    or

  - his or her person is touched in such a way that he or she is made aware that he or she is under compulsion in relation to a criminal matter.[410]

---

405 See *R v Mackintosh* (1983) 76 Cr App R 177, per Lawton LJ at 182.

406 See *The State v Andrew Maurup* (1991) N1033.

See also: section 26 of the *Arrest Act* (Ch. 339), section 22 of the *Juvenile Courts Act 1991* and the provisions of the *Claims By and Against the State Act 1996.*

407 See for example, *Kawi Yawi v Torepa Nenga; Anton Sinawai and The State* (2002) N2209.

See also: section 26 of the *Arrest Act* (Ch. 339).

408 See section 14(1)(a)(i) of the *Arrest Act* (Ch. 339).

409 See section 14(1)(b) of the *Arrest Act* (Ch. 339).

410 See *SCR No. 5 of 1987; The State v Songke Mai and Gai Avi* [1988-89] PNGLR 56, [1988] PGSC 22 and *The State v Dakoa* (2009) N3586, [2009] PGNC 8.

See also: *R v O'Donoghue* (1988) 34 A Crim R 397 at 401.

Once a suspect is taken by the elbow or told 'come with me' or 'stay here' or prevented from continuing to go about his or her business he or she is arrested in real terms. A suspect does not have to be charged at a police station in order to be under arrest.[411]

An arrest also occurs whenever it is made plain by what is said by a police officer that the suspect is no longer a free person[412], however, no formal words of arrest are required[413].

Irrespective, a police officer should make it plain to a suspect by what is said and done that he or she is no longer free[414];

- should advise the suspect as to the reason for his or her arrest[415] or detention in a language that the suspect understands[416];

- shall advise the suspect of the reason why he or she was arrested by outlining what the suspect did or did not do that was illegal.[417]

The fact that:

  - a person is not informed of the charge for which he or she was arrested;

    or

---

411 See *The State v Andrew Maurup* (1991) N1033, [1991] PGNC 25.

412 See *R v Inwood* [1973] 2 All ER 645, (1973) 57 Cr App R 529 and *Alderson v Booth* [1969] 2 QB 216, per Parker LCJ at 220-221.

See also: *R v Latimer* [1997] 1 SCR 217 and *R v O'Donoghue* (1988) 34 A Crim R 397 at 401.

413 See *R v Inwood* [1973] 2 All ER 645 at 649, (1973) 57 Cr App R 529.

See also: *R v Conley* (1982) 30 SASR 226 at 239 and *Norton v R* (2001) 24 WAR 488, [2001] WASCA 207.

414 See *R v Inwood* [1973] 2 All ER 645 at 649, (1973) 57 Cr App R 529.

415 See section 14(1)(a)(ii) of the *Arrest Act* (Ch. 339).

416 See section 42(2) of the *Constitution of the Independent State of Papua New Guinea*.

See also: *Meyauzin v Volo* [2012] PGSC 9, (2012) SC1173; *The State v Andrew Maurup* (1991) N1033, [1991] PGNC 25 and *The State v Lakio Tambai* (1980) N235.

417 See *R v Kulynycz* [1970] 3 All ER 881, [1970] 3 WLR 1029, [1971] 1 QB 367, (1971) 55 Cr App R 34 and *Christie v Leachinsky* [1947] AC 573, per Lord Simon at 587.

See also: *Abbassay and another v Commissioner of Police of the Metropolis and others* [1990] 1 WLR 385, [1990] 1 All ER 193, (1990) 90 Cr App R 250.

- there were no reasonable grounds under section 3 of the *Arrest Act* (Ch. 339) for effecting the arrest

does not alter the fact that the person is, for practical purposes, 'arrested'.[418]

What that raises is whether the arrest was lawful or wrongful.[419]

Hence the provisions in section 26 of the *Arrest Act* (Ch. 339) and the civil remedy for wrongful imprisonment or breach of section 42(1) of the *Constitution of the Independent State of Papua New Guinea* are available to persons if they have been:

- arrested;

  or

- deprived of their liberty

without legal cause[420];

- is not obliged to use precise or technical language regarding the offence.[421]

  Such information does not have to be conveyed to the suspect in the precise words and terms of the *Criminal Code* (Ch. 262), the *Summary Offences Act* (Ch. 264) or some other legislation[422];

- does not have to be able to specify the specific details of the particular offence for which he or she had in mind[423];

- shall:

  - advise the suspect of the substance of a warrant of arrest if such a warrant is being executed;

    and

---

[418] See *The State v Andrew Maurup* (1991) N1033, [1991] PGNC 25.

[419] See *The State v Andrew Maurup* (1991) N1033, [1991] PGNC 25.

[420] See *The State v Andrew Maurup* (1991) N1033, [1991] PGNC 25.

[421] See *Abbassay and another v Commissioner of Police of the Metropolis and others* [1990] 1 WLR 385, [1990] 1 All ER 193, (1990) 90 Cr App R 250.

[422] See *The State v Andrew Maurup* (1991) N1033, [1991] PGNC 25.

[423] See *Chapman v Director of Public Prosecutions* (1989) 89 Cr App R 190, [1988] Crim LR 843.

- produce it upon request to the suspect.[424]

However, when a warrant of arrest is being executed it does not have to be shown to the suspect at the time of the arrest[425];

- shall immediately inform the suspect of his or her rights as provided for by section 42(2) of the *Constitution of the Independent State of Papua New Guinea*[426];

and

- shall request the suspect to accompany him or her to a police station.

However, depending on the circumstances at the time of the arrest it may not be practicable to provide such information.[427]

If a suspect:

- resists the arrest, whether by force or by refusing to move;

or

- seeks to evade arrest, whether by running away or by other means,

the arresting officer may use all reasonable means to make the arrest.[428]

---

[424] See section 15 of the *Arrest Act* (Ch. 339).

[425] See section 15 of the *Arrest Act* (Ch. 339).

Refer also to the section titled 'Institution Of Proceedings' in the chapter titled 'Charges' in the text titled 'Injia on Criminal Practice and Procedure in Papua New Guinea and the Pacific'.

[426] See *Meyauzin v Volo* [2012] PGSC 9, (2012) SC1173; *The State v Paro Wampa* [1987] PNGLR 120 and *The State v Dakoa* (2009) N3586, [2009] PGNC 8.

Those rights include communicating, without delay and in private, with a member of his or her family, a personal friend and a lawyer of his or her choice, see section 42(2) of the *Constitution of the Independent State of Papua New Guinea*.

See also: section 18(2) of the *Arrest Act* (Ch. 339).

Refer also to the section titled 'Confessional Evidence' in the chapter titled 'Evidence' in the text titled 'Injia on Criminal Practice and Procedure in Papua New Guinea and the Pacific'.

[427] See *Christie v Leachinsky* [1947] AC 573.

[428] See section 14(1)(c) of the *Arrest Act* (Ch. 339).

However, the arresting officer is not justified in using greater force than is reasonable in the circumstances.[429]

A police officer who applies excessive physical force will then be liable for assault.[430]

What amounts to reasonable force is a question of fact that depends on the circumstances of the particular case.

[4.0] COMMON LAW AUTHORITY TO ENTER

A police officer has the same powers as a Constable under the underlying law[431], except as those powers are modified by or under an Act.[432]

A police officer may only enter private property if he or she is exercising very clear:

- statutory power;

  or

- common law power.[433]

Every unauthorised entry upon private property is a trespass, ie., the right of a person in possession or entitled to possession of premises to exclude others from those premises.[434]

---

429 See section 14(2) of the *Arrest Act* (Ch. 339).

430 See *Bennett v Commissioner of Police* (1997) 10 Admin LR 245 at 264 and *Tahche v Abboud* [2002] VSC 42.

431 Refer also to the chapter titled 'Sources Of Law' in the text titled 'Injia on Criminal Practice and Procedure in Papua New Guinea and the Pacific'.

432 See section 140 of the *Police Act 1998.*

433 See *Kuru v State of New South Wales* [2008] HCA 26; *Halliday v Nevill* [1984] 155 CLR 1 at 10 and *Director of Public Prosecutions v Jeremiah* [2011] NRSC 14.

434 See *Entick v Carrington* (1765) 2 Wils KB 275 at 291, [1765] EWHC J98, 95 ER 807 at 817.

See also: *Halliday v. Nevill* (1984) 155 CLR 1, per Brennan J at 10, [1984] HCA 80; *Plenty v Dillon* (1991) 171 CLR 635, [1991] HCA 5; *Colet v R* (1981) 119 DLR (3d) 521 at 526 and *Coco v R* (1994) 179 CLR 427 at 435-436, [1994] HCA 15.

The occupier of any dwelling-house, however, gives an 'implied licence' to any member of the public, including a police officer, coming on his or her legitimate business to enter upon his or her property.[435]

The scope of the implied license for a police officer to pursue legitimate business will not necessarily be the same as that for members of the public.[436]

The scope of the authority to enter may vary so as to permit that which having regard to the occupant's reasonable expectation of privacy is reasonable in the circumstances.[437]

Generally prior to entering a person's property a police officer should identify himself or herself in the interests of personal safety and respect for the privacy of the owner or occupier.[438]

When the implied license is revoked by the licensee, ie., the occupier of the dwelling-house, a reasonable time must be given to leave the property.[439]

However, if a police officer is invited into a dwelling-house by a co-occupier for the purpose of investigating an offence that officer is entitled to remain on the premises for a reasonable period of time in order to carry out that investigation to his or her satisfaction, notwithstanding that the officer may have been told to leave by another occupant.[440]

---

[435] See *Davis v Lisle* [1936] 2 KB 434.

See also: *Plenty v Dillon* (1991) 171 CLR 635 at 639, [1991] HCA 5; *Halliday v Nevill* (1984) 155 CLR 1 at 10, [1984] HCA 80; *Howden v Mot* [1987] 2 NZLR 747 at 751; *Coster v Police* (1992) 10 CRNZ 54; *R v Evans* [1996] 1 SCR 8 and *R v Tricker* (1995) 21 OR (3d) 575 (CA) at 579.

[436] See *Davis v Lisle* [1936] 2 KB 434.

See also: *R v Bradley* (1997) 15 CRNZ 363 at 367-369; *Howden v Mot* [1987] 2 NZLR 747 and *Coster v Police* (1992) 10 CRNZ 54.

[437] See *Davis v Lisle* [1936] 2 KB 434.

See also: *R v Bradley* (1997) 15 CRNZ 363 at 367-369; *Howden v Mot* [1987] 2 NZLR 747 and *Coster v Police* (1992) 10 CRNZ 54.

[438] See *Eccles v Bourque* (1974) 19 CCC (2d) 129, per Dickson J at 133-134.

[439] See *Davis v Lisle* [1936] 2 KB 434; *R v Davies* [1937] 2 All ER 213; *R v Waterfield* [1963] 3 All ER 659, per Ashworth J at 661-662 and *Robson and Robson v Hallett* [1967] 3 WLR 28, [1967] 2 QB 939, [1967] 2 All ER 407, (1967) 51 Cr App R 307.

See also: *Lambert v Roberts* (1981) 72 Cr App R 223; *Howden v Mot* [1987] 2 NZLR 747 and *Coster v Police* (1992) 10 CRNZ 54.

[440] See *R v Thornley* (1981) 72 Cr App R 302.

A police officer who enters or remains on private property without the leave or licence of the person in possession or entitled to possession commits a trespass, unless the entry or presence is authorised or excused by the law.[441]

In such circumstances such a person may commence legal proceedings in the Supreme Court and National Court under 57 of the *Constitution of the Independent State of Papua New Guinea* because his or her fundamental right as provided for by section 44 has been unlawfully breached.

[5.0] SEARCH AND SEIZURE

[5.1] INTRODUCTION

The fundamental human right to protection against unlawful searches and seizures is a basic right guaranteed by the *Constitution of the Independent State of Papua New Guinea*[442], and is part of the English common law[443].

In broad terms:

- a 'search' is an examination of a person or property;

  and

- a 'seizure' is the taking of what is discovered.[444]

A police officer has the same powers as a Constable under the underlying law[445], except as those powers are modified by or under an Act.[446]

The *Search Act* (Ch. 341) is of an Act permitted by sections 44 and 49 of the *Constitution of the Independent State of Papua New Guinea* to regulate or restrict the freedom from arbitrary search and entry.[447]

---

441 See *Coco v R* (1994) 176 CLR 427 at 435-436, [1994] HCA 15; *Plenty v Dillon* (1991) 171 CLR 635 at 639, [1991] HCA 5 and *Halliday v Nevill* (1984) 155 CLR 1 at 10, [1984] HCA 80.

442 See sections 44 and 49.

443 See *Attorney General of Jamaica v Williams and another* [1998] AC 351, per Lord Hoffmann at 354-355.

444 See *R v Grayson and Taylor* [1997] 1 NZLR 399 at 300.

445 Refer also to the chapter titled 'Sources Of Law' in the text titled 'Injia on Criminal Practice and Procedure in Papua New Guinea and the Pacific'.

446 See section 140 of the *Police Act 1998*.

447 See *The State v James Bero Popo* [1987] PNGLR 286 at 291.

However, depending on the circumstances an application for the issuance of a search warrant may need to be made under section 74 of the *Firearms Act* (Ch. 310).[448]

Subject to the provisions of the *National Intelligence Organisation Act 1984* and *Civil Aviation Act 2000*, the *Search Act* (Ch. 341) applies to and in relation to any search whether by or under that Act or any other law[449].[450]

By virtue of the *Search Act* (Ch. 341):

- all powers at common law to issue search warrants;

  and

- all duties and responsibilities imposed by the common law in relation to searches and search warrants

are abolished.[451]

The provisions of the *Search Act* (Ch. 341) that specify the circumstances in which a person may be searched are in addition to and not in derogation of a provision of any other Act or subordinate enactment that confers a power of search.[452]

The police have no general right to enter a house and seize property.

This is the very reason for the right under section 44 of the *Constitution of the Independent State of Papua New Guinea*.

A police officer can only enter a dwelling-house:

- under the exceptions provided for by section 44;

- under the provisions of the *Search Act* (Ch. 341)[453];

---

448 Refer also to the section titled 'Police Powers' in the chapter titled 'Firearms Offences' in the text titled 'Injia on Criminal Offences in Papua New Guinea and the Pacific'.

449 See for example, section 74 of the *Firearms Act* (Ch. 310) and Division 1 of Part 4 of the *Proceeds of Crime Act 2005*.

450 See section 2 of the *Search Act* (Ch. 341).

451 See section 19 of the *Search Act* (Ch. 341).

452 See section 16 of the *Search Act* (Ch. 341).

453 See *John Alex v Martin Golu* [1983] PNGLR 117 at 120 and *The State v Iga* [1990] PNGLR 146.

See also: *In the Matter of the Constitution S. 44 and 57 and In the Matter of the Application of Chai Chen Sheng and In the Matter of the Application of Kiang Chin Chee* [1993] PNGLR 105, (1993) N1145, (1993) PGNC 100.

or

- with the consent of the owner or occupier.

Entering and searching premises without a lawfully obtained search warrant amounts to a breach of the fundamental right to freedom from arbitrary search and entry secured in section 44 of the *Constitution of the Independent State of Papua New Guinea*[454].

Evidence obtained in breach of:

- section 44 of the *Constitution of the Independent State of Papua New Guinea*;

  or

- the *Search Act* (Ch. 341)

may be ruled inadmissible.[455]

A police officer however does not have to comply with the provisions of the *Search Act* (Ch. 341) if the owner or occupier of the property consents. In such circumstances the consent should be obtained in writing.

When conducting a search a police officer should explain to the person to be searched the reason for the search, unless the circumstances rendered the giving of the reasons:

- unnecessary;

  or

- impracticable.[456]

---

[454] See *The State v Kevin Evertius and Thomas Kundi* [1985] PNGLR 109.

See also: *The State v James Bero Popo* [1987] PNGLR 286.

[455] See *The State v Benny Buen Iga* [1990] PNGLR 146 and *The State v James Bero Popo* [1987] PNGLR 286.

See also: section 57 of the *Constitution of the Independent State of Papua New Guinea* and *John Alex v Martin Golu* [1983] PNGLR 117.

See also: *Bunning v Cross* (1978) 141 CLR 54, [1978] HCA 22; *R v Ireland* (1970) 126 CLR 321 at 335; *King (Herman) v R* (1968) 52 Cr App R 353, per Lord Hodson at 365; *Jeffrey v Black* [1977] 3 WLR 895, [1978] 1 All ER 555, [1978] QB 490, [1977] Crim LR 555, (1978) 66 Cr App R 81; *Finnigan v Sandiford; Clowser v Chaplin* (1981) 73 Cr App R 153; *R v Coombs* [1985] 1 NZLR 318; *R v Jeffries* [1994] 1 NZLR 290 and *McLorie v Oxford* (1982) 75 Cr App R 137.

Refer also to the section titled 'Introduction To Evidence' in the chapter titled 'Evidence' in the text titled 'Injia on Criminal Practice and Procedure in Papua New Guinea and the Pacific'.

[456] See *Brazil v Chief Constable of Surrey* [1983] 1 WLR 1155 and *Lens v King* [1988] WAR 76.

The extent of any search must be reasonable, having regard to the circumstances that exist for the search at the time.[457]

A police officer who is lawfully on premises, other than to execute a search warrant, may seize property found in the course of being there lawfully, such as by consent or in order to execute a warrant of arrest.[458]

[5.2] SEARCH ACT

[5.2.1] INTRODUCTION

The long title of the *Search Act* (Ch. 341) is as follows:

'Being an Act –

(a) to regulate or restrict certain rights or freedoms referred to in Subdivision III.3.C (qualified rights) of the Constitution, namely –

(i) the freedom from arbitrary search and entry conferred by Section 44 of the Constitution; and

(ii) the right to privacy conferred by Section 49 of the Constitution,

so as to –

(iii) provide for searches of individuals, premises and property in certain cases; and

(iv) confer on persons making searches certain powers and duties; and

(b) to abolish certain rules of common law,

and for related purposes'.

---

[457] See *Frank Truman Export Ltd v Metropolitan Police Commissioner* [1977] 1 QB 952 at 965-966; *Crowley v Murphy* (1981) 52 FLR 123 at 129, 137 and 154 and *Baker v Campbell* (1983) 49 ALR 385.

[458] See section 10(1)(a) and (c) of the *Search Act* (Ch. 341).

See also: *Pringle v Bremner and Stirling* (1867) 5 Macph HL 55, per Chelmsford LC at 60; *Chic Fashions (West Wales) Ltd v Jones* [1968] 2 QB 299; *Ghani v Jones* [1970] 1 QB 693; *R v Governor of Pentonville Prison; ex parte Osman* [1990] 1 WLR 277 at 311 and *R v Commissioner of Police for the Metropolis; ex Parte Rottman* [2002] ACD 69, [2002] 2 WLR 1315, [2002] 2 All ER 865, [2002] HRLR 32, 12 BHRC 329, [2002] 2 AC 692, [2002] UKHL 20.

[5.2.2] SEARCH OF A PERSON[459]

Section 3 of the *Search Act* (Ch. 341) states:

'(1) Where a policeman believes on reasonable grounds[460] that a person has in his possession –

(a) anything that has been stolen or otherwise unlawfully obtained; or

(b) anything used or intended to be used in the commission of an indictable offence[461],

he may stop and search that person in accordance with Section 4 and, where applicable, exercise the power of seizure under Section 10(1)[462].

(2) Subject to Section 4, where a policeman believes on reasonable grounds that it is necessary to do so, he may, at the time of arresting a person, search his person, the clothing he is wearing and any property under his immediate control –

---

[459] **Citizen's Power To Search**

Section 3 of the *Search Act* (Ch. 341) states (in part):

'(4) The owner of a craft or a person in command of a craft or a person authorized by either of them or a policeman may in accordance with Section 4, search a person intending to board the craft and, where applicable, may exercise the power of seizure under Section 10(3).

(5) Where a person in command of a craft suspects that a person on board the craft constitutes a danger to the safety of the craft he may, or persons authorized by him may, search that person in accordance with Section 4 and, where applicable, may exercise the power of seizure under Section 10(4)'.

See also: L. Kalinoe, Citizen's Arrests and the Lawfulness of Routine Searches by Security Guards: *McKenzie v The State* (1998) SC596, [1998] MLJ 8, [1998-99] 26 MLJ 178.

[460] 'For the purposes of this Act, a person believes something on reasonable grounds if --
(a) he personally has that belief; and
(b) there are reasonable grounds for that belief', see section 1(2) of the *Search Act* (Ch. 341).

[461] Section 21 of the *Interpretation Act* (Ch. 2) states:
'An offence --
(a) declared to be treason, crime, misdemeanor or indictable offence; or
(b) punishable by imprisonment for a term exceeding 12 months,
is an indictable offence'.

[462] Section 10(1) of the *Search Act* (Ch. 341) states:
'Where, during the course of a search that is authorised by this Act, a policeman finds any thing that he believes on reasonable grounds --
(a) has been stolen or otherwise unlawfully obtained; or
(b) has been used or is intended to be used in the commission of any indictable offence; or
(c) will provide evidence of an offence,
he may seize that thing'.

(a) for the purpose of ascertaining whether he is concealing a firearm[463] or other offensive weapon; or

(b) for the purpose of preventing the loss or destruction of evidence relating to the offence for which he was arrested, and, where applicable,

may exercise the power of seizure under Section 10(2)[464].

(3) Where a person in lawful custody is to be detained in a place of confinement he may, immediately before he is so detained, be searched at that place of confinement by a policeman or a member of the Correctional Service, as the case requires in accordance with Section 4, who may, where applicable, exercise the power of seizure under Section 10(3)[465].

(4) The owner of a craft[466] or a person in command of a craft or a person authorised by either of them or a policeman may in accordance with Section 4, search a person intending to board the craft and, where applicable, may exercise the power of seizure under Section 10(3).[467]

(5) Where a person in command of a craft suspects that a person on board the craft constitutes a danger to the safety of the craft he may, or persons authorised by him may, search that person in accordance with Section 4 and, where applicable, may exercise the power of seizure under Section 10(4)'.

---

463 See also: section 68 of the *Firearms Act* (Ch. 310).

Refer also to the section titled 'Police Powers' in the chapter titled 'Firearms Offences' in the text titled 'Injia on Criminal Offences in Papua New Guinea and the Pacific'.

464 Section 10(2) of the *Search Act* (Ch. 341) states:
'For the purposes of Sections 3(2), 5(2) and 5(3), where the person searching finds a firearm or offensive weapon he may seize it'.

465 Section 10(3) of the *Search Act* (Ch. 341) states:
'For the purposes of Sections 3(3) and 3(4), where the person searching finds any thing which in his opinion may be dangerous or inexpedient to leave in the possession of the person searched he may seize that thing'.

466 Section 1(1) of the *Search Act* (Ch. 341) defines the term 'craft' as meaning:
(a) an aircraft or part of an aircraft; or
(b) a vessel or part of a vessel'.

467 There is no suggestion in section 3(4) of the *Search Act* (Ch. 341) that the power must follow a reasonable suspicion or grounds or be with authority in the form of a warrant from a Court. However, the term 'intending to board the craft' limits it to persons who are about to go on board a craft and does not extend to persons who are already aboard the craft or have not reached the stage of intending or showing an intention to go aboard, see *The State v Benny Buen Iga* [1990] PNGLR 146.

Section 4 states:

'(1) Subject to this section, a person conducting a search of a person may touch the body and clothing of the person being searched.

(2) Searches of the person shall be conducted with due regard to decency.

(3) A person conducting a search of another person shall not use any greater force than is reasonable in the circumstances.

(4) Subject to Subsection (5), a search of a female shall only be carried out by or in the presence of an adult female.

(5) Where a policeman has reasonable grounds to believe[468] that a female he has arrested is carrying a firearm[469] or other offensive weapon he may, with due regard to decency, seize the weapon.

(6) Subsection (5) does not justify the use of greater force than is reasonable in the circumstances'.

[5.2.3] SEARCH OF A VEHICLE, CRAFT AND IN IMMEDIATE PURSUIT[470]

Section 5 of the *Search Act* (Ch. 341) states:

'(1) Where a policeman has reasonable grounds to believe[471] that a vehicle[472] or anything in a vehicle –

---

468 'For the purposes of this Act, a person believes something on reasonable grounds if --
(a) he personally has that belief; and
(b) there are reasonable grounds for that belief', see section 1(2) of the *Search Act* (Ch. 341).

469 See also: section 68 of the *Firearms Act* (Ch. 310).

Refer also to the section titled 'Police Powers' in the chapter titled 'Firearms Offences' in the text titled 'Injia on Criminal Offences in Papua New Guinea and the Pacific'.

470 See also: section 68 of the *Firearms Act* (Ch. 310).

Refer also to the section titled 'Police Powers' in the chapter titled 'Firearms Offences' in the text titled 'Injia on Criminal Offences in Papua New Guinea and the Pacific'.

471 'For the purposes of this Act, a person believes something on reasonable grounds if --
(a) he personally has that belief; and
(b) there are reasonable grounds for that belief', see section 1(2) of the *Search Act* (Ch. 341).

472 Section 1(1) of the *Search Act* (Ch. 341) defines the term 'vehicle' as meaning:
'any description of vehicle on wheels or runners'.

(a) has been stolen or otherwise unlawfully obtained; or

(b) has been used or is intended to be used in the commission of an indictable offence[473],

he may stop and search that vehicle and, where applicable, exercise the power of seizure under Section 10(1)[474].

(2) Where a policeman believes on reasonable grounds that a person has in a vehicle that he is using at the time, a firearm or other offensive weapon, he may search the vehicle for the firearm or offensive weapon and, where applicable, exercise the power of seizure under Section 10(2)[475].

(3) Where a policeman believes on reasonable grounds that it is necessary to do so, he may, at the time of arresting a person, search any vehicle the arrested person was using at the time of his arrest, for the purpose of preventing the loss or destruction of evidence relating to the offence for which he was arrested and, where applicable, may exercise the power of seizure under Section 10(2).

(4) Where the owner or the person in command of a craft[476] or a policeman has reasonable grounds to suspect that a situation has arisen or is likely to arise involving the safety of the craft he may or persons authorised by him may search –

(a) the craft; and

(b) any luggage and freight on board or about to be placed on board the craft,

---

[473] Section 21 of the *Interpretation Act* (Ch. 2) states:
'An offence --
(a) declared to be treason, crime, misdemeanor or indictable offence; or
(b) punishable by imprisonment for a term exceeding 12 months,
is an indictable offence'.

[474] Section 10(1) of the *Search Act* (Ch. 341) states:
'Where, during the course of a search that is authorised by this Act, a policeman finds any thing that he believes on reasonable grounds --
(a) has been stolen or otherwise unlawfully obtained; or
(b) has been used or is intended to be used in the commission of any indictable offence; or
(c) will provide evidence of an offence,
he may seize that thing'.

[475] Section 10(2) of the *Search Act* (Ch. 341) states:
'For the purposes of Sections 3(2), 5(2) and 5(3), where the person searching finds a firearm or offensive weapon he may seize it'.

[476] Section 1(1) of the *Search Act* (Ch. 341) defines the term 'craft' as meaning:
'(a) an aircraft or part of an aircraft; or
(b) a vessel or part of a vessel'.

and, where applicable, may exercise the power of seizure under Section 10(4)[477].[478]

(5) Where a policeman is in immediate pursuit[479] of a person whom he believes on reasonable grounds[480] to have committed an indictable offence[481], he may, or persons authorised by him may, search any building or place in which he believes on reasonable grounds that the person being pursued –

(a) is concealed; or

(b) has, in the course of his pursuit, concealed or deposited anything[482].

---

[477] Section 10(4) of the *Search Act* (Ch. 341) states:
'For the purposes of Sections 3(5) and 5(4), where the person searching finds anything that in his opinion --
(a) constitutes a danger or is capable of constituting a danger to the safety of the craft; or
(b) is capable of being used to threaten a person on the craft,
he may seize that thing'.

[478] Refer also to section 9 of the *Search Act* (Ch. 341).

[479] The term 'immediate pursuit' in section 5(5) of the *Search Act* (Ch. 341) means immediate pursuit there and then physically, analogous to the notion of 'hot pursuit' where there is no opportunity or time to take any other course of action otherwise the opportunity for apprehension, seizure of property, prevention of concealment of property or prevention of escape will be lost, see *The State v James Bero Popo* [1987] PNGLR 286 at 288.

[480] 'For the purposes of this Act, a person believes something on reasonable grounds if --
(a) he personally has that belief; and
(b) there are reasonable grounds for that belief', see section 1(2) of the *Search Act* (Ch. 341).

[481] Section 21 of the *Interpretation Act* (Ch. 2) states:
'An offence --
(a) declared to be treason, crime, misdemeanor or indictable offence; or
(b) punishable by imprisonment for a term exceeding 12 months,
is an indictable offence'.

[482] Refer also to section 9 of the *Search Act* (Ch. 341).

[6.0] SEARCH WARRANT

[6.1] STATUTORY PROVISIONS[483]

Section 6 of the *Search Act* (Ch. 341) states:

'(1) If a court, other than a Local Court, is satisfied by information on oath[484] that there are reasonable grounds for suspecting that there is in any building, craft[485], vehicle[486] or place –

(a) any thing with respect to which any offence has been or is believed on reasonable grounds[487] to have been committed; or

(b) any thing as to which there are reasonable grounds for believing[488] it is likely to afford evidence of the commission of any such offence; or

(c) any thing as to which there are reasonable grounds for believing[489] it is intended to be used to commit any such offence,

it may issue a warrant to search that building, craft, vehicle or place.

---

483 All powers at common law to issue search warrants and all duties and responsibilities imposed by the common law in relation to searches and search warrants are abolished, see section 19 of the *Search Act* (Ch. 341).

484 Section 3(1) of the *Interpretation Act* (Ch. 2) defines the term 'oath' as including:
'the making of a solemn declaration or affirmation'.

485 Section 1(1) of the *Search Act* (Ch. 341) defines the term 'craft' as meaning:
'(a) an aircraft or part of an aircraft; or
(b) a vessel or part of a vessel'.

486 Section 1(1) of the *Search Act* (Ch. 341) defines the term 'vehicle' as meaning:
'any description of vehicle on wheels or runners'.

487 'For the purposes of this Act, a person believes something on reasonable grounds if --
(a) he personally has that belief; and
(b) there are reasonable grounds for that belief', see section 1(2) of the *Search Act* (Ch. 341).

488 'For the purposes of this Act, a person believes something on reasonable grounds if --
(a) he personally has that belief; and
(b) there are reasonable grounds for that belief', see section 1(2) of the *Search Act* (Ch. 341).

489 'For the purposes of this Act, a person believes something on reasonable grounds if --
(a) he personally has that belief; and
(b) there are reasonable grounds for that belief', see section 1(2) of the *Search Act* (Ch. 341).

(2) If a court is satisfied by information on oath by a commissioned officer of the Police Force that there are reasonable grounds for suspecting that there is in any building or buildings in a village or in any part of a village or village garden any thing specified in Subsection (1)(a), (b) or (c), it may issue a warrant to search the building, buildings, village, part of the village or village garden.

(3) Where a warrant has been issued under Subsection (2) the person, policeman or policemen to whom the warrant is directed shall, where it is practicable to do so, before executing the warrant, endeavour to obtain the co-operation of those persons who, by custom, are regarded as the leaders of the village in respect of which the warrant has been issued.

(4) Subsection (1) or (2) does not justify the use of greater force than is reasonable in the circumstances'.

Section 7 states:

'A warrant may be directed to all or any of the following: –

(a) to a named person;

(b) to the officer for the time being in charge of police in a particular province or place;

(c) to all members of the Police Force'.

Section 8 states:

'A warrant shall –

(a) describe the place to be searched; and

(b) state briefly the offence or matter of the information on which it is founded; and

(c) order the person to whom it is directed to search the place and seize any thing he may find in that place which relates–

(i) to the offence or the matter of the information on which the warrant is founded; or

(ii) to any other offence'.[490]

---

[490] As regards the form of a search warrant, see section 2 of the *Search Regulation* (Ch. 341).

[6.2] GENERAL PRINCIPLES

The Court issuing a search warrant has to be satisfied as to the matters that are specified in:

- section 6(1) of the *Search Act* (Ch. 341);

  or

- section 6(2) of the *Search Act* (Ch. 341),

and not just the informant.[491]

The Court must:

- form its own independent view on the material put before it;
  and
- act judicially.[492]

A Court does not however have to itself suspect and believe the matters set out in sections 6(1) or 6(2).[493]

The Court must, however, be satisfied that:

- reasonable grounds exist for the suspicion and belief[494];
  and
- there is some factual basis for the suspicion and belief[495].

---

491 See *Jimmy Tjeong and another v Ombudsman Commission and Boroko District Court* (1993) OS No. 29 of 1993.

See also: *El-Zarw v Nickola; ex parte El-Zarw* [1992] 1 Qd R 145.

492 See *Jimmy Tjeong and another v Ombudsman Commission and Boroko District Court* (1993) OS No. 29 of 1993.

See also: *El-Zarw v Nickola; ex parte El-Zarw* [1992] 1 Qd R 145.

493 See *Jimmy Tjeong and another v Ombudsman Commission and Boroko District Court* (1993) OS No. 29 of 1993.

494 See *Jimmy Tjeong and another v Ombudsman Commission and Boroko District Court* (1993) OS No. 29 of 1993.

495 See *Jimmy Tjeong and another v Ombudsman Commission and Boroko District Court* (1993) OS No. 29 of 1993.

The Court is therefore required to exercise its discretion by reference to the terms of the Information laid before it, and not by any other extraneous material not properly before it.[496]

The test to be applied is:

> whether the Information discloses sufficient facts and circumstances upon which the Court can be satisfied that there exists reasonable grounds for suspecting that there is in any building, craft, vehicle or place the further circumstances as described by paragraphs (a), (b) and (c) of section 6(1) of the *Search Act* (Ch. 341).[497]

When interpreting section 6(1) it should be noted that there is an important difference between subsections (a) and (b).

The following is a simple example to illustrate that difference:

> Suppose A commits a robbery on a bank with the use of a firearm and steals a quantity of money.

Subsection 6(1)(a)

Referring to subsection (a) which states:

> 'any thing (ie., the 'fruits' of the offence, such as the quantity of money) with respect to which any offence (ie., the robbery) has been or is believed on reasonable grounds to have been committed.

That subsection does not apply in respect of the firearm because it was not 'respect to which the offence was committed'.

Subsection 6(1)(b)

Referring to subsection (b) which states:

> 'any thing (ie., both the tools used to commit the offence, such as the firearm and the fruits of the offence such as the quantity of money) as to which there are reasonable grounds for believing it is likely to afford evidence of the commission of any such offence.

Therefore, if a police officer has any doubts he or she should rely on subsection (b).

Subsection (c) is self-explanatory.

---

[496] See *Jimmy Tjeong and another v Ombudsman Commission and Boroko District Court* (1993) OS No. 29 of 1993.

[497] See *Jimmy Tjeong and another v Ombudsman Commission and Boroko District Court* (1993) OS No. 29 of 1993.

Furthermore, it should be noted that:

- section 6 applies to any offence, and not just indictable offences;

  and

- an application for a search warrant under section 6(2) must be made by a commissioned officer.

The respective search warrants must be marked in either (a), (b) or (c).

A search warrant is valid and effective in law, unless and until it is set aside.[498]

Whilst the National Court has no power to revoke or quash a search warrant issued by the District Court, the District Court that issued the search warrant may do so.[499]

If a search warrant is lost or destroyed, a duplicate warrant may be issued.[500]

A search warrant must have the degree of particularity demanded by the legislation. It is sufficient for a search warrant to repeat the words of the section itself.[501] If a search warrant issued does not precisely follow the language of the enabling statute it will be a question of fact and degree as to whether it is valid on its face.[502]

The validity of a search warrant may be challenged in 'voir dire proceedings'.[503]

---

498 See *R v Grayson and Taylor* [1997] 1 NZLR 399 at 409.

499 See *Soh Chiam Bee v George Avali* (2001) N2148.

500 See *R v Leish Justices; ex parte Kara* (1981) 72 Cr App R 327, [1981] Crim LR 628.

501 See *R v Conley* (1979) 21 SASR 166 and *R v Inland Revenue Commissioner; ex parte Ross Minster Ltd* [1980] AC 953.

502 See *Selby v Pennings* (1998) 19 WAR 520 per Ipp J at 527; *Egarr v Registrar of Board of Optical Registration* [1952] SASR 163, per Napier CJ at 166 and *Myer Queenstown Garden Plaza Pty Ltd and another v Corporation of the City of Port Adelaide and Attorney-General* (1975) 11 SASR 504 at 545.

503 See *R v A* [2000] SASC 51.

[6.3] PROCEDURE

[6.3.1] INTRODUCTION

Section 1 of the *Search Regulation* (Ch. 341) states:

> 'Information sufficient to issue a warrant shall be on oath[504] –
>
> (a) by a person in respect of any building, craft, vehicle or place – in Form 1; and
>
> (b) by a commissioned officer of the Police Force in respect of any building or buildings in a village, or in any part of a village or village garden – in Form 2'.

Considering that the Information must disclose sufficient facts and circumstances upon which the Court can be satisfied that there exists reasonable grounds for suspecting that there is in:

- any building, craft, vehicle or place [section 6(1)];

  or

- any building or buildings in a village or in any part of a village or village garden [section 6(2)]

the further circumstances as described by paragraphs (a), (b) and (c) of section 6(1)[505] an informant should:

- complete an Information;

  and

- arrange for it to be sworn before the Court because the section requires that the Information be on oath or solemn declaration or affirmation.

Although an Information will often be prepared at an early stage of an investigation and may need to be completed in haste, it must comply with the requirements of the law if it is to be valid.[506]

Therefore, it is important that careful preparation is conducted prior to applying for the issuance of a search warrant.[507]

---

[504] Section 3(1) of the *Interpretation Act* (Ch. 2) defines the term 'oath' as including:
'the making of a solemn declaration or affirmation'.

[505] See *Jimmy Tjeong and another v Ombudsman Commission and Boroko District Court* (1993) OS No. 29 of 1993.

[506] See *Zalao v Attorney-General and the Commissioner of Police* [1997] SBCA 6.

[507] See *R v Reading JJ; ex parte South West Meat Ltd* [1992] Crim LR 672.

[6.3.2] FULL AND ACCURATE DETAILS[508]

There should be no:

- rumours;
- assumptions;

  or
- conclusions,

just facts.

The Information must be capable of satisfying the Court that there is the need to issue a search warrant.

In order to satisfy the Court the following must be included:

- details of the alleged offence 'known to law';

  and
- details of the names of the suspect/s, if known;

  and
- details of the thing/s sought;

  and
- details of the building or place where it is believed on reasonable grounds that there are the thing/s sought [section 6(1)];

  or
- details of the craft or vehicle in which it is believed on reasonable grounds that there are the thing/s sought [section 6(1)];

  or
- details of the building or buildings in a village or in any part of a village or village garden in which it is believed on reasonable grounds that there are the thing/s sought [section 6(2)];

---

508 As regards mistakes, refer to *El-Zarw v Nickola; ex parte El-Zarw* [1992] 1 Qd R 145 at 148 and *Malayta* (1996) 87 A Crim R 492 at 495-496.

and

- details of the names of the occupiers or owners, if known;

  and

- details of the relationship between the thing/s sought and the statutory requirements as outlined in section 6(1)(a), (b) or (c).

If the details provided that are the basis for the issuance of a search warrant are false then the evidence seized as a consequence of the execution of such a search warrant may be ruled to be inadmissible.[509]

[6.3.3] OFFENCE

It is not necessary that the statement of the alleged offence be as precise as would be required by a Court in compliance with section 30(2) of the *District Courts Act* (Ch. 40).[510]

However, the offence should be specified:

- in conformity with a wording of a charge;

  and

- with as much detail as is known at that stage of the investigation.

Such details that should be included are:

- the date of the alleged offence;

- the location of the alleged offence;

  and

- a brief description of the alleged offence.

The alleged offence must be an offence 'known to law', as specified in a statute, such as the *Criminal Code* (Ch. 262).

---

509 See *Solicitor-General v Schroder* (1996) 3 HRNZ 157; *R v Dally* [1990] 2 NZLR 184 at 192 and *R v McColl* (1999) 17 CRNZ 136.

510 See *Inland Revenue Commissioners v Rossminster Ltd* [1980] AC 952, [1979] UKHL 5 and *Zalao v Attorney-General and the Commissioner of Police* [1997] SBCA 6.

Refer also to the section titled 'Wording Of Charges' in the chapter titled 'Charges' in the text titled 'Injia on Criminal Practice and Procedure in Papua New Guinea and the Pacific'.

It should be remembered that there is no such offence as 'fraud', the actual offences are either 'False Pretences', 'Valueless Cheques', etc.[511]

[6.3.4] SUSPECT

In many cases the name of the suspect will not be known or capable of being determined before the issuance of a search warrant. Therefore, it is not considered necessary to identify in an Information the name of the suspect involved.[512]

The name of the suspect should however be included, if known.[513]

[6.3.5] THING/S SOUGHT

The thing/s sought must be accurately identified.

All available details must be included.

The search warrant must identify sufficiently specifically what thing/s are authorised to be searched for and seized.[514]

[6.3.6] LOCATION

There must be full and accurate details of the location for which the search warrant is sought.

The term 'place' is not defined in either the *Search Act* (Ch. 341) or the *Interpretation Act* (Ch. 2). The natural and ordinary meaning of that term in the context of the section 6 of the *Search Act* (Ch. 341) would include:

parks and other areas of land as distinct from buildings.

---

511 See *Bradrose Pty Ltd v Commissioner of Police; ex parte Bradrose Pty Ltd* [1989] 2 Qd R 304.

512 See *Coward v Allen* (1984) 52 ALR 320 at 330; *McIntyre v Sing* (1979) 43 FLR 89; *Trimboli v Onley (No. 2)* (1981) 56 FLR 317 at 320 and *R v Tillett* (1969) 14 FLR 101 at 112-114.

See however: *Harrison v Sing* (1979) 36 FLR 322 at 326.

513 See *Gregory Ryan, Stephen Haggerty, Francisca Tagi, Bertha Tingipu and Stotick Kamya v The Madang District Court* (1994) OS No. 277 of 1994.

514 See *Jones v German* [1896] 2 QB 418.

See also: *Arno v Forsyth* (1986) 65 ALR 125; *R v A* [2000] SASC 51 and *Re B.X. Development Inc v R* (1976) 70 DLR (3d) 366).

This means that it is necessary to describe the location with sufficient particularity to enable the owner or occupier objectively to determine that the search warrant relates to their property.[515]

A police officer executing a search warrant should be able to identify and locate the location to be searched by reading the description on the search warrant. Failure to sufficiently describe the place to be searched may result in police executing the search warrant attending to the wrong premises.

If the executing police realise that the address is incorrect then they are required to apply for another search warrant.[516]

If it is sought to search more than one location for the same thing/s then such locations should be specified in the Information. In such circumstances a single search warrant may be issued, provided:

- each location is properly identified;

  and

- there are specific details in the Information as to why it is believed that the thing/s sought may be in more than one location.

[6.4] SOURCE OF INFORMATION[517]

Informer privilege is an ancient and hallowed protection that plays a vital role in law enforcement.[518]

The rule relating to informer privilege is that the identity of a police informer may not be disclosed in most legal proceedings.[519]

---

515 See *Pressler v Holzberger* (1989) 44 A Crim R 261.

516 See *R v Atkinson* [1976] Crim LR 397.

517 See also: *R v William Taupa Tovarula and others* [1973] PNGLR 140 [not in relation to a search warrant].

518 See *Trial of Thomas Hardy for High Treason* (1794) 24 State Tr 199.

See also: *R v Leipert* [1997] 1 SCR 281, 143 DLR (4th) 38, [1997] 3 WWR 457, 112 CCC (3d) 385, 4 CR (5th) 259, 41 CRR (2d) 266 and *R v Basi* 2009 SCC 52, [2009] 3 SCR 389.

519 See section 142 of the *Police Act 1998*.

See also: *Marks v Beyfus* (1890) 25 QBD 494; *D v National Society for the Prevention of Cruelty in Children* [1978] AC 171, [1977] 1 All ER 589, [1977] 2 WLR 201, [1977] UKHL 1; *Tipene v Apperley* [1978] 1 NZLR 761; *R v McNicol* (1994) 12 CRNZ 668 at 670; *R v Hughes* [1986] 2 NZLR 129, (1986) 2 CRNZ 18 at 146 and 35; *Police v Masame* [2007] WSSC 83; *Bisaillon v Keable* (1983) 7 CCC (3d) 385; *Signorotto v Nicholson* [1982] VR 413 and *Smith v Illonois* (1968) 390 US 129.

A police informer is a person who:

- is not a member of the Bougainville Police Service or Royal Papua New Guinea Constabulary;

  and

- informs a police officer of facts relating to:

  - the proposed commission of an offence and the criminal/s involved;

    or

  - the identity of a person involved in the commission of a criminal offence already committed.[520]

The privilege arises where a police officer, in the course of an investigation, guarantees:

- protection;

  and

- confidentiality

to a prospective informer in exchange for useful information that would otherwise be difficult or impossible to obtain.[521]

Informer privilege prevents:

- disclosure of the name of the informant;

  and

- disclosure of any information which might implicitly reveal the identity of the informant[522].[523]

---

[520] See *Re Gibson* (1991) 57 A Crim R 322, per Ambrose J at 331.

[521] See *R v Basi* 2009 SCC 52, [2009] 3 SCR 389.

[522] Refer also to the chapter titled 'Public Interest Immunity' in the text titled 'Injia on Criminal Practice and Procedure in Papua New Guinea and the Pacific'.

See also: *R v Raymond Urbin Strawbridge* [2002] NZCA 332.

[523] See *R v Garofoli* [1990] 2 SCR 1421, per Sopinka J at 1460 and *R v Leipert* [1997] 1 SCR 281, 143 DLR (4th) 38, [1997] 3 WWR 457, 112 CCC (3d) 385, 4 CR (5th) 259, 41 CRR (2d) 266.

Courts have acknowledged that the smallest details may be sufficient to reveal identity.[524]

It is premised on the duty of all citizens to aid in enforcing the law. The discharge of this duty carries with it the risk of retribution from those involved in crime. The rule of informer privilege was developed to protect citizens who assist in law enforcement and to encourage others to do the same.[525]

If their identity were liable to be disclosed in a court of law, these sources of information would stop and the police would be hindered in their duty of preventing and detecting offences.[526]

The rule is therefore of fundamental importance to the workings of a criminal justice system.[527]

The balance has fallen upon the side of non-disclosure, except where:

> upon the trial of an accused person disclosure of the identity of a police informer could help to show that the accused person was innocent of the offence.[528]

However, mere speculation that the information might assist the defence is insufficient.[529]

---

[524] See *R v Garofoli* [1990] 2 SCR 1421, per Sopinka J at 1460 and *R v Leipert* [1997] 1 SCR 281, 143 DLR (4th) 38, [1997] 3 WWR 457, 112 CCC (3d) 385, 4 CR (5th) 259, 41 CRR (2d) 266.

[525] See *R v Hunter* (1987) 57 CR (3d) 1, per Cory JA at 5-6 and *R v Leipert* [1997] 1 SCR 281, 143 DLR (4th) 38, [1997] 3 WWR 457, 112 CCC (3d) 385, 4 CR (5th) 259, 41 CRR (2d) 266.

[526] See *D v National Society for the Prevention of Cruelty in Children* [1978] AC 171, [1976] 2 All ER 993, [1977] 2 WLR 201, [1977] UKHL 1 and *Tipone v Apperley* [1978] NZLR 761.

[527] See *Bisaillon v Keable* [1983] 2 SCR 60 at 105 and *R v Leipert* [1997] 1 SCR 281, 143 DLR (4th) 38, [1997] 3 WWR 457, 112 CCC (3d) 385, 4 CR (5th) 259, 41 CRR (2d) 266.

[528] See *Marks v Beyfus* (1890) 25 QBD 494, per Lord Esher MR at 498.

See also: *D v National Society for the Prevention of Cruelty in Children* [1978] AC 171, [1977] 1 All ER 589, [1977] 2 WLR 201, [1977] UKHL 1; *R v Lewes Justices; ex parte Home Secretary* [1973] AC 388, per Lord Simon at 407-408; *R v Leipert* [1997] 1 SCR 281, 143 DLR (4th) 38, [1997] 3 WWR 457, 112 CCC (3d) 385, 4 CR (5th) 259, 41 CRR (2d) 266 and *R v Basi* 2009 SCC 52, [2009] 3 SCR 389.

For a slightly more restricted test, see *Jarvie v The Magistrates Court of Victoria* [1995] 1 VR 84, per Brooking J at 89; *Sankey v Whitlam* (1978) 142 CLR 1, per Gibbs ACJ at 42 and *R v Meissner* (1994) 76 A Crim R 81, per Carruthers J at 88.

[529] See *R v Leipert* [1997] 1 SCR 281, 143 DLR (4th) 38, [1997] 3 WWR 457, 112 CCC (3d) 385, 4 CR (5th) 259, 41 CRR (2d) 266.

A more flexible rule that would leave disclosure up to the discretion of the individual trial judge or magistrate would rob informers of that assurance and sap their willingness to cooperate.[530]

However, the importance of informer privilege should not be allowed to trump the right of an accused person to establish his or her innocence by raising a reasonable doubt as to guilt which has always remained paramount.[531]

The Courts will enforce the privilege where it is applicable whether it is claimed or not[532] without the balancing of competing interests that applies to some other forms of privilege such as public interest privilege generally[533], unless the protection is waived by the informer and the State.[534]

Information from a police informer alone may be enough in order to obtain a search warrant.[535]

Hearsay evidence is admissible for the purpose of determining whether a search warrant should be issued.[536]

But once a police informer goes into the 'field' and acts as a police agent, the informer privilege is no longer applicable to prevent disclosure of his or her identity in respect of the events in which he or she acted as an agent provocateur.[537]

---

530 See *Bisaillon v Keable* [1983] 2 SCR 60; *R v Hunter* (1987) 57 CR (3d) 1 (Ont CA); *R v Scott* [1990] 3 SCR 979; *Named Person v Vancouver Sun* 2007 SCC 43, [2007] 3 SCR 253; *R v Leipert* [1997] 1 SCR 281, 143 DLR (4th) 38, [1997] 3 WWR 457, 112 CCC (3d) 385, 4 CR (5th) 259, 41 CRR (2d) 266 and *R v Basi* 2009 SCC 52, [2009] 3 SCR 389.

531 See *R v Scott* [1990] 3 SCR 979 at 995-996.

532 See *Bisaillon v Keable* [1983] 2 SCR 60 at 84 and 88 and *R v Basi* 2009 SCC 52, [2009] 3 SCR 389.

533 See *Carey v Ontario* [1986] 2 SCR 637.

Refer also to the chapter titled 'Public Interest Immunity' in the text titled 'Injia on Criminal Practice and Procedure in Papua New Guinea and the Pacific'.

534 See *R v Basi* 2009 SCC 52, [2009] 3 SCR 389; *Named Person v Vancouver Sun* 2007 SCC 43, [2007] 3 SCR 253; *R v Leipert* [1997] 1 SCR 281, 143 DLR (4th) 38, [1997] 3 WWR 457, 112 CCC (3d) 385, 4 CR (5th) 259, 41 CRR (2d) 266 and *Bisaillon v Keable* [1983] 2 SCR 60 at 93.

535 See *O'Hara v Chief Constable of Royal Ulster Constabulary* [1997] AC 286.

536 See *Malayta* (1996) 87 A Crim R 492 and *R v Smith* [2001] 2 Cr App R 1.

537 See *R v Broyles* [1991] 3 SCR 595 at 607-609; *R v Davies* (1982) 1 CCC (3d) 299 (Ont CA) at 303 and *R v Babes* (2000) 146 CCC (3d) 465 (Ont CA).

[6.5] BRIEFING

Prior to the execution of a search warrant, there should be a briefing to the police officers participating in the search.[538]

In a briefing the following issues should be discussed:

- the location of the thing to be searched for;
- the name of the occupier/s and/or owner/s of the location to be searched, if known;
- how the location to be searched is to be entered, if applicable;
- what thing/s is being searched for;
- how that thing/s relates to the offence in question;
- the roles of each police officer participating in the search;

  and
- any dangers which may arise whilst searching the location in question.

[6.6] BUSINESS PREMISES -- LEGAL REPRESENTATIVE[539]

A police officer should be particularly careful if a search warrant is being sought to be executed on the office of a legal representative.

In that regard the issue of legal professional privilege:

- is important;

  and
- must be respected.

---

538 See *R v Reading JJ; ex parte South West Meat Ltd* [1992] Crim LR 672.

539 See also: *Propend Finance Ltd v The Commissioner, Australian Federal Police* (1995) 79 A Crim R 453.

Legal professional privilege is however confined to a document that has been brought into existence for the sole purpose of it being:

- submitted to a legal representative for advice

  or

- used in legal proceedings.[540]

A document which would in any event have been brought into existence for another purpose is not privileged from production.[541]

Therefore, in determining whether legal professional privilege exists the purpose for which the document was brought into existence, and not the purpose for which it was given to a legal representative is the fundamental consideration.

Mere delivery of a document to a legal representative is not sufficient to confer immunity where the document was not of a privileged nature.

Prior to applying to a Court for the issuance of a search warrant to search the business premises of a legal representative advice should be sought from the office of the Public Prosecutor.

The Court that issues a search warrant should be made aware of any thing that may be the subject of legal professional privilege.[542]

A police officer does not have to accept at face value that any document is subject to legal professional privilege.[543]

A police officer executing a search warrant at the business premises of a legal representative may conduct a preliminary search at the premises prior to taking the document/s the subject of the search warrant to a police station for more comprehensive examination. However, the legal representative should be present when the document is examined.[544]

---

[540] See *Grant v Downes* (1976) 135 CLR 674.

[541] See *Grant v Downes* (1976) 135 CLR 674.

[542] See *R v Southhampton Crown Court; ex parte J and P* [1993] Crim LR 962.

As regards the law in relation to 'Legal Professional Privilege', refer to the section titled 'Right To Representation' in the chapter titled 'Rights Of An Accused Person' in the text titled 'Injia on Criminal Practice and Procedure in Papua New Guinea and the Pacific'.

[543] See *R v Chesterfield Justices; ex parte Bramley* [2000] 2 WLR 409, [2000] QB 576, [2000] 1 All ER 411, [2000] 1 Cr App R 486, [2000] Crim LR 385.

[544] See *R v Chesterfield Justices; ex parte Bramley* [2000] 2 WLR 409, [2000] QB 576, [2000] 1 All ER 411, [2000] 1 Cr App R 486, [2000] Crim LR 385.

If during the course of the search there is a dispute as to the seizure of a particular thing it should:

- not be read in detail;
- be placed into a sealed container;

  and

- be immediately conveyed as soon as reasonably practicable to the Court who issued the search warrant for a determination as to whether legal professional privilege apples to the thing in question.

[6.7] EXECUTION

The owner or occupier of the property should be advised as to:

- the identity of the officers executing the search warrant;

  and

- the purpose of the search.

The search warrant should be shown to the owner or occupier.

The owner or occupier has no legal right to consult a legal representative prior to the conduct of a search.[545]

A record should be provided to the owner or occupier in relation to the thing/s taken possession of.

All property seized shall be recorded in a permanent register.[546]

A search warrant may only be executed on a single occasion.[547]

---

[545] See *Mackenzie v R* [2004] WASCA 146.

[546] See section 12 of the *Search Act* (Ch. 341) and section 3 and Form 5 of the *Search Regulation* (Ch. 341).

[547] See *Adams* [1980] QB 575 and *Larsson v Commissioner of Police for New South Wales* (1989) 40 A Crim R 301.

[6.8] EXAMPLE

For the basis of this example the alleged facts and circumstances are as follows:

'On Friday the 7th day of January 2010 Danny Bosing decided to rob a bank.

He obtained a Smith and Wesson handgun from his temporary residence at Room 7, Kuri Resort, Buka.

He decided to wear a blue shirt and brown trousers to commit the robbery.

He then drove a Toyota Hilux Utility Reg. No. A1111 that he had stolen to the Bank of South Pacific situated in Buka.

He entered the bank at 10am with the firearm loaded and a see through plastic bag in his right hand. He approached a teller and said 'This is a hold-up give me your money or I'll kill you'. The teller, Mrs. Joanne Pinia, went to the safe and obtained K1000 in K50 notes and handed it to the offender. At the time there were no other customers in the bank.

He then left and got into the stolen car and drove back to the Kuri Resort. Whilst driving there he was followed by a customer of the bank, Mr. John Kit, who noticed that he was carrying a firearm and a plastic bag containing a quantity of cash when he left the bank.

Mr. Kit followed the offender to the Kuri Resort and observed him enter room 7. There Mr. Kit saw the offender carrying a firearm and a quantity of money in a plastic bag.

On the following day Mr. Kit decided to contact Constable Melchior Sabuin of the Buka CID and he told him what he saw.

Detective Sabuin had previously arrested the offender for the offence of Armed Robbery five years earlier.'

THE INDEPENDENT STATE OF PAPUA NEW GUINEA
Search Act (Ch. No. 341)

INFORMATION

Act, **Sec., 6(1)** Form 1
Reg., Section 1(a)

To the **Buka District** Court

I, **Melchior Sabuin** (name) **Constable of Police** (occupation)
of **Buka CID** (address)

declare that:

1. **I have received information and hereby declare that there is a Smith and Wesson handgun, K1000, blue shirt, brown pair of trousers and a Toyota Hilux Utility Reg. No. A1111** [SECTION 6(1)(b)] [THINGS SOUGHT] **which will afford evidence of the commission of the alleged offence** [SECTION 6(1)(b)] **of Armed Robbery committed at the Bank of South Pacific at Buka at 10am on 7th January 2010** [OFFENCE] **by Danny Bosing** [SUSPECT].

2. **At 10am on 7th January 2010 Danny BOSING** [SUSPECT] **was observed to enter the Bank of South Pacific at Buka wearing a blue shirt and a brown pair of trousers** [SECTION 6(1)(b)] [THINGS SOUGHT].

3. **At that time Danny BOSING** [SUSPECT] **was carrying a Smith and Wesson handgun** [SECTION 6(1)(b)] [THINGS SOUGHT] **that he used to threaten staff.**

4. **As a consequence of the threat an employee of the bank handed to Danny BOSING** [SUSPECT] **K1000 in K50 notes** [SECTION 6(1)(b)] [THINGS SOUGHT].

5. **The suspect was observed to walk from the bank carrying a firearm and a plastic bay containing a quantity of cash.**

6. **The suspect was observed by a police informer** [CONFIDENTIAL SOURCE OF INFORMATION] **to drive a Toyota Hilux Utility Reg. No. A1111** [SECTION 6(1)(b)] [THINGS SOUGHT] **to the Kuri Resort, Buka before entering Room 7 immediately after the commission of this alleged offence.**

7. **It has been confirmed by the management of the Kuri Resort that the suspect is currently residing by himself in that room.**

(here state belief in respect of commission, or likely commission, of offence)

being the grounds for which a search warrant may be issued in respect of:

Room 7, Kuri Resort, Buka and Toyota Hilux Utility Reg. No. A1111.

(here state particulars of building, craft, vehicle or place)

Declared at **Buka**

Dated **8th January 2010**

....
Magistrate
Buka District Court

[6.9] VILLAGES SPECIFICALLY

[6.9.1] STATUTORY PROVISION

Section 6 of the *Search Act* (Ch. 341) states (in part)

> '(2) If a court is satisfied by information[548] on oath[549] by a commissioned officer of the Police Force that there are reasonable grounds for suspecting that there is in any building or buildings in a village or in any part of a village or village garden any thing specified in Subsection (1)(a), (b) or (c), it may issue a warrant to search the building, buildings, village, part of the village or village garden.
>
> (3) Where a warrant has been issued under Subsection (2) the person, policeman or policemen to whom the warrant is directed shall, where it is practicable to do so, before executing the warrant, endeavour to obtain the co-operation of those persons who, by custom, are regarded as the leaders of the village in respect of which the warrant has been issued.
>
> (4) Subsection (1) or (2) does not justify the use of greater force than is reasonable in the circumstances'.

[6.9.2] GENERAL PRINCIPLES

In *The State v James Bero Popo*[550] Amet J (as he then was) stated:

> 'It will also be noted that unlike s 6(1) where the information on oath is not specified to be necessarily by a commissioned officer of the police force, under s 6(2) it is. A further requirement of a search warrant issued under s 6(2) is that under s 6(3), the person, policeman or policemen to whom the warrant is directed shall, where it is practicable to do so, before executing the warrant, endeavour to obtain the co-operation of those persons who, by custom, are regarded as the leaders of the village in respect of which the warrant has been issued.

---

548 The Information to ground a search warrant for a village is same format as an Information under section 6(1), except that it is headed:
Act, Sec., 6(2), Form 2
Reg., Section 1(b)

549 The term 'oath' includes the making of a solemn declaration or affirmation, see section 3(1) of the *Interpretation Act* (Ch. 2).

550 [1987] PNGLR 286, [1987] PGNC 59.

See also: *Acting Public Prosecutor v Richard Saronduo and others* [1988-89] PNGLR 17 at 19.

These rather more stringent and special conditions for the issue of a search warrant for any search relating to a village are for sound practical reasons that the village community should not be unnecessarily disturbed and its peace violated without valid reasons, thus the special requirement that the information on oath shall be by a commissioned officer of the police as distinct from s 6(1), and where practicable, to first seek co-operation of village leaders. The village is protected and placed at a higher plane than any other building or place under s 6(1)'.

[6.10] POWERS AND DUTIES RELATING TO A SEARCH

Section 9 of the *Search Act* (Ch. 341) states:

'(1) A person conducting a search under Sections 5 and 6 in any place (other than in a baggage or freight container) and his assistants (if any) –

(a) have power –

(i) to enter and be in that place for the duration of the search and for that purpose to use such force as is reasonably necessary; and

(ii) to the least extent necessary with the least amount of damage – to interfere with the structure of the place for the purpose of search; and

(iii) to touch any article in that place; and

(iv) to stop and search any person found in that place in accordance with Section 4; and

(b) shall, within a reasonable period after the conclusion of the search, restore the place or cause the place to be restored as nearly as possible to the same state of cleanliness and neatness that existed immediately before the commencement of the search.

(2) A person conducting a search under Sections 5 and 6 in any baggage or freight container and his assistants (if any) –

(a) have power –

(i) to enter and be in the place where the baggage or freight container is situated and for that purpose to use such force as is reasonably necessary; and

(ii) to the least extent necessary and with the least amount of damage – to interfere with the structure of the container for the purpose of search; and

(iii) touch any article in the container; and

(b) shall, within a reasonable period after the conclusion of the search, restore the container and any article in the container as nearly as possible to the same state of cleanliness and neatness that existed immediately before the commencement of the search.

(3) Where a search of a container under Subsection (2) cannot otherwise be made, a person conducting a search referred to in that subsection and his assistants may destroy the container for the purpose of search.

(4) This section does not require the restoration of the structure of any place or container interfered with by virtue of the powers conferred by this section'.

[6.11] PROPERTY LOCATED DURING SEARCH

Section 10 of the *Search Act* (Ch. 341) states:

'(1) Where, during the course of a search that is authorised by this Act, a policeman finds any thing that he believes on reasonable grounds –

(a) has been stolen or otherwise unlawfully obtained; or

(b) has been used or is intended to be used in the commission of any indictable offence; or

(c) will provide evidence of an offence,

he may seize that thing.

(2) For the purposes of Sections 3(2), 5(2) and 5(3), where the person searching finds a firearm or offensive weapon he may seize it.

(3) For the purposes of Sections 3(3) and 3(4), where the person searching finds any thing which in his opinion may be dangerous or inexpedient to leave in the possession of the person searched he may seize that thing.

(4) For the purposes of Sections 3(5) and 5(4), where the person searching finds any thing that in his opinion –

(a) constitutes a danger or is capable of constituting a danger to the safety of the craft; or

(b) is capable of being used to threaten a person on the craft,

he may seize that thing'.

Section 12 states:

'Where any thing is seized by a policeman under this Act or is handed to a policeman, he shall enter in a permanent register of property[551] –

(a) a full description of the thing including where appropriate, a note of any identification marks; and

[551] 'A record of things seized by, or handed to, a policeman shall be kept in a register of property in Form 5', see section 3 of the *Search Regulation* (Ch. 341).

(b) the time and date the thing was seized or received by him and in the case of things received by him the name and address of the person who handed the thing to him; and

(c) the place and the person from whom the thing was seized; and

(d) other details as are prescribed'.

[6.12] POSSESSION OF CERTAIN PROPERTY

Section 13 of the *Search Act* (Ch. 341) states:

'(1) Where any thing is seized under this Act by a policeman or is handed to policeman, the thing shall be deemed to be in the possession of the State.

(2) Where any thing is seized under Section 10(4) by a person, other than a policeman, the thing shall be deemed to be in the possession of the owner of the craft.

(3) Where any thing is seized under this Act, other than under Section 10(4), by a person other than a policeman –

(a) in the course of his employment – the thing shall be deemed to be in the possession of his employer; or

(b) in any other case – the thing shall be deemed to be in the possession of that person.

(4) Anything referred to in Subsection (1), (2) or (3) may be retained in possession in accordance with that subsection for the purpose of examination and investigation and in the event that a person is charged with an offence in relation to that thing or in relation to which that thing is evidence the thing may, subject to any order to the contrary of a court, be retained in that possession until the charge and any subsequent proceedings on that charge have been determined'.

CASE FILE

[1.0] CONTENTS

When an investigation has been completed it is the responsibility of an investigating officer to complete his or her Case File prior to submitting it to a Prosecutions Office.

A completed Case File is comprised of the following documentation:

- Copy of the Information(s);

  An Information must have the correct wording of charge;

- Statement Of Facts[552];
- Bail Refusal Form, if applicable[553];
- Bail Certificate[554] or Certificate Of Refusal To Grant Bail[555];
- Witness List[556];
- Original statements of all police officers involved in the investigation[557];
- Original statements of all civilian witnesses[558];
- Exhibit List[559];
- Original Record Of Interview[560];

---

552 See Appendix 12.

553 See Appendix 13.

554 See Appendix 14.

555 See Appendix 15.

556 See Appendix 16.

557 See Appendix 17.

558 Refer also to the chapter titled 'Witness Statements'.

As regards the law in relation to 'Witnesses', refer also to the chapter titled 'Witnesses' in the text titled 'Injia on Criminal Practice and Procedure in Papua New Guinea and the Pacific'.

559 See Appendix 10.

560 Refer also to the chapter titled 'Interviewing Suspects'.

As regards the law in relation to 'Confessional Evidence', refer also to the chapter titled 'Evidence' in the text titled 'Injia on Criminal Practice and Procedure in Papua New Guinea and the Pacific'.

- Original Voluntary Statement[561];
- Crime Report[562];
- Supplementary Crime Report (if applicable)[563];
- Antecedent Report[564];
- Victim Impact Statement[565];
- Other documentary exhibits;

  and
- Check List[566].

However, if an investigation is incomplete then a written report is to be attached to the Case File advising:

- what is required to be done in order to complete the investigation;

  and
- what time-period is requested for that purpose.

Irrespective, all available documentation is to be submitted to the Prosecutions Office.

---

561 Refer also to the chapter titled 'Interviewing Suspects'.

As regards the law in relation to 'Confessional Evidence', refer also to the chapter titled 'Evidence' in the text titled 'Injia on Criminal Practice and Procedure in Papua New Guinea and the Pacific'.

562 Refer also to the chapter titled 'Court Proceedings'.

As regards the law in relation to 'Court Procedure', refer also to the text titled 'Injia on Criminal Practice and Procedure in Papua New Guinea and the Pacific'.

563 Refer also to the chapter titled 'Court Proceedings'.

As regards the law in relation to 'Court Procedure', refer also to the text titled 'Injia on Criminal Practice and Procedure in Papua New Guinea and the Pacific'.

564 See Appendix 18.

565 Refer also to the chapter titled 'Victims of Crime' and Appendix 5.

566 See Appendix 19.

[2.0] STATEMENT OF FACTS

A Statement of Facts must contain the following:

- Details covering each element of the offence whilst explaining how the offence was committed, including:
    - the extent of the injuries suffered;

      and
    - value of any property unlawfully obtained,

  if applicable;
- Details of the explanation given by the accused person for committing the offence;
- Details of any court orders sought in relation to the case, including the destruction of illegal drugs and firearms;
- Details of compensation:
    - already paid;

      or
    - that is being sought[567];

  and
- The antecedents of the accused person.

[3.0] BAIL[568]

[3.1] INTRODUCTION

It is unlawful to keep an accused person in custody for any period longer then they should be in compliance with the law.

The arrest and detention of a suspect during a period that a Court is closed for business may be an abuse of power and is in certain circumstances unlawful, such as the arrest of a suspect on a Friday afternoon and detention over the week-end period without bail when the arrest was not necessary and/or bail should have been granted.

[567] Refer also to the chapter titled 'Victims Of Crime'.

[568] As regards the law in relation to 'Right To Bail', refer also to the chapter titled 'Rights Of An Accused Person' in the text titled 'Injia on Criminal Practice and Procedure in Papua New Guinea and the Pacific'.

The only officers authorised to grant or refuse bail are:

- the Officer-in-Charge[569] of a police station at the time the decision as to bail is to be made[570], and referred to as the 'Officer-in-Charge';

  and

- a commissioned officer[571].

Such officers are referred to as a 'Bail Authority'.

The decision as whether to grant bail is to be made as soon as practicable upon the arrival of an accused person at a police station.[572]

Whenever possible, all bail documentation is to be typed.

When this is not possible, such documentation must be written neatly and legibly in English.

[3.2] CAPITAL OFFENCES

A police officer is not to grant bail to an accused person charged with:

- wilful murder, murder, piracy, attempted piracy or treason;

  or

- rape, abduction, burglary, stealing with violence or robbery, kidnapping, assault with intent to steal or breaking and entering a building or dwelling-house that was committed with the use of a firearm.[573]

---

569 See section 1(1) of the *Arrest Act* (Ch. 339).

570 See section 18 of the *Arrest Act* (Ch. 339) and section 5 of the *Bail Act* (Ch. 340).

See also: section 50(2) of the *District Courts Act* (Ch. 40).

571 See section 5 of the *Bail Act* (Ch. 340).

572 See section 42(7) of the *Constitution of the Independent State of Papua New Guinea* and section 18(1)(d) of the *Arrest Act* (Ch. 339).

573 See section 4(1) of the *Bail Act* (Ch. 340) and section 104 of the *District Courts Act* (Ch. 40).

[3.3] RESPONSIBILITIES OF A BAIL AUTHORITY

The Officer-in-Charge is to:

- as soon as practicable after an accused person has been arrested and brought to the Police Station consider whether bail should be granted[574];
  and
- cause the accused person to be taken before a Court without delay if an accused person is not granted bail[575].

  The need to:

  - interview an accused person;

    or

  - take statements from witnesses

  are not a lawful reason for not taking an accused person to Court without delay.

  However, the urgency of travel which in the circumstances are reasonable may, without taking away any other protection available to the accused person, be such a ground.[576]

If, however, a commissioned officer considers that it is not practicable to arrange to bring an accused person before a Court within a reasonable time that officer is to consider whether bail should be granted.[577]

An officer who fails to ensure that an accused person is taken before a Court without delay:

- shall be liable to be charged with a disciplinary offence;
- may depending on the circumstances be dismissed;

  and
- may be found guilty of committing a criminal offence[578].

---

574 See section 18(1)(d) of the *Arrest Act* (Ch. 339).

575 See section 42(3) of the *Constitution of the Independent State of Papua New Guinea* and section 18(1)(e) of the *Arrest Act* (Ch. 339).

576 See section 42(4) of the *Constitution of the Independent State of Papua New Guinea.*

577 See section 5 of the *Bail Act* (Ch. 340).

578 See section 133 of the *Criminal Code* (Ch. 262) as a party to that offence.

[3.4] DECISION AS TO BAIL

A Bail Authority is not to refuse bail unless:

- the investigating officer has correctly completed a Bail Refusal Form[579];
- and
- the officer is satisfied on reasonable grounds[580] that:
    - the accused person is unlikely to appear in court if granted bail[581];
    - the offence for which the accused person has been charged was committed whilst he or she was on bail[582];
    - the offence for which the accused person has been charged involved a serious assault[583];
    - the offence for which the accused person has been charged involved a threat of violence to another person[584];
    - the accused person did possess a firearm, imitation firearm, other offensive weapon or an explosive[585];
    - the accused person is likely to commit an indictable offence[586] if granted bail[587];

---

[579] See Appendix 13.

[580] See section 9 of the *Bail Act* (Ch. 340).

[581] See section 9(1)(a) of the *Bail Act* (Ch. 340).

[582] See section 9(1)(b) of the *Bail Act* (Ch. 340).

[583] See section 9(1)(c)(i) of the *Bail Act* (Ch. 340).

[584] See section 9(1)(c)(ii) of the *Bail Act* (Ch. 340).

[585] See section 9(1)(c)(iii) of the *Bail Act* (Ch. 340).

[586] An offence that is:

- declared to be treason, crime, misdemeanour or indictable offence; or
- punishable by imprisonment for a term exceeding 12 months,

is an indictable offence, see section 21 of the *Interpretation Act* (Ch. 2).

[587] See section 9(1)(d) of the *Bail Act* (Ch. 340).

- t is necessary for the accused person's own protection[588];
- the accused person is likely to interfere with witnesses[589];
- the alleged offence involved property of a substantial value that has not been recovered and the accused person if released would make efforts to conceal or otherwise deal with the property[590];
- that there are, in progress or pending, extradition proceedings made under the *Extradition Act 2005*[591] against the person in custody[592];
- that the alleged offence involved the possession, importation or exportation of a narcotic drug[593], other than for the personal medical use by the accused person under prescription only[594];

  or
- that the alleged offence involves a breach of parole[595].[596]

But the list of considerations under section 9 is not exhaustive in relation to offences, other than capital offences, as specified in section 4 of the *Bail Act* (Ch. 340).[597]

---

588 See section 9(1)(e) of the *Bail Act* (Ch. 340).

589 See section 9(1)(f) of the *Bail Act* (Ch. 340).

590 See section 9(1)(g) of the *Bail Act* (Ch. 340).

591 Refer also to the chapter titled 'Extradition Proceedings'.

592 See section 9(1)(h) of the *Bail Act* (Ch. 340).

593 'For the purposes of Subsection (1)(i), "narcotic drug" has the meaning given to it in the *Customs Act 1951*', see section 9(3) of the *Bail Act* (Ch. 340).

Section 1(1) of the *Bail Act* (Ch. 340) defines the term 'narcotic drug' as meaning:

> 'any goods consisting of, or of a mixture containing, bufotenine, dimethyltryptamine, lysergide, mescaline, psilocin or psilocybin, or any goods declared under Section 2 to be narcotic drugs for the purposes of this Act'.

594 See section 9(1)(i) of the *Bail Act* (Ch. 340).

595 Refer also to the *Parole Act 1991*.

596 See section 9(1)(j) of the *Bail Act* (Ch. 340).

597 Refer also to the section titled 'Right To Bail' in the chapter titled 'Rights Of An Accused Person' in the text titled 'Injia on Criminal Practice and Procedure in Papua New Guinea and the Pacific'.

The other considerations that may be taken into account before deciding whether to grant bail, include:

- the nature of the offence itself and the consequences that flow, or could flow from it;
- the strength of evidence against the accused person;
- whether the accused person is an habitual criminal;
- whether the accused person is a trustworthy person and will comply with any conditions of bail that may be imposed;
- the number of bench warrants outstanding for the kind of offence that the accused person has been charged;
- the costs and expenses the State may be put through in trying to bring the accused person to justice if he or she breaches his or her bail conditions which may mean delays in a speedy trial and the resultant risk of the State losing vital evidence supporting the charge against the accused person;
- whether the proposed guarantors are serious in their proposal having regard to the amount of money they are able to pay in sureties;
- whether the amount of cash bail proposed by the accused person has any relative correlation to the offence with which he or she has been charged;
- whether the accused person would have already served his or her penalty without a trial by reference to the offence with which he or she has been charged and the possible date for his or her trial;
- whether the welfare of the family of the accused person will suffer;
- the length of time that the accused person has been remanded in custody;
- the standard of conditions of the place of custody that the accused person is being held;

  and

- the interest of the accused person to be released on bail and returning to his or her community balanced against the interests of the law-abiding citizens of the society at large.

If a Bail Authority decides to grant bail that officer is to:

- complete a Bail Certificate[598];
- collect the cash bail;
- ensure that the cash bail together with a copy of the Bail Certificate to handed to the OIC, Prosecutions;
- give a copy of the Bail Certificate to the investigating officer, accused person and accused person's legal representative, if present;

  and
- verbally explain the conditions of bail to the accused person.

An accused person may be bailed to appear no later than one week after he or she has been arrested.

[3.5] REFUSAL AS TO BAIL

A Bail Authority who refuses to grant bail shall:

- complete all relevant details in the Cells Register;
- give his or her reasons verbally to:
  - the accused person;

    and
  - his or her legal representative[599];

---

[598] See section 5 of the *Bail Act* (Ch. 340) and section 1 and Form 1 of the *Bail Regulation* (Ch. 340).

See also: Appendix 14.

[599] See section 16 of the *Bail Act* (Ch. 340).

- record his or her reasons in the Cells Register[600] by attaching a copy of:
    - the Bail Refusal Form;

      and
    - the Certificate Of Refusal To Grant Bail[601]

  to the Cells Register;
- give a copy of the Certificate Of Refusal To Grant Bail to the investigating officer;

  and
- give a copy of:
    - the Bail Refusal Form;

      and
    - the Certificate Of Refusal To Grant Bail

  to:
    - the accused person;

      and
    - his or her legal representative.

[3.6] BAIL CONDITIONS

A Bail Authority may release an accused person subject to complying with specified conditions.[602]

---

600 See section 42(7) of the *Constitution of the Independent State of Papua New Guinea* and sections 18(1)(b) and 18(1)(c) of the *Arrest Act* (Ch. 339).

601 See sections 13(3) and 16 of the *Bail Act* (Ch. 340) and section 3 and Form 3 of the *Bail Regulations* (Ch. 340).

See also: Appendix 15.

602 See section 18(1) of the *Bail Act* (Ch. 340).

However, a Bail Authority is not to impose bail conditions that[603]:

- will cause undue interference with the accused person's domestic life;
- will interfere with the accused person's legitimate means of:
  - earning a living;

    or

  - making himself or herself available for work;
- will interfere with the accused person's rights to political freedom of action or movement, except insofar as it is necessary to ensure that he or she appears at court when required;
- will cause the accused person financial hardship;

  and

- are unreasonable in all of the circumstances.

When a Bail Authority fixes a bail condition to be complied with before release from custody, the officer shall, in the Bail Certificate, specify the condition that must be complied with.[604]

Bail conditions that may be imposed include:

- the payment of specified cash bail.

  Cash bail is to be set as follows:

  - K100 -- non-indictable offence; and
  - K250 -- indictable offence[605].[606]

  The Bail Authority is to ensure that all cash bail, together with a copy of the Bail Certificate, is handed to the OIC, Prosecutions.

---

603 See section 18(1) of the *Bail Act* (Ch. 340).

604 See section 18(2) of the *Bail Act* (Ch. 340).

605 The term 'indictable offence' is defined in section 21 of the *Interpretation Act* (Ch. 2) as meaning:
'an offence either declared to be treason, a crime, a misdemeanor, an indictable offence or an offence that is punishable by imprisonment for a term exceeding 12 months'.

606 The amounts specified are only suggested guidelines in order to standardise the amount of cash bail set by police officers.

The OIC, Prosecutions is to ensure that all cash bail is deposited:

- at the Treasury and the receipt received from the Treasury, together with a copy of the Bail Certificate, is handed to the Clerk of a District Court;

  or

- with the Clerk of a District Court, if there is no office of Treasury;

- a requirement to reside at a particular address or in the case of a juvenile[607] under the age of 18 years being placed into the care of a parent or responsible person who agrees to accept the juvenile[608];
- a reporting condition to a police station;
- the surrender of a passport[609];
- no contact with the complainant and/or other witnesses to be called by the prosecution;
- no interference with the on-going police investigation;
- and
- the appointment of no more than two guarantors.

A guarantor[610] must be:

- a neutral person, ie., not related by blood or marriage;

  and

- of some standing in the community.

A guarantor must depose in an affidavit as to:

- who he or she is in the community;
- his or her relationship with the accused person;

[607] See section 2 of the *Juvenile Courts Act 1991*.

[608] See section 21(5) of the *Juvenile Courts Act 1991*.

[609] See section 23 of the *Bail Act* (Ch. 340).

[610] Section 1(1) of the *Bail Act* (Ch. 340) defines the term 'guarantor' as meaning:
'a person who undertakes to see that a person granted bail complies with his bail obligations'.

- his or her knowledge of the accused person;
- his or her ability to ensure compliance by the accused person with any conditions of bail that may be imposed[611];

  and

- his or her financial means, source and ability to pay an amount of money in support of his or her undertaking that the accused person will comply with his or her conditions of bail[612].

A guarantor may seek the assistance from the office of the Public Solicitor in order to prepare the affidavit.

---

[611] See section 19(1) of the *Bail Act* (Ch. 340).

[612] See sections 19(5) and 21(3) of the *Bail Act* (Ch. 340).

[1.0] INITIAL RECORDING OF OFFENCES

[1.1] INTRODUCTION

The initial receipt of a complaint alleging the commission of an offence is the starting point of the investigatory process.

The officer who initially takes a complaint should:

- record the complaint in the Station Occurrence Book;
- record the complaint in a Crime Report in compliance with policy;
- record further details in a Supplementary Crime Report, if required;

  and

- obtain a detailed statement from the victim or complainant.

The accurate recording of facts relating to each individual offence has an important bearing on a number of matters, including:

- accurate criminal histories;
- accurate criminal statistics;

  and

- the effective and efficient conduct of investigations.

[1.2] CRIME REPORT

A Crime Report is divided into the following sections:

- the name and address of the person bringing the facts to the notice of the police;
- the particulars of the victim or complainant;
- the details of the offence, including:
  - when;
  - where;

    and

  - how

it was committed;

- the details of property that was unlawfully obtained, including all available identifying particulars;
- the details of a person who has been arrested;
- a brief report of the offence, including the result of initial inquiries;

  and
- an Investigation Report, including details of any suspect.

Each Crime Report is completed in triplicate as follows:

- the white original copy is issued to the investigating officer and when an arrest is made it becomes part of the Case File;
- the yellow copy is forwarded to the NCRO;

  and
- the green copy remains in the Crime Report book and is referred to as the Bookfast Station Record.

  Upon completion of each book it is forwarded to OIC, Supply for a replacement register.

[1.3] SUPPLEMENTARY CRIME REPORT

A Supplementary Crime Report is only required to be completed when:

- there is insufficient space in the Crime Report for any particular information;
- further details of unlawfully obtained property is reported;
- property is recovered;

  and
- the details of suspects are obtained and need to be circulated.

[1.4] STATION OCCURRENCE BOOK

The following details should be recorded in the Station Occurrence Book in order to develop criminal intelligence:

- the short title of the alleged offence, for example, Stealing;
- the details of the offence, including:
  - date;
  - time;
  - where;

    and
  - how

  it was committed;
- the particulars of the victim or complainant;
- the details of the offender;
- the name, address and mobile telephone number of the person bringing the facts to the notice of the police;
- the date and time of the report;

  and
- action taken.

[1.5] CRIME REPORT REGISTER

The details of each offence are entered into the Crime Report Register based on the details in the Crime Reports.

The CO No. is allocated from the Crime Report Register.

[2.0] DELEGATION OF INVESTIGATIONS

A Shift Supervisor/OIC, Traffic is responsible for either:

- delegating a reported offence to an officer under his or her command;

  or

- advising the OIC, CID depending on the seriousness of the offence.

[3.0] CASE MANAGEMENT

Each Shift Supervisor, OIC, Traffic and OIC, CID is responsible for:

- recording and monitoring all investigations conducted by officers under their command;
- ensuring that all complaints and offences for which an accused person has been arrested are not being investigated by an officer who has a close relationship with the offender, complainant or victim;
- ensuring that all complaints and offences for which an accused person has been arrested are comprehensively investigated as soon as is reasonably possible;

  and

- ensuring that all victims of crime are advised as to what charges the offender has been or will be charged with and how those charges will be instituted, ie., whether by arrest or summons[613].

If a complaint does not constitute an offence then the investigating officer is to submit a report, together with the white original copy of the Crime Report.

All investigating officers should maintain an:

- accurate;

  and

- current

record of each of their ongoing investigations.

[613] Refer also to the section titled 'Institution Of Proceedings' in the chapter titled 'Charges' in the text titled 'Injia on Criminal Practice and Procedure in Papua New Guinea and the Pacific'.

[4.0] TRIAL PREPARATION

[4.1] DISTRICT COURT

In respect to trials prosecuted in the District Court, it is the responsibility of the OIC, Prosecutions to ensure that all investigating officers are advised as to the dates of their trial.

It is the responsibility of an investigating officer to ensure that:

- all their witnesses are advised as to the date for trial;
- all witnesses are advised as to the date for trial.

  In relation to those witnesses whom there is a concern as to whether they will attend court they should be served with a 'Summons to Witness';

  and
- arrangements are made for the transportation of witnesses, as required.

[4.2] NATIONAL COURT

In relation to trials prosecuted in the National Court it is the responsibility of the office of the Public Prosecutor and the informant to arrange attendance of witnesses.

[4.3] WITNESS NON-ATTENDANCE

A witness who fails to attend court to give evidence:

- can be held in contempt of court[614], if it is the National Court[615];

  and
- can be arrested on a warrant of arrest if he or she has been served with a summons to attend court, if it is the District Court[616].

A police officer may also be the subject of disciplinary proceedings.[617]

---

[614] Refer also to the chapter titled 'Contempt Of Court' in the text titled 'Injia on Criminal Practice and Procedure in Papua New Guinea and the Pacific'.

[615] See *The State v Foxy Kia Tala; Re Corney Winjan* (1994) N1192.

[616] See section 68 of the *District Courts Act* (Ch. 40).

[617] See section 20(1)(c) of the *Police Act 1998.*

[5.0] TRIAL COURT PROCEDURE[618]

The procedure in the conduct of a trial, although not necessarily always in the following order, is as follows:

Formal Opening Of The Court

Plea Of Not Guilty

Opening Addresses

Formal Admissions

Examination Of Prosecution Witnesses

Submission Of No Case To Answer

Examination Of Defence Witnesses

Final Addresses

Decision

Unless called solely to give the opinion of an expert a witness should not be in court prior to giving evidence.

[6.0] REFRESHING MEMORY IN COURT

The fundamental importance of note-taking is:

the memory and recollection of every person will fade over time.

[618] As regards the law in relation to 'Court Procedure', refer to the chapter titled 'Court Procedure' in the text titled 'Injia on Criminal Practice and Procedure in Papua New Guinea and the Pacific'.

Obviously notes should be made:

- ideally at the time of the incident;

  or

- as soon as possible thereafter.

Notes may be referred to in Court for the purpose of:

- accuracy;

  and

- refreshing the memory of a witness,

with leave of the Court

A Court is only concerned with hearing the truth.

Giving evidence in court is not a memory test.

In the exercise of its discretion and in the interests of justice, a Court may permit a police officer and any other witness who has begun to give evidence to refresh his or her memory from a statement or notes made near to the time of the events in question, provided:

- that the witness indicates that he or she cannot now recall the details of events because of the lapse of time since those events took place;

- that the witness made a statement much nearer the time of the events and that the contents of the statement represented his or her recollection at the time he or she made it;

- that the witness had not read the statement before coming into the witness box;

  and

- that the witness wished to have an opportunity to read the statement before he or she continued to give evidence.[619]

[619] See *R v Da Silva* [1990] 1 All ER 29, (1990) 90 Cr App R 233, [1990] 1 WLR 31, [1990] Crim LR 192.

All police officers should use the following application to apply to a Court to use notes in order to refresh their memory:

> 'Your [Worship/Honour], I have some further recollection of what happened and the conversations which I had in relation to the matter before the court. I recorded my recollection on [ie. describe the type of notes] approximately [how long after the incident were the notes recorded] after the incident. In order to refresh my memory and for the purpose of accuracy I seek the permission of the Court to refer to those notes.'

A witness who has forgotten what had occurred, may refresh his or her memory from notes, provided that:

- the notes accurately depict what occurred;

  and

- at the time of writing the notes the witness was satisfied with its accuracy.[620]

If an officer wishes to refer to the notes of another officer then he or she should:

- read the notes when the facts were fresh in his or her memory;

  and

- initial the notes as being accurate.

It is irrelevant who wrote the notes, the issue is whether the witness had:

- read the notes when the facts were fresh in his or her memory;

  and

- agreed with the content of the notes as being accurate.

If the original notes have been lost or destroyed, an accurate copy of the notes may be referred to in order to refresh the memory of a witness.[621]

The practice of police officers collaborating in the making of notes is permissible.[622]

---

[620] See *R v Bryant and Dickson* (1946) 31 Cr App R 146.

See also: *R v Alexander* [1975] VR 741.

[621] See *R v Chang* (1976) 63 Cr App R 20, [1976] Crim LR 379.

[622] See *R v Bass* [1953] 1 QB 680, [1953] 2 WLR 825, [1953] 1 All ER 1064, (1953) 37 Cr App R 51.

[1.0] INTRODUCTION

It is vital that all policing organisations are able to:

- identify offences occurring and that may potentially occur in their area of operation;

  and

- effectively and efficiently organise resources, including personnel, to deal with such offences.

It is essential that all police officers contribute to the intelligence system, thereby enabling policing to be successful.

In community policing the need for ethical decision-making is based, among other reasons, on the need to develop trust between the police and community. Without this trust, the public will not provide the critical information necessary for effective crime control.

Public education is critical for the fight against crime. The public encompasses many different groups and different public initiatives need to be considered and implemented. However, all public initiatives should incorporate the following factors that are related to the intelligence function:

- Know how to observe;
- Know what is suspicious;
- Know how to report;
- Know what to report;

  and

- Know what happens next.

[2.0] WHAT IS CRIMINAL INTELLIGENCE?

Often there is confusion as regards the difference between:

- 'information';

  and

- 'criminal intelligence'.

CRIMINAL INTELLIGENCE

'Information' is pieces of raw and unanalysed data that:

- identifies persons, evidence or events;

  or

- illustrates processes that indicate:

  - the incidence of a criminal event;

    or

  - evidence of a criminal event.

Whereas criminal intelligence is:

> information that is recorded, reported, gathered, collated, evaluated, analysed and disseminated by a policing organisation.

Criminal intelligence may be in relation to:

- specific types of offences;
- identified criminals;

  and

- known or suspected criminal groups.

Criminal Intelligence, therefore, is:

> a planned product intended to provide significant direction to police decision-makers about crime and criminals, community crime and safety concerns and including road trauma.

While a criminal investigation is clearly part of the information collection process, the intelligence function is often more exploratory and broadly focused than a criminal investigation.

For example, a policing organisation may have a reasonable suspicion to believe that a person or group of people have the intent, capacity and resolve to commit an offence.

Evidence collected as part of the criminal intelligence function, however, may fall short of being able to prove an offence.

[3.0] PURPOSES OF CRIMINAL INTELLIGENCE

There are essentially two broad purposes of the intelligence function:

- **Short-term Prevention**

  Includes gaining or developing information related to threats of crime and using this information to develop strategies that will eliminate or mitigate the threat.

  This is referred to as 'tactical intelligence'.

- **Long-term Prevention**

  Providing information to police decision-makers about the changing nature of threats, characteristics and methodologies of threats and emerging threats for the purpose of developing response strategies and reallocating resources, as necessary, in order to accomplish effective prevention.

  This is referred to as 'strategic intelligence'.

[4.0] INTELLIGENCE-LED POLICING

Intelligence-led Policing is a strategic intelligence model for policing where criminal intelligence is crucial to an objective, decision-making framework that enables:

- crime and road trauma reduction;

  and

- a disruption and prevention of offences through strategic management and effective strategies that target prolific and serious offenders and locations.

The aim of Intelligence-led Policing is:

> for police decision-makers to have a strategic overview so that they can better allocate resources to the most important crime priorities.

Intelligence-led Policing requires:

- police intelligence officers to interpret the criminal environment;

  and

- the police decision-makers to use the criminal intelligence in order to have an impact on the criminal environment.

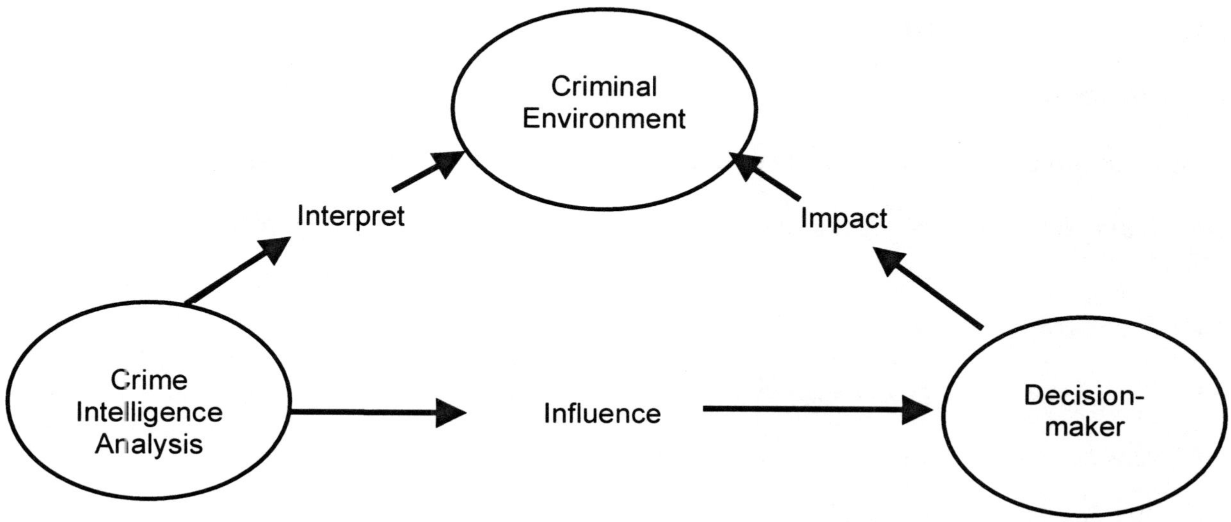

3i Model

[5.0] INTELLIGENCE CYCLE

[5.1] INTRODUCTION

Criminal intelligence is:

> the result of a logical intellectual process, often referred to as the 'intelligence cycle', which produces new actionable knowledge designed to assist in developing a plan of action in order to accomplish a desired goal.

Often it also includes learning from mistakes.

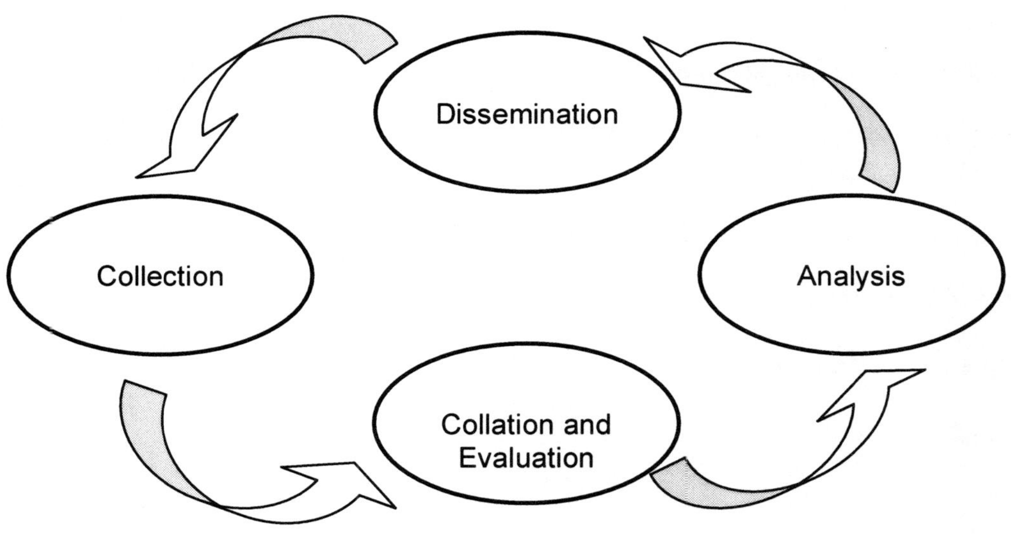

Intelligence Cycle

[5.2] COLLECTION PHASE

The Collection Phase is:

where information is collected from a person or place, and is referred to as a source.

One of the key views of Intelligence-led Policing is that every police officer is a collector of intelligence.

Information is obtained by:

- building a good relationship with the general public;
- talking to the general public;
- listening to what the general public has to say;
- taking notice of what is occurring when patrolling;

  and
- questioning accused persons as to their associates.

All information is good information.

The onus is on all police officers to:

- record any information relating to emerging crime and road trauma;

  and
- advise the appropriate Intelligence officer in relation to such information.

Intelligence can be evaluated and analysed from information entered into all operational policing records, including:

- an entry in the Station Occurrence Book;
- a Crime Report entry;
- a Supplementary Crime Report entry;
- an Intelligence Report;

  and
- an Intelligence Noting Sheet entry [BPS only].

However, all information that is recorded must be:

- complete;

  and

- accurate.

An officer may think that a piece of information is not of importance and ignore it. However, that one piece of information could be the one piece which is needed to complete the picture. An Intelligence Officer may need that piece of information in order to develop intelligence that could:

- prevent an offence from occurring;

  and/or

- lead to accused persons being arrested.

[5.3] COLLATION AND EVALUATION PHASE

[5.3.1] INTRODUCTION

All of the information that is collected needs to be collated in order to be evaluated.

An information's usefulness largely depends on:

- its reliability;
- its validity;

  and

- its relevance.

[5.3.2] RELIABILITY

When the source of the information is scrutinised then the reliability of the information is also being scrutinised.

The following questions should be answered:

- Has the information come from a reliable person?;
- Has the information come from an anonymous phone call?;
- What is the relationship between the source of information and the information that has been provided?;

and

- Is it possible for the information to be known to that person?

[5.3.3] VALIDITY

The next step is to determine the validity of the information.

The following questions should be answered:

- Is the information sound in itself?;

  and

- Can the information be sought by other independent sources?

[5.3.4] GRADING

When contemplating the grading of information the Admiralty Grading System is used:

SOURCE		INFORMATION	
A	Completely reliable	1	Confirmed
B	Usually reliable	2	Probably true
C	Fairly reliable	3	Possibly true
D	Not usually reliable	4	Doubtful
E	Unreliable	5	Improbable
F	Reliability unknown	6	Truth cannot be judged

For example,

- If a fairly reliable informant passes information that is confirmed by other sources then this would be graded/evaluated as C1;

- If a usually reliable source passes doubtful information then this would be graded/evaluated as B4;

  and

- If a new source passes information that cannot be confirmed by other sources and provides no clue as to its accuracy then this would be graded/evaluated as F6.

  However, if the information is confirmed by another source then it could be graded/evaluated as F1.

[5.4] ANALYSIS PHASE

Intelligence analysis is a complex task involving:

- examination;

  and

- assessment

of information in order to draw conclusions about a particular topic.

This task is undertaken by intelligence officers by applying:

- proven sound methodologies;

  and

- common sense.

[5.5] DISSEMINATION PHASE

Criminal intelligence is disseminated through a written confidential report.

As a general rule, the following are intelligence reports that may be needed by a policing organisation:

- a report that can aid in the investigation and apprehension of offenders;

- a report that provides threat advisories as regards potential threats;

  and

- a strategic analysis report that can aid in the strategic:

  - planning;

    and

  - allocation

  of resources.

However, criminal intelligence is usually disseminated on a needs-to-know basis.

Dissemination leads to planning.

[1.0] INTRODUCTION

The principles relating to:

- diplomatic immunity;

  and

- consular immunity

are distinct.

The principles relating to diplomatic immunity are covered by:

> the Vienna Convention on Diplomatic Relations, subject to the provisions of the Part II of the *Diplomatic and Consular Privileges and Immunities Act* (Ch. 83).

Whereas the principles relating to consular immunity are covered by:

> the Vienna Convention on Consular Relations, subject to the provisions of the Part III of the *Diplomatic and Consular Privileges and Immunities Act* (Ch. 83).

[2.0] DIPLOMATIC IMMUNITY

[2.1] DIPLOMATIC AGENT

A diplomatic agent[623] is inviolable[624], and therefore he or she may not be:

- detained;

  or

- arrested.[625]

This principle is the most fundamental rule of diplomatic law and is the oldest established rule of diplomatic law.[626]

---

[623] Article 1 of the Vienna Convention on Diplomatic Relations defines the term 'diplomatic agent' as meaning:

> 'the head of the mission or a member of the diplomatic staff of the mission, including administrative, technical and service staff'.

[624] See Article 29 of the Vienna Convention on Diplomatic Relations.

[625] See sections 4(1) and 4(3) of the *Diplomatic and Consular Privileges and Immunities Act* (Ch. 83).

[626] See M. Shaw, 'International Law', 5th edition, 2003, Cambridge University Press, page 681.

Article 29 states:

> 'The person of a diplomatic agent shall be inviolable. He shall not be liable to any form of arrest or detention. The receiving State shall treat him with due respect and shall take all appropriate steps to prevent any attack on his person, freedom or dignity.'

As a consequence a diplomatic agent is entitled to complete immunity from the legal system of Papua New Guinea.[627]

The only remedies that Papua New Guinea has in relation to a diplomatic who commits a criminal offence are to:

- request the sending State to institute criminal proceedings against the diplomatic agent[628];

  and/or

- request the sending State to waive the immunity of the diplomatic agent[629].

Furthermore, a diplomatic agent cannot be required to give evidence as a witness.[630]

---

[627] See *Dickinson v De Solar* [1930] 1 KB 376.

See also: M. Shaw, 'International Law', 5th edition, 2003, Cambridge University Press, page 682.

[628] See section 4(1) of the *Diplomatic and Consular Privileges and Immunities Act* (Ch. 83).

See also: Article 31(4) of the Vienna Convention on Diplomatic Relations and M. Shaw, 'International Law', 5th edition, 2003, Cambridge University Press, page 682.

[629] See section 4(1) of the *Diplomatic and Consular Privileges and Immunities Act* (Ch. 83).

See also: Article 32 of the Vienna Convention on Diplomatic Relations.

[630] See section 4(1) of the *Diplomatic and Consular Privileges and Immunities Act* (Ch. 83).

See also: Article 31(2) of the Vienna Convention on Diplomatic Relations.

[2.2] MISSION PREMISES

The premises of a diplomatic mission[631] shall be inviolable.[632]

The agents of the receiving State, including a police officer, may not enter the premises of a diplomatic mission, except with the consent of the head of the mission.[633]

The premises of the mission, their furnishings and other property thereon are immune from search, requisition, attachment or execution.[634]

[2.3] MISSION CORRESPONDENCE

The archives and documents of a diplomatic mission shall be inviolable:

- at any time;

  and
- whatever they may be.[635]

The official correspondence of a diplomatic mission which includes all correspondence relating to:

- the mission;

  and
- its functions[636]

---

[631] Article 1 of the Vienna Convention on Diplomatic Relations defines the term 'premises of the mission' as meaning:

> 'the buildings or parts of buildings and the land ancillary thereto, irrespective of ownership, used for the purposes of the mission including the residence of the head of the mission'.

[632] See section 4(1) of the *Diplomatic and Consular Privileges and Immunities Act* (Ch. 83).

See also: Article 22(1) of the Vienna Convention on Diplomatic Relations.

[633] See section 4(1) of the *Diplomatic and Consular Privileges and Immunities Act* (Ch. 83).

See also: Article 22(1) of the Vienna Convention on Diplomatic Relations.

[634] See section 4(1) of the *Diplomatic and Consular Privileges and Immunities Act* (Ch. 83).

See also: Article 22(3) of the Vienna Convention on Diplomatic Relations.

[635] See section 4(1) of the *Diplomatic and Consular Privileges and Immunities Act* (Ch. 83).

See also: Article 24 of the Vienna Convention on Diplomatic Relations.

[636] See Article 3 of the Vienna Convention on Diplomatic Relations.

- is inviolable[637],

and including the contents of a diplomatic bag[638].[639]

[2.4] PRIVATE RESIDENCE

The private residence of a diplomatic agent shall enjoy the same inviolability and protection as the premises of a diplomatic mission.[640]

Temporary absence would not lead to a loss of immunity, whereas permanent absence would.[641]

[2.5] MEANS OF TRANSPORT

The means of transport of a diplomatic mission is immune from search, requisition, attachment or execution.[642]

[2.6] PERSONAL BAGGAGE

The personal baggage of a diplomatic agent is exempt from inspection, unless there are serious grounds for presuming that it contains articles not covered by the specified exemptions in Article 36(1) of the Vienna Convention on Diplomatic Relations.[643]

---

[637] See section 4(1) of the *Diplomatic and Consular Privileges and Immunities Act* (Ch. 83).

See also: Article 27(2) of the Vienna Convention on Diplomatic Relations.

[638] See section 4(1) of the *Diplomatic and Consular Privileges and Immunities Act* (Ch. 83).

See also: Article 27(3) of the Vienna Convention on Diplomatic Relations.

[639] See section 4(1) of the *Diplomatic and Consular Privileges and Immunities Act* (Ch. 83).

See also: Article 30(2) of the Vienna Convention on Diplomatic Relations.

[640] See section 4(1) of the *Diplomatic and Consular Privileges and Immunities Act* (Ch. 83).

See also: Article 30(1) of the Vienna Convention on Diplomatic Relations.

[641] See *Agbor v Metropolitan Police Commissioner* [1969] 2 All ER 707.

See also: M. Shaw, 'International Law', 5th edition, 2003, Cambridge University Press, page 682.

[642] See section 4(1) of the *Diplomatic and Consular Privileges and Immunities Act* (Ch. 83).

See also: Article 22(1) of the Vienna Convention on Diplomatic Relations.

[643] See M. Shaw, 'International Law', 5th edition, 2003, Cambridge University Press, page 684.

Such inspections can only take place in the presence of:

- the diplomatic agent;

  or

- his or her authorised representative.[644]

The articles referred to are:

- articles for the official use of a diplomatic mission;

  and

- articles for the personal use of a diplomatic agent or members of his or her family forming part of his or her household, including articles intended for his or her establishment.[645]

[2.7] DIPLOMATIC STAFF

Section 7 of the *Diplomatic and Consular Privileges and Immunities Act* (Ch. 83) states:

> 'In respect of acts performed in the course of their duties –
>
> (a) members of the administrative and technical staff, and members of the service staff of the mission of an overseas country who are citizens or are ordinarily resident in Papua New Guinea; and
>
> (b) private servants of members of such a mission,
>
> are entitled to the immunity from jurisdiction, and inviolability to which persons referred to in paragraph 1 of Article 38 of the Vienna Convention on Diplomatic Relations[646] as having the force of law under this Act are entitled.'[647]

---

[644] See sections 4(1) and 4(2)(e) of the *Diplomatic and Consular Privileges and Immunities Act* (Ch. 83).

See also: Article 36(2) of the Vienna Convention on Diplomatic Relations and M. Shaw, 'International Law', 5th edition, 2003, Cambridge University Press, page 684.

[645] See section 4(2)(e) of the *Diplomatic and Consular Privileges and Immunities Act* (Ch. 83).

See also: Article 36(1) of the Vienna Convention on Diplomatic Relations.

[646] The persons referred to are a diplomatic agent and member of his or her family forming part of his or her household.

[647] See also: Articles 31 and 37 of the *Vienna Convention on Diplomatic Relations* and sections 4(1) and 4(2)(g) of the *Diplomatic and Consular Privileges and Immunities Act* (Ch. 83).

The rationale behind this is to ensure that a diplomatic agent's:

- independence;

  and

- ability to function free from harassment.[648]

[2.8] WAIVER OF IMMUNITY

The sending State may waive the immunity from jurisdiction, and therefore prosecution.[649]

However, such waiver must be express and is generally unusual.[650]

A diplomatic agent has no authority to waive the immunity.[651]

[3.0] CONSULAR IMMUNITY

[3.1] CONSULAR OFFICER

Consular officers are of the following categories:

- career consular officers;

  and

- honorary consular officers.

A consular officer:

- represents their State in many administrative ways such the issuing of visas and passports;

  and

---

[648] See M. Shaw, 'International Law', 5th edition, 2003, Cambridge University Press, page 684.

[649] See Article 32 of the Vienna Convention on Diplomatic Relations and section 4(1) of the *Diplomatic and Consular Privileges and Immunities Act* (Ch. 83).

[650] See M. Shaw, 'International Law', 5th edition, 2003, Cambridge University Press, page 687.

[651] See *Fayed v Al-Tajir* [1987] 2 All ER 396 at 411.

- may assist nationals in distress.[652]

A career consular officer may not be:

- arrested;

  or

- detained pending trial,

except in the case of a grave crime[653] and following a decision by the competent judicial authority, ie., a court of law.[654]

However, if a consular officer is:

- arrested;

  or

- detained in custody

then criminal proceedings may be instituted, provided that the proceedings are not in relation to acts performed in the exercise of consular functions[655].[656]

Whilst a career consular officer may be called upon to give evidence, no action can be taken against a career consular officer if he or she declines to give evidence.[657]

---

[652] See M. Shaw, 'International Law', 5th edition, 2003, Cambridge University Press, page 688.

See also: section 10(2)(g) of the *Diplomatic and Consular Privileges and Immunities Act* (Ch. 83) and Article 58(1) of the Vienna Convention on Consular Relations.

[653] Section 10(2)(d) of the *Diplomatic and Consular Privileges and Immunities Act* (Ch. 83) defines the term 'grave crime' as meaning:

> 'any offence punishable on a first conviction by imprisonment for a term that may extend to five years or by a more severe sentence'.

[654] See section 10(3) of the *Diplomatic and Consular Privileges and Immunities Act* (Ch. 83).

See also: Article 41(1) of the Vienna Convention on Consular Relations.

[655] See Article 5 of the Vienna Convention on Consular Relations.

[656] See section 10(2)(g) of the *Diplomatic and Consular Privileges and Immunities Act* (Ch. 83).

See also: Articles 43(1) and 58(2) of the Vienna Convention on Consular Relations.

[657] See Article 44(1) of the Vienna Convention on Consular Relations.

However, a consular officer is not under any obligation to:

- give evidence concerning matters connected with the exercise of their functions;

  or

- produce official correspondence or documents relating thereto.[658]

[3.2] CONSULAR POST

The consular premises[659] of a career consular officer is inviolable.[660]

It may not be entered by the authorities of Papua New Guinea, including a police officer[661], without consent, except in the case of fire or other disaster requiring prompt protective action.[662]

---

[658] See sections 10(2)(g) and 10(2)(h) of the *Diplomatic and Consular Privileges and Immunities Act* (Ch. 83).

See also: Articles 44(3), 51 and 58(2) of the Vienna Convention on Consular Relations.

[659] Article 1 of the Vienna Convention on Consular Relations defines the term 'consular premises' as meaning:

> 'the buildings or parts of buildings and the land ancillary thereto, irrespective of ownership, used exclusively for the purposes of the consular post'.

[660] See Article 31 of the Vienna Convention on Consular Relations.

As regards:

- the furnishings of a consular post of a consular officer, see Article 31(4) of the Vienna Convention on Consular Relations; and

- a consular post that is headed by an honorary consular officer, see section 10(2)(h) of the *Diplomatic and Consular Privileges and Immunities Act* (Ch. 83) and Article 51 of the Vienna Convention on Consular Relations.

[661] See section 10(2)(c) of the *Diplomatic and Consular Privileges and Immunities Act* (Ch. 83).

[662] See Article 31 of the Vienna Convention on Consular Relations.

As regards:

- the furnishings of a consular post of a consular officer, see Article 31(4) of the Vienna Convention on Consular Relations; and

- a consular post that is headed by an honorary consular officer, see section 10(2)(h) of the *Diplomatic and Consular Privileges and Immunities Act* (Ch. 83) and Article 51 of the Vienna Convention on Consular Relations.

[3.3] CONSULAR CORRESPONDENCE

The consular archives[663] and documents of a consular officer are inviolable:

- at any time;

  and

- whatever they may be.[664]

The official correspondence of a consular post which is all correspondence relating to:

- the consular post;

  and

- its functions,

and including the contents of a consular bag are inviolable.[665]

However, if an authority of Papua New Guinea, including a police officer[666], has a serious reason to believe that a consular bag contains, other than official correspondence, documents or articles, a request may be made for the bag to be opened and if refused, the bag shall be returned to its place of origin.[667]

---

663 Article 1 of the Vienna Convention on Consular Relations defines the term 'consular premises' as including:

> 'all the papers, documents, correspondence, books, films, tapes and registers of the consular post, together with the ciphers and codes, the card-indexes and any article of furniture intended for their protection or safekeeping'.

664 See Article 33 of the Vienna Convention on Consular Relations.

As regards an honorary consular officer, see section 10(2)(h) of the *Diplomatic and Consular Privileges and Immunities Act* (Ch. 83) and Article 51 of the Vienna Convention on Consular Relations.

665 See section 10(2)(g) of the *Diplomatic and Consular Privileges and Immunities Act* (Ch. 83).

See also: Articles 35(2), 58(1) and 58(3) of the Vienna Convention on Consular Relations.

666 See section 10(2)(c) of the *Diplomatic and Consular Privileges and Immunities Act* (Ch. 83).

667 See section 10(2)(g) of the *Diplomatic and Consular Privileges and Immunities Act* (Ch. 83).

See also: Articles 35(3), 58(1) and 58(3) of the Vienna Convention on Consular Relations.

[3.4] MEANS OF TRANSPORT

The means of transport of a consular post of a career consular officer is immune from requisition as a public utility.[668]

[3.5] PERSONAL BAGGAGE

The personal baggage accompanying:

- a career consular officer;

  and

- members of his or her family forming part of his or her household

shall be exempt from inspection, except if there is a serious reason to believe that it contains articles:

- that are not for the official use of the consular post;

  or

- that are for the personal use of the consular officer or members of his or her family forming part of his or her household, including articles intended for his or her establishment.[669]

The personal baggage accompanying an honorary consular officer shall be exempt from inspection, except if there is a serious reason to believe that it contains articles:

- that are not for the official use of the consular post;

  or

- that are for the personal use of the consular officer or members of his or her family forming part of his or her household, including articles intended for his or her establishment.[670]

---

[668] See Article 31(4) of the Vienna Convention on Consular Relations.

[669] See Article 50(3) of the Vienna Convention on Consular Relations.

[670] See section 10(2)(g) of the *Diplomatic and Consular Privileges and Immunities Act* (Ch. 83).

See also: Articles 58(1) and 60(3) of the Vienna Convention on Consular Relations.

[3.6] CONSULAR STAFF

Consular employees of a consular post who are:

- citizens of;

  or

- are ordinarily resident in

Papua New Guinea are entitled to immunity from jurisdiction in respect of official acts performed in the exercise of their functions.[671]

[3.7] WAIVER OF IMMUNITY

The sending State may waive consular immunity in relation to:

- the prosecution for an offence[672];

  and

- the giving of evidence[673].[674]

---

[671] See section 14 of the *Diplomatic and Consular Privileges and Immunities Act* (Ch. 83).

[672] See section 10(2)(g) of the *Diplomatic and Consular Privileges and Immunities Act* (Ch. 83).

See also: Articles 41, 43 and 58(2) of the Vienna Convention on Consular Relations.

[673] See section 10(2)(g) of the *Diplomatic and Consular Privileges and Immunities Act* (Ch. 83).

See also: Articles 44 and 58(2) of the Vienna Convention on Consular Relations.

[674] See section 10(2)(e) of the *Diplomatic and Consular Privileges and Immunities Act* (Ch. 83).

EXTRADITION PROCEEDINGS

[1.0] INTRODUCTION

The *Extradition Act 2005* applies to all foreign countries.[675]

That Act however only applies to an 'extradition offence'.

An offence is an 'extradition offence' if:

- it is an offence against a law of the requesting country, for which the maximum penalty is death or imprisonment for a period of not less than 12 months;

  and

- the conduct that constitutes the offence, if committed in Papua New Guinea, would constitute an offence in Papua New Guinea for which the maximum penalty is death or imprisonment for a period of not less than 12 months.[676]

An offence is also an 'extradition offence' if, under an extradition treaty between:

- the requesting country;

  and

- Papua New Guinea,

the conduct that constitutes the offence is required to be treated as an offence for which the surrender of persons is permitted by the requesting country and Papua New Guinea.[677]

An extradition request and any supporting documents must be:

- in writing;

  and

- in English.[678]

---

[675] See section 5(1) of the *Extradition Act 2005.*

See also: sections 42(1)(g) and 52(2) of the *Constitution of the Independent State of Papua New Guinea*.

[676] See section 7 of the *Extradition Act 2005.*

[677] See section 7 of the *Extradition Act 2005.*

[678] See section 3 of the *Extradition Act 2005.*

The procedure to be applied in relation to an extradition depends on whether:

- the country making the request is a Forum country, ie., a country that is a member of the Pacific Islands Forum[679];

  or

- the country making the request is a non-Forum country for which there is an extradition treaty[680].

An extradition may be objected to on a number of grounds.[681]

[2.0] EXTRADITION TO A FORUM COUNTRY

Upon a request to extradite a person to a Forum country a magistrate may:

- issue a provisional arrest warrant[682];

  or

- endorse the original warrant of arrest issued in the Forum country[683].

Such a person:

- must be brought before a magistrate, as soon as practicable, after being arrested[684];

  and

---

[679] See section 5(2) of the *Extradition Act 2005*.

[680] See section 5(3) of the *Extradition Act 2005*.

Section 2 of the *Extradition Act 2005* defines:

- the term 'treaty country' as meaning:
  a country with which Papua New Guinea has an extradition treaty;

  and

- the term 'treaty' as including:
  a convention, protocol, or agreement between 2 or more countries.

[681] See section 8 of the *Extradition Act 2005*.

[682] See section 10 of the *Extradition Act 2005*.

[683] See section 12 of the *Extradition Act 2005*.

[684] See sections 11(1) and 13 of the *Extradition Act 2005*.

- may be:
    - remanded in custody;

      or
    - released on bail in special circumstances[685];

  and
- may consent to surrender into custody for extradition to the Forum country as soon as practicable[686];

  or
- may refuse to consent to surrender into custody and as a consequence an extradition proceedings will then have to be conducted by a magistrate[687].

[3.0] EXTRADITION TO A NON-FORUM COUNTRY

Upon a request to extradite a person to a non-Forum country a magistrate may:

- issue a provisional arrest warrant[688];

  or
- issue a warrant of arrest[689].

Such a person:

- must be brought before a magistrate as soon as practicable after being arrested[690];

  and

---

685 See sections 11(2) and 13 of the *Extradition Act 2005*.

686 See Division 3 of Part 2 of the *Extradition Act 2005*.

687 See Division 3 of Part 2 of the *Extradition Act 2005*.

688 See section 24 of the *Extradition Act 2005*.

689 See section 27 of the *Extradition Act 2005*.

690 See sections 25(1) and 13 of the *Extradition Act 2005*.

- may be:
    - remanded in custody;

      or
    - released on bail in special circumstances[691];

  and
- may consent to surrender into custody for extradition to the requesting country as soon as practicable[692];

  or
- may refuse to consent to surrender into custody and as a consequence an extradition proceedings will then have to be conducted by a magistrate[693].

[4.0] SEARCH AND SEIZURE

If a police officer who arrests a person under the *Extradition Act 2005* has reasonable grounds for suspecting that property in the vicinity of such a person:

- may be evidence in proving an offence for which the warrant was issued;

  or
- has been acquired by the person as a consequence of the commission of the offence for which the warrant was issued,

then the officer may seize the property.[694]

If a police officer:

- arrests a person under the *Extradition Act 2005*;

  and

[691] See sections 25(2) and 13 of the *Extradition Act 2005*.

[692] See Division 4 of Part 3 of the *Extradition Act 2005*.

[693] See section 31 of the *Extradition Act 2005*.

[694] See section 40(2) of the *Extradition Act 2005*.

- has reasonable grounds for suspecting that there is:
  - on the person;
  - in the clothing that the person is wearing;

    or
  - in or on any property in the vicinity of the person that is under the apparent control of the person,

  anything (including a sum of money) that:
  - may be evidence in proving any offence for which:
    - the warrant was issued;

      or
    - surrender of the person is sought;

    or
  - has been acquired by the person as a consequence of the commission of that offence,

then the officer may search the person, the person's clothing or the property and may seize any thing found as a result of the search.[695]

However, such a person:

- cannot be required to remove any clothing that he or she is wearing[696];

  and
- must be searched by a police officer of the same sex[697].

The police officer must retain in safe-keeping any property or thing seized pending a direction from the Minister as to how the thing is to be dealt with.[698]

---

[695] See section 40(3) of the *Extradition Act 2005.*

[696] See section 40(4) of the *Extradition Act 2005.*

[697] See section 40(5) of the *Extradition Act 2005.*

[698] See section 40(6) of the *Extradition Act 2005.*

Upon being admitted to a prison after having been arrested then:

- the person;
- any clothing worn by the person;

  and

- any property under the immediate control of the person,

may be searched.[699]

A magistrate may issue a search warrant under the *Extradition Act 2005* if he or she is informed by affidavit that there are reasonable grounds for suspecting that there may be in a place:

- a thing that may be material as evidence in proving an offence for which;
  - a provisional arrest warrant has been issued;

    or

  - the surrender of a person in relation to a provisional warrant is sought;

  or

- a thing that has been acquired by a person as a result of such an offence,

and the affidavit sets out those grounds.[700]

The magistrate may issue a warrant authorising a police officer, with such assistance, and by such force, as is necessary and reasonable:

- to seize the thing;
- to enter the place and seize the thing;

  and

- to enter the place, search the place for a thing of that kind and seize any thing of that kind found in that place.[701]

---

[699] See section 40(7) of the *Extradition Act 2005*.

[700] See section 41(1) of the *Extradition Act 2005*.

[701] See section 41(2) of the *Extradition Act 2005*.

A police officer may arrest:

- a person without a warrant if the officer has reasonable grounds for believing that the person has escaped from custody that was authorised under the *Extradition Act 2005*[702];

  and

- a person who has been remanded on bail under the *Extradition Act 2005* if the officer has reasonable grounds for believing that the person:

  - has contravened;

    or

  - is about to contravene,

  a condition subject to which bail was granted[703].

[5.0] EXTRADITION TO PAPUA NEW GUINEA

A person surrendered to Papua New Guinea for an offence against a law of Papua New Guinea of which the person:

- is accused;

  or

- has been convicted,

must be brought into Papua New Guinea and delivered to the appropriate authorities to be dealt with according to law.[704]

The person may be:

- remanded in custody;

  or

- granted bail

until he or she can be brought to trial.[705]

---

[702] See section 43 of the *Extradition Act 2005*.

[703] See section 44 of the *Extradition Act 2005*.

[704] See section 47(1) of the *Extradition Act 2005*.

[705] See section 47(2) of the *Extradition Act 2005*.

FAMILY VIOLENCE

[1.0] INTRODUCTION

Most families experience some conflict and tension. There will be quarrels, arguments and shouting between family members. This is not unusual.

This is not what is referred to as 'Family Violence'.

Family Violence happens all over the world and 98% of the victims of Family Violence are women.

Family Violence is also common in Papua New Guinea.

The threat and reality of gender-based violence continue to damage the:

- physical health;

  and

- mental health

of women across the country who live with permanent injuries and scars that are both:

- seen;

  and

- unseen.[706]

Family and Sexual Violence is:

- a protection issue[707];
- a public health issue[708];

---

[706] See Amnesty International, 2006, 'Papua New Guinea – Violence Against Women: Not Inevitable, Never Acceptable!', September.

[707] See also: Background documentation for: 61st session of the General Assembly, Item 60(a) on advancement of women, 'Secretary-General's study on violence against women', forthcoming as document A/61/122/Add. 1, page 54 and UNICEF Papua New Guinea, (2008), Child Protection Situational Analysis 2008, Port Moresby, UNICEF, page 7.

An application may be made to the District Court for the issuance of an Interim Protection Order and Protection Order.

An application made be made to the Village Court for the issuance of a Preventative Order.

[708] See also: Law Reform Commission, 1996, 'Final Report on Domestic Violence', Report 14 cited in UNICEF Papua New Guinea, (2008), Child Protection Situational Analysis 2008, Port Moresby, UNICEF, page 1.

- a cause and a consequence of HIV and AIDS[709];
- a barrier to development with dire economic costs[710];
- an education issue;

and, by many stakeholder accounts, an affront to traditional values.[711]

In many parts of Papua New Guinea, it is believed (by women as well as men) that men have the right to control women, by force if necessary.[712]

The most common form of Family Violence is 'wife beating'. However, sexual violence is also common within families. Many men have the mistaken belief that they are entitled to have sex with their wife, irrespective of her wishes[713].[714]

---

[709] See also: Institute of Medical Research study, cited in Amnesty International, (2006), Papua New Guinea: Violence Against Women: Not Inevitable, Never Acceptable!.

Available at: http://www.amnesty.org/en/library/info/ASA34/002/2006, page 5.

[710] See also: Inter-Agency Standing Committee (IASC), (2005), Guidelines for Gender-based Violence Interventions in Humanitarian Settings: Focusing on Prevention of and Response to Sexual Violence in Emergencies.

Available at: http://www.humanitarianinfo.org/iasc/publications/asp.

[711] See 'The GoPNG National Strategy and Implementation Program to Reduce Family and Sexual Violence 2010-2020'.

[712] See Guidelines for hospital based One Stop Centres for family and sexual violence (draft), Health Improvement Branch, National Department of Health, dated 6/11/08.

Refer also to:

- the fundamental rights and freedoms that are guaranteed to all persons in Papua New Guinea as specified in Division 3 of Part III of the *Constitution of the Independent State of Papua New Guinea*;
- the fundamental rights and freedoms that are guaranteed to all persons in the Autonomous Region of Bougainville as specified Part 14 of the *Constitution of the Autonomous Region of Bougainville*;

  and

- the International Human Rights Instruments titled 'Declaration of Basic Principles of Justice for Victims of Crime and Abuse of Power' and 'Declaration on the Elimination of Violence Against Women'.

[713] Refer also to the chapter titled 'Sexual Offences' in the text titled 'Injia on Criminal Offences in Papua New Guinea and the Pacific'.

[714] See Amnesty International, 2006, 'Papua New Guinea – Violence Against Women: Not Inevitable, Never Acceptable!', September.

It is also not widely known that all forms of violence against women and children are against the laws of Papua New Guinea, including forced sex in marriage[715], regardless of brideprice or other customs.[716]

Many women who are a victim of gender-based violence do not realise that they are entitled to seek help.[717]

The victims of gender-based violence are victims of crime, and should be treated as such, rather than treating it as a family issue.[718]

Papua New Guinea has some of the highest rates of Family Violence in the world for a country not at war.[719]

Case reports represent only a tiny fraction of actual incidents, but reliable research shows that:

- on average, two out of three women have been beaten by their husbands or partners, with the figure rising close to 100% in some areas.[720]

  This is higher than in any of the 15 studies conducted by the World Health Organisation in 10 countries;

- one in two women have been forced to have sex against their will;

- 60% of men admit to participating in 'group sex', most likely gang rape[721];

- around half of the victims of rape representing:

  - one in three or four are under 12 years old;

  and

[715] Refer also to the chapter titled 'Sexual Offences' in the text titled 'Injia on Criminal Offences in Papua New Guinea and the Pacific'.

[716] See Guidelines for hospital based One Stop Centres for family and sexual violence (draft), Health Improvement Branch, National Department of Health, dated 6/11/08.

[717] See Guidelines for hospital based One Stop Centres for family and sexual violence (draft), Health Improvement Branch, National Department of Health, dated 6/11/08.

[718] Refer also to the chapters titled 'Client Service' and 'Victims Of Crime'.

[719] See Guidelines for hospital based One Stop Centres for family and sexual violence (draft), Health Improvement Branch, National Department of Health, dated 6/11/08.

[720] Refer also to the chapter titled 'Offences Against The Person' in the text titled 'Injia on Criminal Offences in Papua New Guinea and the Pacific'.

[721] Refer also to the chapter titled 'Sexual Offences' in the text titled 'Injia on Criminal Offences in Papua New Guinea and the Pacific'.

   - one in ten are under 8 years old[722];

- 75% of children report that they live in a home where violence is endemic, mostly against the mother;

  and

- 50% of children are estimated to be at risk of sexual abuse[723].[724]

Violence against women, in all its forms:

- violates;

  and

- impairs or nullifies

the enjoyment of women of human rights and fundamental freedoms.[725]

Violence against women may be:

- physical[726];
- sexual[727];

[722] Refer also to the chapter titled 'Sexual Offences' in the text titled 'Injia on Criminal Offences in Papua New Guinea and the Pacific'.

[723] Refer also to the section titled 'Sexual Offences Involving Children' in the chapter titled 'Sexual Offences' in the text titled 'Injia on Criminal Offences in Papua New Guinea and the Pacific'.

[724] See Amnesty International, 2006, 'Papua New Guinea – Violence Against Women: Not Inevitable, Never Acceptable!', September.

[725] See International Human Rights Instrument titled 'Declaration on the Elimination of Violence Against Women', Preambular paragraph 5.

[726] See International Human Rights Instrument titled 'Declaration on the Elimination of Violence Against Women', Article 2.

Refer also to the chapter titled 'Offences Against The Person' in the text titled 'Injia on Criminal Offences in Papua New Guinea and the Pacific'.

[727] See International Human Rights Instrument titled 'Declaration on the Elimination of Violence Against Women', Article 2.

Refer also to the chapter titled 'Sexual Offences' in the text titled 'Injia on Criminal Offences in Papua New Guinea and the Pacific'.

- social[728];
- economic[729];

  or

- psychological[730],

and includes assaults, sexual abuse, dowry violence, harmful traditional practices, non-spousal rape and violence, sexual harassment, forced prostitution, trafficking in women and exploitation-related violence.[731]

In the performance of their duty, police officers should:

- respect and protect human dignity[732];
- maintain and uphold the human rights of all persons[733];
- exercise due diligence to prevent, investigate and make arrests for all acts of violence against women, whether perpetrated by public officials or private persons, in the home, the community and in official institutions[734];

  and

---

[728] See International Human Rights Instrument titled 'Declaration of Basic Principles of Justice for Victims of Crime and Abuse of Power, Principle 1.

[729] See International Human Rights Instrument titled 'Declaration of Basic Principles of Justice for Victims of Crime and Abuse of Power, Principle 1.

[730] See International Human Rights Instrument titled 'Declaration of Basic Principles of Justice for Victims of Crime and Abuse of Power, Principle 1.

[731] See International Human Rights Instrument titled 'Declaration on the Elimination of Violence Against Women', Article 2.

[732] See section 148(2)(a) and Part 14 of the *Constitution of the Autonomous Region of Bougainville.*

See also: International Human Rights Instrument titled 'Code of Conduct for Law Enforcement Officials', Article 2.

[733] See section 148(2)(a) and Part 14 of the *Constitution of the Autonomous Region of Bougainville.*

See also: International Human Rights Instrument titled 'Code of Conduct for Law Enforcement Officials', Article 2.

[734] See International Human Rights Instrument titled 'Declaration on the Elimination of Violence Against Women', Articles 4(c) and 4(i).

- take rigorous official action to prevent the victimisation of women, and shall ensure the victimisation does not occur as a result of the omissions of police, or gender-insensitive enforcement practices.[735]

The victims of gender-based violence are victims of crime, and should be treated as such, rather than treating it as a family issue.[736]

Some men in Papua New Guinea are also subjected to violence from their female partners, although such violence is less common and less likely to result in serious injury.[737]

It is the policy of the Bougainville Police Service and Royal Papua New Guinea Constabulary to prosecute those offenders who commit acts of family violence, irrespective of their gender.

[2.0] TYPES OF ABUSE

Family Violence can be:

- 'physical', including personal violence, such as punching, slapping, hitting, shoving, throwing things, pulling hair, twisting arms and legs and choking and the use of weapons, such as knives, sticks and stones and damage to property;
- 'sexual', including sexual abuse or assault;
- 'psychological', including emotional and mental abuse and threats to women and children;
- 'social', including verbally abusing or putting the victim down in front of others;

  or

- 'economic', including where the abuser or offender takes control of financial resources and may forbid the victim to work thus controlling all the finances and being denied basic needs such as food and money.

---

[735] See International Human Rights Instrument titled 'Declaration on the Elimination of Violence Against Women', Article 4(f).

[736] See International Human Rights Instrument titled 'Declaration on the Elimination of Violence Against Women', Preambular paragraph 8 and Articles 1, 2(a) and 4(c).

Refer also to the chapters titled 'Client Service' and 'Victims Of Crime'.

[737] See Amnesty International, 2006, 'Papua New Guinea – Violence Against Women: Not Inevitable, Never Acceptable!', September.

[3.0] CYCLE OF VIOLENCE

[3.1] INTRODUCTION

It is not always easy for outsiders to see that Family Violence is happening. In most abusive families, the violence is not going on all the time -- it goes in cycles.

For most victims, when they begin a relationship with an abuser or offender, they have no way of knowing that he or she might become violent.

The victims are then, terribly shocked the first time they are subjected to Family Violence.

Family Violence can often begin during the first year of marriage.

Quite a lot of victims report that the abuser or offender started to beat her when she first became pregnant.

[3.2] THE PHASES

[3.2.1] INTRODUCTION

The cycle of physical violence in a relationship often follows this pattern.

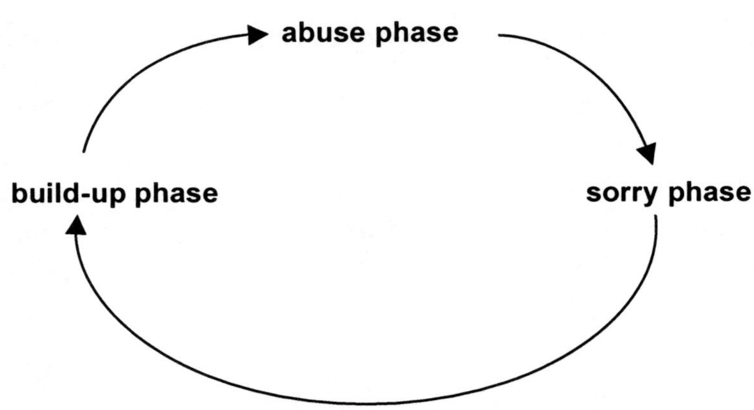

Cycle Of Violence

[3.2.2] BUILD - UP PHASE

Tension builds up.

The abuser or offender starts to abuse the victim.

For example, a male abuser or offender may swear at his wife or girlfriend, threaten her or slap or push her.

The victim feels as though he or she is walking in a minefield, waiting for the explosion.

Victims feel a loss of control as no matter how much they try to please the abuser or offender, they are still abused.

[3.2.3] ABUSE/VIOLENCE PHASE

When the abuser or offender actually attacks, the victim feels totally unable to stop the violence.

The victim feels helpless.

Some victims say even though the physical abuse is bad, the on-going emotional abuse (telling him or her that he or she's nothing, he or she's worthless, etc) kills him or her inside, as a person.

[3.2.4] SORRY PHASE

After the violence, sometimes the abuser or offender feels remorse, and promises it will never happen again.

The abuser or offender does this especially if the victim has threatened to leave.

The abuser or offender usually comes up with lots of excuses.

The victim so badly wants to believe the promises of the abuser or offender that he or she stays.

Another version of this phase is when the abuser or offender behaves as if nothing happened.

The abuser or offender expects life to just go on as it used to.

Then the tension starts to build again and the cycle continues on to the build-up phase yet again.

[3.3] CONTINUOUS CYCLE

The time frame of the cycle varies greatly.

In some relationships, it may take months to get through a cycle.

In others, a whole cycle might happen in a day.

Remember, it is the abuser or offender who controls the cycle, not the victim.

This cycle will go on and on unless:

- the abuser or offender takes responsibility for his or her behaviour and genuinely changes (he or she will need help);

  or

- the victim leaves the violent situation and/or takes legal steps to halt the violence or abuse.

[4.0] VICTIMS

[4.1] WHO ARE THE VICTIMS?

Victims of Family Violence are everywhere.

Some victims have survived and are now living free of abuse.

Many victims continue to suffer.

Some victims have not survived -- they have been killed.

Women from all social and cultural groups can be victims of Family Violence.

This is true overseas as well as in Papua New Guinea.

The old or young, the rich or poor, can all be victims.

[4.2] WHY DO WOMEN STAY IN VIOLENT RELATIONSHIPS?

Victims of Family Violence are usually afraid or unable to seek help, for a variety of social, cultural and economic reasons.[738]

Some people illogically think that victims do not leave their husbands because they like being beaten.

No one likes being beaten!

There are a number of factors which trap them in their relationships.

---

[738] See Guidelines for hospital based One Stop Centres for family and sexual violence (draft), Health Improvement Branch, National Department of Health, dated 6/11/08.

FAMILY VIOLENCE

Many victims:

- are financially dependent on their abusers or offenders.

  Even if the victims can find somewhere else to live, the victims know that if they do leave, they and their children may have to live in poverty;

- fear the social disgrace of being known to be a battered wife or a divorced woman;

- feel powerless because the physical abuse is often accompanied by other forms of abuse and controlling behaviours.

  As a consequence a victim of Family Violence often finds it difficult to make decisions and follow through[739];

- feel worthless;

- have no confidence in their ability to cope on their own;

- have been convinced by the abuser or offender that the abuse is their own fault and they deserve what is happening to them;

- feel guilty and ashamed;

- fear what will become of their children without a father;

- are scared because the abuser or offender has threatened to hurt people the victim cares about.

  Many abusers or offenders threaten victims with worse violence if they leave.

  For example, the abuser or offender may threaten to beat their children.

  Often the victim's fears are realistic;

- still love their abuser or offender but just want the violence to stop -- not the relationship;

- keep hoping that the abuser or offender will change;

  and

- are at home with dependent children, unaware that there is assistance available to them.

---

[739] See Guidelines for hospital based One Stop Centres for family and sexual violence (draft), Health Improvement Branch, National Department of Health, dated 6/11/08.

Some of the victims seek help to leave a violent relationship, but are advised by the priest or pastor and others in their community to go back home.

They tell her that it is her duty to stay with her husband.

[5.0] ABUSERS/OFFENDERS

It is not easy to tell if a person is an abuser or offender - just by looking at him or her.

Often men who appear to be Mr. Nice Guy to everyone outside the home, are cruel and brutal to their families.

As with victims, abusers or offenders come from all racial and cultural groups and may be rich or poor, young or old.

Surveys reveal that men convicted of committing Family Violence:

- have little pride in themselves (low self-esteem);
- cannot communicate well;
- are emotionally inadequate (unwilling to acknowledge emotion);
- find it hard to trust others;
- are extremely jealous of their partners and resent any other influence on them;
- want to control their partners;
- are insecure;
- sometimes were, themselves, abused as children;

  and
- are usually not mentally ill, although they can show big character changes.

  For example, charming and funny to other people (and, sometimes, even to the victim) but brutal and vicious at other times.

Abusers or offenders are abusive in various ways.

Some victims report that the abuser or offender is totally unpredictable.

Many abusers or offenders:

- explode into violence over just small things, such as the dinner not being warm enough.

The victims wait in fear until they know that the abuser or offender is in a good mood;

- seem to conduct a cold and calculated reign of terror over their victims by abusing them in a controlled way whilst showing no remorse;
- deny that they are responsible for what they are doing;
- deny that any family violence is happening at all;
- attempt to justify their behaviour by blaming others;
- blame the victim by saying that the victim deserved it because he or she is inadequate, ineffectual, irritating and/or always depressed or that the victim provoked them;
- play down the seriousness of the incidents of family violence by referring to such incidents as arguments or problems even though the abuser or offender has committed a serious criminal assault;
- blame many outside factors, including alcohol consumption, a hard day at work, unemployment or stress;

  and

- feel remorse after they have beaten their partners.

  Victims say their partners cry, and ask for forgiveness.

  The abusers or offenders say they will never do it again.

  However, this remorse lasts only a short time.

  The anger flares up again, the violence begin again and the cycle continues.

[6.0] EFFECTS

[6.1] INTRODUCTION

The effects of Family Violence on victims are extremely damaging.

Research shows that, compared to other people, Family Violence victims are more likely to:

- suffer physical injuries and disabilities;
- suffer mental health problems, including being anxious, depressed and suicidal;
- have miscarriages (twice as likely);

- contribute unwillingly to the spread of HIV and AIDS as a consequence of unwanted sex[740];
- have fewer skills for coping and solving problems;
- be cut off from other people (social isolation);
- abuse their own children;

  and
- suffer from headaches, asthma and other stress related illnesses.

It is important not to confuse the effects of Family Violence with the causes.

That is, some abusers or offenders will say they abuse their partner because he or she is inadequate, ineffectual, irritating and/or always depressed.

But the truth is usually that the victim was not like that before the abuse began.

The victim is like this as a result of the abuse.

Years of intimidation and abuse grind a person down.

[6.2] EFFECTS ON CHILDREN

It is not only the victims who suffer as a result of Family Violence.

Think about the children.

Some children suffer directly -- they are beaten too.

Some suffer indirectly -- they have to watch while the violence occurs.

At least half of all children whose mothers are abused are also abused.

Most are physically abused, some are sexually abused, and all suffer emotional abuse.

Quite a large number of women report that the violence began when they were pregnant.

It seems that some violent and possessive men resent the thought of children because they do not want to share their wife's attention.

Usually, having children in the house does not discourage male abusers or offenders from abusing their wives.

[740] See Amnesty International, 2006, 'Papua New Guinea – Violence Against Women: Not Inevitable, Never Acceptable!', September.

FAMILY VIOLENCE

There are cases where male abusers or offenders have deliberately forced their children to watch while they beat up their wives.

Some male abusers or offenders use this as another way of tormenting and humiliating their wives.

Observing such violence is profoundly traumatic for children.

Often they are frozen with fear and shock, and do nothing while their father attacks their mother.

Some children try to stop the violence or call for help.

There are cases of older children finally killing the father after years of helplessly watching the abuse.

Not all children are affected in the same way.

Often, children who witness Family Violence:

- are nervous and withdrawn;
- are full of anxiety;
- wet their beds;
- are restless;
- do not do well at school;
- suffer from headaches, stomach complaints, asthma, and stuttering;
- are cruel to animals;
- copy aggressive language and behaviour in their play;
- run away from home;

  and

- boys beat their girlfriends up when they are teenagers.

Children can learn the wrong things, when they grow up in a violent home.

They can learn that violence is a normal part of family life.

They can learn:

- the only way to cope with stress and pressure is through the use of violence;
- that it is okay to use violence to solve problems;
- that it is okay to use physical force to get what you want;

  and
- to disrespect women.

Other damage to children includes:

- having to change school and home often as their mothers try to get away from the violence;
- not being able to make or keep friends if the father cuts them off from the community;

  and
- suffering emotional neglect if parents are caught up in their own turmoil and if the mother is struggling just to survive.

Quite often, children in violent homes may grow up to be violent themselves.

Research suggests that 50-80 per cent of men who beat their wives and/or children, grew up in violent homes.

These children are more likely to believe that violence against women is acceptable.

They may also have suffered emotional damage as children and this often reduces their ability to feel things appropriately as adults.

[6.3] EFFECT ON COMMUNITY

As well as the impact on individuals and families of survivors, family and sexual violence has enormous consequences for Papua New Guinea, in terms of:

- the costs to the nation of providing health care and other services;
- the losses to the economy when women are unable to care properly for their families or carry out their jobs or other duties;
- the effect on development, when women cannot participate freely because of fear of rape or other violence;
- the perpetuation of a culture of violence, when children learn violence at home;

and

- the consequences to communities of the continuing spread of HIV and AIDS.[741]

[7.0] CAUSES

Alcohol does not cause people to be violent.

It is important that that is understood.

Alcohol is often present with abuse -- but it is not the cause.

It is a symptom of the problem.

Alcohol is often the trigger that allows them to do what they want to do anyway.

Men still believe that women are their possessions and they can do what they like with them.

If they feel angry or aggressive, they think they can take it out on their wives -- and no-one has the right to tell them they cannot.

This belief is supported by the community, which turns a blind eye and permits them to get away with it.

That is the major cause of Family Violence.

[8.0] MYTHS AND REALITIES

People have a lot of false ideas or myths about Family Violence.

x False idea

Family Violence does not happen often.

√ Fact

One in three wives is likely to suffer Family Violence at some time in her marriage.

[741] See Guidelines for hospital based One Stop Centres for family and sexual violence (draft), Health Improvement Branch, National Department of Health, dated 6/11/08.

x **False idea**

Marriage is private and what happens in that relationship is no-one else's business.

√ **Fact**

Assault is a crime, and society as a whole is responsible for criminal behaviour.

Violence is not a normal part of marriage.

x **False idea**

If a woman does not like being hit, she can always leave.

√ **Fact**

It is usually extremely hard for a battered woman to leave.

She does not leave because she:

- is afraid the abuser or offender will do something to her or someone she cares for;
- depends on abuser or offender for financial support and does not have any other support;
- does not have anywhere to go;
- is worried about the children's future;
- lacks self-esteem;
- is afraid the man will do something to her and her children;

  and
- does not want to break up the family.

The following are some more 'myths' and 'realities' about Family Violence:

Myths	Realities
Family Violence isn't a big problem	It is difficult to know because those involved often do not report it.
Family Violence happens mostly in poor people's homes	Violence happens in all kinds of homes, towns and villages.
Family Violence is worse in certain cultures/ethnic communities	People in all cultures and communities are subject to Family violence.
If a woman doesn't like it she can leave	The victim feels she is forced to stay because of financial matters, children, fear of reprisals, lack of knowledge or access to help, cultural/social isolation, emotional dependence, shame.
Women only get beaten when they ask for it	Violence is never an acceptable method of solving conflict in relationships. Partners do not have a legal right to assault one another, whatever they claim to have provoked them.
Alcohol is the most common cause of Family Violence	Alcohol is not the cause of Family Violence. Many cases do not involve the consumption of alcohol at all.
Some women seek out abusive men	No person is able to tell an abusive person from looking at them.
Violent men are psychiatrically ill. They can't control themselves	Violent people are ordinary people and capable of being charming and loving as well as violent. They often present well in public and are not usually violent elsewhere.
Violent men come from violent homes	Some offenders come from violent homes but not all children become offenders. However, not all offenders have been subjected to violence themselves or are from a violent childhood.

Some Myths And Realities Of Family Violence[742]

[742] See NSW Police Service, 1995, 'Volunteers in Policing'.

[9.0] RESPONDING TO NEEDS OF VICTIMS

[9.1] INTRODUCTION

Often people do not do anything when they find out that a man is assaulting his or her partner.

An excuse is:

> 'the law will protect innocent victims, sometimes this does not happen'.

The truth is:

> the law is supposed to protect everyone, including men and women who are victims of Family Violence.

Despite its limitations, the law in Papua New Guinea does go some way to bringing abusers or offenders to justice.

The fact the incident occurs in a family relationship does not either:

- justify;

  or

- minimize

its significance.[743]

The Courts have long recognised that personal and general deterrence have a heightened significance when sentencing in relation to offences involving family violence.[744]

If an offender has committed a criminal offence then he or she is to be prosecuted for that offence, irrespective of who is the victim.

An application may be made to:

- the District Court for an Interim Protection Order followed by a Protection Order;

  and/or

- the Village Court for a Preventive Order[745].

---

[743] See *Kunia v R* [2005] SBHC 60.

[744] See *R v Lennon* (2003) 86 SASR 295, per Doyle CJ.

Refer also to the section titled 'Comparative Sentences' in the text titled 'Injia on Sentencing in Papua New Guinea and the Pacific'.

[745] See section 51 of the *Village Courts Act 1989*.

Whilst a police officer may, with leave of the Court, apply for a Protection Order on behalf of and with the consent of a victim, a police officer cannot apply for a Preventive Order.

[9.2] ATTITUDE OF THE VICTIM

When a victim does not lay charges, it is often because:

- they are afraid of further beatings if they do;
- they are afraid that if the abuser or offender goes to jail or leaves them, there will be no money to live on;
- they are pressured not to do so by their family;

  or

- they do not really want the abuser or offender to be in trouble.

  They just want the abuse to stop.

[9.3] ATTITUDE OF THE POLICE

One of the major problems is that the law as it relates to Family Violence is not either:

- properly;

  or

- consistently

enforced by the police.

Some police officers do not want to help a victim by instituting criminal proceedings[746] because:

- they know the abuser or offender;
- they are related to the abuser or offender;
- they have negative attitudes to women and believe that women either provoke or deserve the attacks;

  and/or

- they think Family Violence is a private matter that should be solved in the home.

[746] Refer also to the section titled 'Institution Of Proceedings' in the chapter titled 'Charges' in the text titled 'Injia on Criminal Practice and Procedure in Papua New Guinea and the Pacific'.

If, however, a victim reports a Family Violence incident then a police officer has a responsibility to take action on behalf of the victim.

[9.4] POLICY

It is the policy of the Bougainville Police Service and Royal Papua New Guinea Constabulary to:

- prosecute those offenders who commit acts of family violence, irrespective of their gender;

  and

- assist a victim of Family Violence to apply for an Interim Protection Order and/or Protection Order, if requested.

[9.5] CUSTOMER CARE

Many victims will require counselling and other assistance, but are unaware of what is available to them.

In order to assist victims of Family Violence, all police officers need to:

- have knowledge of support agencies within their community that can provide extra assistance;
- refer victims to the appropriate agency and provide additional assistance, as deemed appropriate and necessary;

  and

- take the fears of victims seriously.

Violence is never an acceptable method of solving conflict in relationships.

Partners do not have a legal right to assault one another.

[1.0] INTRODUCTION

The *Mutual Assistance in Criminal Matters Act 2005* enables:

- Papua New Guinea[747];

  and

- foreign countries[748]

to make a request for international assistance in a criminal matter.

Such requests have to be approved by the Minister for Justice.

Whilst the Act applies to all foreign countries it only applies to those countries that have entered into a mutual assistance treaty with Papua New Guinea.[749]

[2.0] REQUEST BY PAPUA NEW GUINEA

Papua New Guinea may make a request to a foreign country:

- to arrange for:
  - evidence to be taken in the foreign country under the law of that country;

    or

  - a document or other article in the foreign country to be produced under the law of that country;

  and

- to arrange for the evidence, document or other article to be sent to Papua New Guinea[750];

  and

[747] See section 6 of the *Mutual Assistance in Criminal Matters Act 2005*.

[748] See section 7 of the *Mutual Assistance in Criminal Matters Act 2005*.

[749] See section 2 of the *Mutual Assistance in Criminal Matters Act 2005*.

[750] See section 12 of the *Mutual Assistance in Criminal Matters Act 2005*.

- in relation to a court proceedings or an investigation into a criminal matter involving an indictable[751] or serious offence:
    - to obtain a warrant or other instrument that, under the law of the foreign country, authorises:
        - a search for a thing relevant to the proceeding or investigation;

          and

        - the seizure of the thing or any other thing that is or may be relevant to the proceeding or investigation and is found as a result of the search;

      and

    - to arrange for the thing that has been seized to be sent to Papua New Guinea[752];

  and

- for a prisoner that is in custody in that country, referred to as a 'foreign prisoner[753]' to give evidence in a criminal proceeding in Papua New Guinea with the consent of that prisoner[754].

---

[751] The term 'indictable offence' means an offence against the law of Papua New Guinea:

- that may be prosecuted on indictment; and
- for which the maximum penalty is death or a term of imprisonment for at least one year, see section 3 of the *Mutual Assistance in Criminal Matters Act 2005.*

[752] See section 19 of the *Mutual Assistance in Criminal Matters Act 2005.*

[753] The term 'foreign prisoner' means a person who:

- is being held in custody pending trial or sentence for an offence against a law of a foreign country; or
- is under a sentence of imprisonment for an offence against a law of a foreign country,

but does not include a person who is at large after having escaped from lawful custody, see section 3 of the *Mutual Assistance in Criminal Matters Act 2005.*

[754] See section 24 of the *Mutual Assistance in Criminal Matters Act 2005.*

[3.0] REQUEST BY FOREIGN COUNTRY

A foreign country may make a request:

- that evidence be taken in Papua New Guinea for a court proceedings or investigation into a criminal matter in that country[755];

- that a search warrant be issued in Papua New Guinea and property seized for a court proceedings or investigation into a criminal matter in that country[756];

  and

- that arrangements be made for a prisoner[757] who is in Papua New Guinea to attend at a court proceedings and/or assist in an investigation into a criminal matter in that country[758].

---

[755] See section 13 of the *Mutual Assistance in Criminal Matters Act 2005.*

[756] See section 20 of the *Mutual Assistance in Criminal Matters Act 2005.*

[757] The term 'prisoner' means a person who:

- is being held in custody pending trial or sentence for an offence against a law of Papua New Guinea; or

- is under a sentence of imprisonment for an offence against a law of Papua New Guinea,

but does not include a person who is at large, having escaped from lawful custody, see section 3 of the *Mutual Assistance in Criminal Matters Act 2005.*

[758] See section 32 of the *Mutual Assistance in Criminal Matters Act 2005.*

JUVENILE OFFENDERS

[1.0] INTRODUCTION

The Juvenile Courts Service has been established under the *Juvenile Courts Act 1991*.[759]

That Service is comprised of:

- a Director;

  and

- such number of Juvenile Court Officers as are required,

who shall be officers or employees of the Public Service and shall be officers of the Court.[760]

Juvenile Courts have been established[761] and Juvenile Court Magistrates have been appointed[762].

[2.0] INTERESTS OF JUVENILE PARAMOUNT

In the proceedings and actions under the *Juvenile Courts Act 1991* the interests of a juvenile shall be the paramount consideration.[763]

[3.0] POWERS OF JUVENILE COURT OFFICERS

Section 13 of the *Juvenile Courts Act 1991* states:

> '(1) Juvenile Court Officer may –
>
> (a) enter any police station, lock-up or any other place of detention, for the purpose of interviewing a juvenile or a ward; and
>
> (b) be present at the interrogation of a juvenile or a ward; and
>
> (c) advise a juvenile or a ward of his legal rights and of his right to refuse to answer questions; and

---

759 See section 8 of the *Juvenile Courts Act 1991*.

760 See section 9 of the *Juvenile Courts Act 1991*.

761 See section 5 of the *Juvenile Courts Act 1991*.

762 See section 6 of the *Juvenile Courts Act 1991*.

763 See section 4 of the *Juvenile Courts Act 1991*.

(d) question an arresting officer in respect of a juvenile or a ward who is arrested or who is charged with, or in connection with, an offence; and

(e) attend in any Court and be heard in connection with any charge against a juvenile or a ward to whom he is assigned; and

(f) make submissions in respect of a sentence to be imposed on a juvenile or a ward; and

(g) counsel or advise a juvenile or a ward.

(2) A Juvenile Court Officer may commence, appear in or continue any proceedings or action on behalf of any other Juvenile Court Officer.

(3) A person who hinders or obstructs a Juvenile Court Officer in the exercise of his powers under this Act is guilty of an offence.

Penalty[764]: A fine not exceeding K300.00 or imprisonment for a term not exceeding three months, or both[765].

[4.0] JURISDICTION OF THE JUVENILE COURT[766]

A Juvenile Court has jurisdiction in respect of a juvenile[767]:

- to hear and determine summarily all offences otherwise triable in a District Court or Village Court;

  and

- who is charged with an indictable offence, other than homicide, rape or other offence punishable by death or imprisonment for life, to hear and determine the charge summarily in accordance with the provisions of the *Juvenile Courts Act 1991*.[768]

---

[764] This is not an indictable offence [see section 21(b) of the *Interpretation Act* (Ch. 2)] and therefore can be dealt with summarily [see section 22 of the *Interpretation Act* (Ch. 2)].

Refer also to the chapter titled 'Classification Of Offences' in the text titled 'Injia on Criminal Practice and Procedure in Papua New Guinea and the Pacific'.

[765] As regards the law in relation to 'Sentencing', refer to the text titled 'Injia on Sentencing in Papua New Guinea and the Pacific'.

[766] Refer also to the chapter titled 'Criminal Jurisdiction Of The Courts' in the text titled 'Injia on Criminal Practice and Procedure in Papua New Guinea and the Pacific'.

[767] The term 'juvenile' means a person aged not less than seven years and less than 18 years, see section 2 of the *Juvenile Courts Act 1991*.

[768] See section 15 of the *Juvenile Courts Act 1991*.

Section 3 of the *Juvenile Courts Act 1991* states:

'(1) Where a person apparently under the age of 18 years is arrested or detained and there is doubt or dispute as to the age of the person, the age shall, subject to Subsection (2) and in the absence of evidence to the contrary be as determined by a Juvenile Court Officer.

(2) Where in any proceedings under this Act, there is doubt or dispute as to the age of the defendant, the age shall, in the absence of evidence to the contrary, be as determined by the Court.

(3) In making a determination of age under this section, regard shall be had to –

(a) the development, maturity and conduct of the juvenile; and

(b) any other information that may be available'.

[5.0] ARREST AND DETENTION[769]

[5.1] INFANT

Section 20 of the *Juvenile Courts Act 1991* states:

'(1) Where an infant[770] is detained by a member of the Police Force, or in accordance with Subsection (2), the officer in charge of the police station[771] to which the infant is brought shall immediately –

(a) notify a parent or a responsible person[772], and a Juvenile Court Officer, of the whereabouts and the reasons of the detention of the infant; and

(b) allow access to the infant by all or any of the persons referred to in Paragraph (a),

and shall, as soon as practicable –

(c) release the infant into the care of a parent or responsible person or Juvenile Court Officer; or

(d) where compliance with Paragraph (c) is not practicable–place the infant in a remand centre or in such other place as is approved by the Director for that purpose.

---

[769] Refer also to the section titled 'Arrest And Detain' in the chapter titled 'Police Powers'.

[770] The term 'infant' means a person aged less than seven years, see section 2 of the *Juvenile Courts Act 1991*.

[771] The term 'officer in charge' means the member of the Police Force in charge of the police station at the time of the detention or arrest, see section 19(1) of the *Juvenile Courts Act 1991*.

[772] Where notification etc., of a parent or responsible person is required, and such a parent or person cannot, with reasonable diligence, be found, it is sufficient to notify a Juvenile Court Officer only, see section 19(2) of the *Juvenile Courts Act 1991*.

(2) Where an infant is detained by a person other than a member of the Police Force, the person shall immediately notify a Police Officer, who shall proceed in accordance with Subsection (1).

(3) Where an infant has been placed in a remand centre under Subsection (1)(d), the infant shall, as soon as practicable, be brought before a Magistrate, who shall order the release of the infant to a Juvenile Court Officer, a parent or a responsible person'.

[5.2] JUVENILE

Section 21 of the *Juvenile Courts Act 1991* states:

'(1) In this Section –

"bail authority" means an authority empowered to grant bail in accordance with the Bail Act 1977.

(2) Where a juvenile is arrested by a member of the Police Force, or in accordance with Subsection (3), the officer in charge of the police station[773] shall –

(a) immediately notify a parent or a responsible person[774], and a Juvenile Court Officer, and shall allow access by all or any of them to the juvenile; and

(b) place the juvenile in a remand centre or in such other place as is approved by the Director for that purpose; and

(c) notify a Juvenile Court Officer of the arrest, the reasons for the arrest and the place of detention.

(3) Where a juvenile is arrested by a person other than a member of the Police Force, the person shall immediately notify the police, who shall proceed in accordance with Subsection (2).

(4) Where a juvenile has been charged and placed on remand under Subsection (2), the Juvenile Court Officer notified shall –

(a) where the parent or responsible person has not yet been notified–notify a parent of the juvenile or a responsible person; and

(b) where the juvenile is on probation–notify a probation officer,

of the arrest of the juvenile.

---

[773] The term officer in charge' means the member of the Police Force in charge of the police station at the time of the detention or arrest, see section 19(1) of the *Juvenile Courts Act 1991*.

[774] Where notification etc., of a parent or responsible person is required, and such a parent or person cannot, with reasonable diligence, be found, it is sufficient to notify a Juvenile Court Officer only, see section 19(2) of the *Juvenile Courts Act 1991*.

(5) Where a juvenile is granted bail, the bail authority may require, as a condition of bail, that the juvenile be placed in the care of a parent or responsible person who agrees to accept him'.

[6.0] JUVENILE COURT

At a sitting of the Juvenile Court, the Court shall:

- conduct proceedings in camera;

  and

- reduce to a minimum contacts between:
  - a juvenile and the public;

    and

  - a juvenile and an offender appearing before the court.[775]

In all hearings under the *Juvenile Courts Act 1991* a Court:

- shall allow proceedings to be conducted so as to receive all matters, facts and opinions into evidence and shall not be bound by strict rules of evidence;

  and

- where it considers it necessary or desirable, may adjourn the proceedings and discuss any relevant matter with the juvenile or any other person immediately concerned with the matter.[776]

[7.0] JUVENILE CORRECTIONAL INSTITUTION

The Minister for Justice may, by notice in the National Gazette, approve the following institutions for the purposes of the *Juvenile Courts Act 1991*:

- a juvenile section of a corrective institution;
- a juvenile institution;

  and

- a remand centre.[777]

---

[775] See section 23(1) of the *Juvenile Courts Act 1991*.

[776] See section 25 of the *Juvenile Courts Act 1991*.

[777] See section 47 of the *Juvenile Courts Act 1991*.

[1.0] INTRODUCTION[778]

A coronial inquest may be conducted:

- when a person dies in suspicious or unusual circumstances[779];
- into the cause and origin of any fire by which any property has been destroyed or damaged[780];

  and
- where a person has been reported to a police officer as a missing person and the police have not found the missing person within a period of 6 months after the date of the report[781] [782].

The purposes for holding a coronial inquest include:

- to hold an enquiry and make findings in relation to the facts surrounding a death, fire or missing person;
- to provide a public forum for considering public issues, including health or safety, relating to specific deaths, fires or missing persons;
- to allay rumours and suspicion[783];

  and
- where necessary to commit a person to stand trial in the National Court.

Whenever an expatriate dies or is reported missing and that expatriate is not a permanent resident of Papua New Guinea then the relevant consulate is to be advised.

---

[778] Refer also to the text titled 'Injia on Coronial Proceedings in Papua New Guinea and the Pacific'.

[779] See section 7(1) of the *Coroners Act* (Ch. 32).

[780] See section 17 of the *Coroners Act* (Ch. 32).

[781] See section 20 of the *Coroners Act* (Ch. 32).

[782] See *Nells Aingiris for himself and on behalf of 14 others v Orim Karapo and The State* (2008) N3325.

[783] See *R v Greater Manchester Coroner; ex parte Tal* [1985] QB 67 at 83.

[2.0] DEATH INQUEST

[2.1] INTRODUCTION

Section 7 of the *Coroners Act* (Ch. 32) provides that a Coroner has the jurisdiction to inquire into the manner and cause of the death of a person who:

- was killed;
- drowned;
- died a sudden death of which the cause is unknown;
- died under suspicious or unusual circumstances;
- died while under an anesthetic in the course of a medical, surgical or dental operation or an operation of a like nature;
- died, but no certificate of a medical practitioner has been given as to the cause of death;
- died within a year and a day after the date of an accident where the cause of death is directly attributable to the accident;
- died in a correctional institution[784], rural lock-up[785] or police lock-up[786] or while a prisoner or in custody;
- died in a mental hospital or other institution under such circumstances as to require an inquest under this or any other enactment;
- died in such circumstances that, in the opinion of the Attorney-General, the cause of death and the circumstances of the death should be more clearly and definitely ascertained;

  or
- died, not having been attended by a medical practitioner at any time within three months before his or her death.

---

[784] See section 63 of the *Correctional Service Act 1995*.

[785] See section 64 of the *Correctional Service Act 1995*.

[786] See section 65 of the *Correctional Service Act 1995*.

A police officer who receives notice or otherwise becomes aware of:

- such a death;

  or

- a dead body being found,

must without delay give to the Coroner such information as he or she can obtain concerning the death or dead body.[787]

Upon a death being reported to the Coroner the body of the deceased person is under the control of the Coroner.

The Coroner has to decide whether it is necessary to conduct a post-mortem examination (autopsy) and only the Coroner can release the body of the deceased person for burial.

However, the Coroner has no jurisdiction to determine how a body of a deceased person is to be buried.[788]

[2.2] REPORT OF A DEATH

When a police officer is advised of a death that officer is to obtain the following information:

- the full name, address and mobile telephone number of the person reporting the death;
- the identity of the deceased person, if known;
- the location of the last residence of the deceased person, if known;
- the location of the body of the deceased person;

  and

- the circumstances of the death.

Such information is to be entered into the Station Occurrence Book.

That officer is also to complete an 'Initial Report Of Death To Coroner' form.[789]

---

787 See section 9 of the *Coroners Act* (Ch. 32).

788 See *Nells Aingiris for himself and on behalf of 14 others v Orim Karapo and The State* (2008) N3325.

789 See Appendix 20.

[2.3] INVESTIGATION -- SUSPICIOUS OR UNUSUAL DEATH[790]

The location in the immediate vicinity of a deceased person is to be treated as a 'crime scene', until it is established to the satisfaction of the Coroner that no criminal offence has been committed.

[2.4] NON-SUSPICIOUS AND NON-UNUSUAL DEATH

A non-suspicious death includes a suicide and death by misadventure.

If, however, there is any doubt as to whether a death was non-suspicious then the death is to be treated as suspicious.

What may appear to be a natural death, without suspicious circumstances, may later prove to be a homicide.

Where there are no suspicious circumstances an investigating officer should attempt to ascertain whether:

- the deceased person had attended a medical practitioner within the previous three months;

  and

- that medical practitioner will certify the 'medical' cause of death.

Where a medical practitioner is prepared to give a 'medical' cause of death certificate, but has not attended the deceased person within the previous three months, the particulars of the death together with the opinion of the medical practitioner is to be forwarded to the Coroner by the investigating officer.

If the Coroner does not accept the opinion of the medical practitioner then a post-mortem examination will need to be conducted.

Section 14(1) of the *Coroners Act* (Ch. 32) provides the Coroner has the power to order that a post-mortem examination be conducted at any time before the termination of an inquest and if necessary, the Coroner may order an exhumation[791].

---

790 As regards how to conduct an investigation into specific deaths, reference should be made to Chapter 30 of the Royal Papua New Guinea Constabulary Investigators Handbook.

791 See section 11 of the *Coroners Act* (Ch. 32).

[2.5] POST-MORTEM EXAMINATION

Prior to a post-mortem examination being conducted an investigating officer should:

- seek the authority of the Coroner for it to be conducted in order to ascertain the 'medical' cause of death, if necessary;

  and

- advise the pathologist conducting the post-mortem as to the identification of the deceased person.

A pathologist may merely conduct a visual inspection of the body of a deceased person to establish a 'medical' cause of death.

However, it is more common for a full post-mortem examination to be carried out.

This will mean that the body of the deceased person will be dissected in order to find a primary, and sometimes secondary cause of death.

A post-mortem examination will usually involve examining certain organs, bones and tissue.

Sometimes other more specific and detailed tests may need to be carried out.

Upon a post-mortem examination being conducted:

- the pathologist should issue a 'Post-Mortem Examination Report'. A copy of that report is to be attached to the investigation file;

  and

- the investigating officer should take possession of the clothing of the deceased person if it is of any evidentiary value.

Whilst the result of a post-mortem examination will assist the Coroner in establishing the 'medical' cause of death, it will not necessarily establish what occurred that resulted in that cause of death.

[2.6] IDENTIFICATION

Before a Coroner is required to determine the name of a deceased person it is important that the investigating officer arrange for a relative or close family friend to identify the body of the deceased and make a formal statement of identification.

However, where a body of a deceased person cannot be recognised, or where the identity of the body of the deceased person is unknown, a simple visual identification will not be possible.

Accordingly, other means will need to be adopted in order to establish the identity of the body of the deceased person, such as:

- fingerprints;
- dental records;
- DNA tests;
- comparison of x-rays of old limb fractures, plates, prostheses, etc. with medical records;
- circumstantial evidence, such as jewellery, clothing and property found on the body of the deceased;

  and

- tattoos, birthmarks and other body marks.

An inquest must be held when a body of a deceased person cannot be identified.[792]

[2.7] VIEWING

The Coroner may view the body of a deceased person if he or she thinks it is advisable.[793]

[3.0] FIRE INQUEST

Any fire:

- involving substantial destruction or damage of property;
- that endangered life;

  or

- that is suspicious in nature,

should be reported to a Coroner.[794]

---

[792] See sections 7(1)(c) and 7(1)(d) of the *Coroners Act* (Ch. 32).

[793] See section 12 of the *Coroners Act* (Ch. 32).

[794] See section 17 of the *Coroners Act* (Ch. 32).

When a police officer is advised of a fire that officer is to obtain the following information:

- the full name, address and mobile telephone number of the person reporting the fire;
- the location of the fire;
- what destruction or damage has been caused by the fire;

  and

- whether any person has been injured or killed as a consequence of the fire.

Such information is to be entered into the Station Occurrence Book.

That officer is also to complete an 'Initial Report Of Fire To Coroner' form.[795]

[4.0] MISSING PERSON INQUEST

Where:

- a person has been reported to a police officer as missing and the police have not found the missing person within the period of six months after the date of the report;
- a Coroner is of the opinion that an inquest into the disappearance of a missing person ought to be held;
- the Attorney-General directs a Coroner to hold such an inquest;

  or

- the Commissioner of Police/Chief of Police, a Superintendent of Police or the husband, wife, father, mother, sister, brother, son, daughter or guardian of the missing person requests a Coroner to hold such an inquest[796],

a Coroner shall inquire into the cause and circumstances of the disappearance of the missing person and into all matters and things that will reveal, or are likely to reveal, whether the missing person is alive or dead, and if the person is alive or likely to be alive his or her whereabouts at the time of the inquiry.[797]

---

[795] See Appendix 21.

[796] See section 20(6) of the *Coroners Act* (Ch. 32).

[797] See section 20(1) of the *Coroners Act* (Ch. 32).

[5.0] INVESTIGATION FILE

[5.1] INTRODUCTION

The Coroner may play an active and pro-active role in the investigation process and therefore, may give directions as to how an investigation is to be conducted.[798]

At least three copies of the investigation file are to be given to the Coroner.

[5.2] DEATH INQUEST

A comprehensive investigation file should be completed that includes a statement under the hand of the investigating officer that should:

- outline the circumstances of the death, including a summary of the evidence of each witness and a chronological sequence of the steps taken to investigate the manner and cause of death of the deceased person;
- specify the identity of the deceased person and how that identity was confirmed;
- specify the details of the person who identified the deceased person;
- specify the details of the investigation conducted;
- specify the details of any suspect or whether any person has been charged in relation to the death of the deceased person;
- specify any possible exhibits that have been taken possession of;
- specify the date and time when life was pronounced extinct and by whom;
- specify the 'medical' cause of death as determined by a medical practitioner or health extension officer;
- outline his or her opinion as to the 'medical' cause of death of the deceased person and the basis thereto, including the injuries observed to have been suffered by the deceased person, if any;
- provide a full description of the circumstances and surroundings in which the body of the deceased person was viewed by police;
- provide a detailed description of the position of the body of the deceased person;
- specify any associated pertinent details, such as a rifle laying beside the body of the deceased person;

[798] See sections 6 and 10(a) of the *Coroners Act* (Ch. 32).

- outline whether the deceased person was the subject of a Missing Person Report;
- outline whether the Coroner was advised of the death and if so, who and when;
- specify how the body of the deceased person was removed from the scene and to where;
- specify the date and location of the burial and who approved the burial;
- specify the names and addresses of relatives who have been advised of the death of the deceased person and when;
- outline what the photographs that are attached to the investigation file depict, together with a list of the photographs;
- specify whether a coronial inquest should be held and the reasons therefore;

  and
- specify whether the relatives of the deceased person have requested that a coronial inquest be held and the reasons therefore.

A statement should also be obtained from:

- the person who identified the body of the deceased person and the basis thereof;
- the police officer to whom the body of the deceased person was identified;
- the person who identified the body of the deceased person to the medical practitioner or health extension officer, if applicable;
- the person/s who located the body of the deceased person, including:
  - the date and time that the deceased person was located;
  - where the deceased person was located;
  - whether in his or her opinion the deceased person was dead at the time of being located and the basis for such an opinion;

    and
  - whether the deceased person said anything prior to dying;

- the person/s who witnessed the death of the deceased person and if no person witnessed the death:
    - o the last person who saw the deceased person alive;
    - o the apparent state of health of the deceased person at that time;

      and
    - o the behaviour of the deceased person at that time;

  and
- any medical practitioner or health extension officer who had been treating the deceased person immediately prior to his or her death, including:
    - o his or her academic qualifications and experience;
    - o any medical condition for which the deceased person was being treated;
    - o the date that the medical practitioner or health extension officer last saw the deceased person and the state of the health of the deceased person at that time;
    - o details of treatment provided;
    - o duration of such treatment;
    - o medication prescribed;
    - o opinion as to 'medical' cause of the death of the deceased person;

      and
    - o whether in his or her opinion there is any need for a post-mortem examination to be performed and the reasons therefore.

The investigation file should also include:

- a list of all witnesses from whom statements have been taken[799];
- a list of potential exhibits, including the original receipt of any property taken possession of;

---

[799] Considering that the rules of evidence do not strictly apply to a coronial inquest such statements may contain hearsay evidence.

The 'Hearsay Rule' states that a witness must only give evidence of what he or she saw and not what he or she was told, subject to a number of exceptions.

As regards the law in relation to 'Hearsay Evidence', refer to the chapter titled 'Evidence' in the text titled 'Injia on Criminal Practice and Procedure in Papua New Guinea and the Pacific'.

- the original statement of the medical practitioner or health extension officer that specifies:
- his or her academic qualifications and experience;
- the date, time and place of the examination of the body of the deceased person;
- that he or she pronounced 'life extinct' and the 'medical' cause of death, if able to do so, after performing such an examination;
- any diagram or plan made in respect of the scene of the death, if considered necessary;
- any photographs taken of the scene of the death;
- any suicide note;
- the original of any Record of Interview conducted and Voluntary Statement obtained;
- any other medical reports, including the original 'Post-Mortem Examination Report';

  and
- any other potentially relevant documentary material.

[5.3] FIRE INQUEST

An investigation file into a fire to be forwarded to the Coroner is to include the following documentation:

- a statement under the hand of the investigating officer that:
  - outlines the circumstances of the fire, including a summary of the evidence of each witness and a chronological sequence of the steps taken to investigate the cause and origin of the fire;
  - specifies the details of the investigation conducted;
  - specifies the details of any suspect;
  - specifies any possible exhibits that have been taken possession of;

    and
  - outlines what photographs that are attached to the file depict, together with a list of the photographs;

- a statement from the person who located the fire, including:
  - the place where the fire was located;
  - the time that the fire was located;
  - the description and any other particulars of any person seen running away from the vicinity of the scene of the fire, if applicable;

    and
  - the description and any other particulars of any person seen acting suspiciously in the vicinity of the scene of the fire, if applicable;
- a statement from the owner of the property, including:
  - the particulars of the last person to use the property;
  - security procedures installed in respect to the property;
  - the extent of damage to the property and the estimated value of loss;

    and
  - any insurance details in respect to the property;
- whether a Fire Inquest is requested to be held and the reasons therefore;
- a statement from the fire officer who is able to give an opinion as to the cause and origin of the fire;

  and
- a statement from a person who has the appropriate forensic qualifications and experience in determining the cause and origin of a fire, if applicable.

The investigation file should also include:

- a brief summary of the circumstances of the fire;
- a list of all witnesses from whom statements have been taken[800];
- a list of potential exhibits;

---

[800] Considering that the rules of evidence do not strictly apply to a Fire Inquest such statements may contain hearsay evidence.

The 'Hearsay Rule' states that a witness must only give evidence of what he or she saw and not what he or she was told, subject to a number of exceptions.

As regards the law in relation to 'Hearsay Evidence', refer to the chapter titled 'Evidence' in the text titled 'Injia on Criminal Practice and Procedure in Papua New Guinea and the Pacific'.

- any reports from relevant experts;
- any diagram or plan made in respect of the scene of the fire;
- any photographs taken of the scene of the fire;
- the original of any Record of Interview conducted and Voluntary Statement obtained, if applicable;

  and
- any other potentially relevant documentary material.

[5.4] MISSING PERSON INQUEST

An investigation file into the disappearance of a missing person to be forwarded to the Coroner is to include the following documentation:

- a statement under the hand of the investigating officer that:
  - specifies the particulars of the missing person, including full name, address, age and mobile telephone number;
  - outlines the circumstances of the disappearance of the missing person, including a summary of the evidence of each witness;
  - specifies the details of the investigation conducted;
  - specifies the details of any suspect;
  - specifies any possible exhibits that have been taken possession of;

    and
  - outlines any photographs that are attached to the file depict, together with a list of the photographs;
- the original statements of all witnesses;
- the original of any Record of Interview conducted and Voluntary Statement obtained;

  and
- any other relevant documentation.

[6.0] PROCEDURE IN A CORONERS COURT

[6.1] INTRODUCTION

An inquest, although it is a Court of Record, is less formal than a Court of Law.

[6.2] PROCEDURE

The Coroner is addressed as 'Sir' or 'Madam'.

The Coroner is not bound by the strict rules of evidence, and may be informed and conduct a coronial inquest in any manner that he or she reasonably thinks fit, provided that there is compliance with the rules of natural justice.

The Coroner is assisted by a Coroners Assistant.

A Coroners Assistant plays a supportive and investigatory role, and is usually a police prosecutor or a lawyer from the Attorney-General's department. Unlike a criminal trial, the Coroners Assistant works closely with the Coroner before, during and after the investigation and inquest.

An 'interested party' may seek leave from the Coroner to appear, or be represented by a lawyer, at an inquest.

A person whose interest is likely to be affected should be given every opportunity to be represented and heard in his or her defence.[801]

It is the Coroner who decides which witnesses will be called to give evidence on oath and in what order. However, the Coroners Assistant usually calls the witnesses.

Witnesses are not necessarily expected to give evidence in full, but rather confirm the correctness of their statement.

The cross-examination of witnesses is at the discretion of the Coroner, provided that there is compliance with the rules of natural justice.

However, the Coroner must give a warning to a witness where there appears to be any evidence that could lead to self-incrimination. Such a witness cannot be required to give evidence.

It is at the discretion of the Coroner as to whether he or she will hear submissions, provided there is compliance with the rules of 'natural justice[802]'.

---

[801] See *Sakawar Kasieng v Andrew Baigry, Magistrate of Wewak District Court and The State* (2004) N2562.

[802] See section 59 of the *Constitution of the Independent State of Papua New Guinea*.

[6.3] FINDINGS

[6.3.1] INTRODUCTION

At the conclusion of an inquest the Coroner is required to make a finding.

[6.3.2] DEATH INQUEST

The Coroner holding a coronial inquest into a death must find, if possible:

- the full name of the deceased;
- how, when and where the death occurred.

  For example, in relation to a drug overdose the finding could be:

  > 'I find that on (date) at (location) the deceased person AB, the subject of this inquest, did die from [specify the 'medical' cause of death] as a consequence of the effects of [for example] self-ingested poisoning, but whether [he or she] had the intention of taking [his or her] own life or otherwise, the evidence adduced does not enable me to say';

  and

- the identity of any person who contributed to the death where there is evidence of Wilful Murder, Murder or Manslaughter.

  In such circumstances that person can be charged by the Coroner and committed to the National Court.[803]

[6.3.3] FIRE INQUEST

The Coroner holding a coronial inquest into a fire must find, if possible:

- the date, time and location where the fire occurred;
- the cause of the fire;

  and

- the identity of any person who contributed to the fire where there is evidence of Arson.[804]

---

[803] See section 19 of the *Coroners Act* (Ch. 32).

[804] As regards the law in relation to the offence of 'Arson', refer to the chapter titled 'Offences Against Property' in the text titled 'Injia on Criminal Practice and Procedure in Papua New Guinea and the Pacific'.

In such circumstances that person can be charged by the Coroner and committed to the National Court.[805]

[6.3.4] MISSING PERSON INQUEST

The Coroner holding a coronial inquest into the disappearance of a missing person must find, if possible:

- the full name of the missing person;
- the last known place of residence of the missing person;
- the sex of the missing person;
- the age, or approximate age, of the missing person;
- the date that the missing person was last seen;
- the place where the missing person was last seen;

  and

- a summary of the circumstances leading up to the person going missing.

The Coroner may make a finding that a specified person did cause the death by the commission of the offence of 'Wilful Murder'[806], 'Murder'[807] or 'Manslaughter'[808] [809].

---

805 See section 19 of the *Coroners Act* (Ch. 32).

806 See section 299 of the *Criminal Code* (Ch. 262).

807 See section 300 of the *Criminal Code* (Ch. 262).

808 See section 301 of the *Criminal Code* (Ch. 262).

809 See section 19 of the *Coroners Act* (Ch. 32).

See also: sections 10(b), 22, 23(3) and 27(b) of the *Coroners Act* (Ch. 32).

A Coroner must follow those specific procedures when committing a person for trial in the National Court.

As regards the law in relation to 'Homicidal Offences', refer to the chapter titled 'Offences Against The Person' in the text titled 'Injia on Criminal Offences in Papua New Guinea and the Pacific'.

[6.4] RECOMMENDATIONS

The Coroner may also make recommendations.

These are usually directed to a government department, private organisation or individual persons, in order to avoid similar deaths or fires from occurring.

[7.0] NO INQUEST

If the Coroner is of the opinion that no good purpose would be served by holding an inquest he or she is required to advise the Attorney-General in writing.[810]

[810] See sections 7(4) and 17(2) of the *Coroners Act* (Ch. 32).

APPENDICES

APPENDIX 1

CODE OF ETHICS

APPENDICES

CODE OF ETHICS

Police officers have a duty to their country and to their Police Force to serve the community by protecting life and property, preserving peace and detecting and apprehending offenders;

Police officers should carry out their duties with integrity and honesty and should at all times make every effort to respect the rights of all people in the community regardless of colour, social status or religion; enforcing the law justly without fear, favour, malice or ill will;

It is incumbent upon all police officers to keep confidential matters of such a nature which they may learn in their official capacity, unless revelation is necessary for the administration of justice;

By their conduct and performance police officers should give high priority to enhancing the reputation of their profession. Police officers should practice self discipline and restraint and should strive to improve their knowledge of the law and contemporary police practice applicable to their community;

Police officers should be aware of these ethics and should accept the desirability of them as an integral part of their personal and professional life.

APPENDIX 2

DISCIPLINE OFFENCES

Section 20 of the *Police Act 1998* states:

'(1) A member of the Force who –

(a) wilfully disobeys or disregards a Standing or Special Order made or given by the Commissioner, or any lawful order given to the member orally or in writing by a member of the Force who is senior to the member, or whose directions the member is required to obey, or fails to carry out such order as soon as practicable; or

(b) fails to carry out any specified duty imposed on the member by this Act or any other Act or Regulation; or

(c) does not promptly and diligently attend to and carry out anything which it is the member's duty to attend to or carry out; or

(d) is insubordinate or disrespectful either by word, act or demeanour to any member senior in rank; or

(e) without reasonable excuse, is absent from duty or is late for parade, court or any other duty; or

(f) while on duty in uniform, smokes in a public place; or

(g) while on duty chews betel nut; or

(h) idles or sleeps while on duty; or

(i) leaves his place of duty, or having left that place of duty for legitimate purposes fails to return without undue delay; or

(j) while on duty acts offensively towards any member of the public; or

(k) while on duty, consumes, or receives from any person, any intoxicating liquor or drug, or is incapable of performing his duties by reason of intoxication caused by alcohol or drugs; or

(l) while on duty is improperly dressed or untidy; or

(m) when wearing uniform in a public place, is dirty or untidy in his person, clothing or equipment; or

(n) unreasonably exercises his powers of arrest or search; or

(o) without good and sufficient cause discharges a firearm; or

(p) uses unnecessary force on any person in the execution of his duty; or

(q) behaves towards another member in an oppressive, offensive, abusive or insulting manner; or

(r) assaults another member or an employee of the Force; or

(s) makes a false or frivolous complaint against another member; or

(t) fails to exercise proper supervision over a member under his control; or

(u) by carelessness or neglect, permits a prisoner to escape; or

(v) negligently makes a false or misleading or inaccurate written statement, or entry in any official document or record; or

(w) negligently omits to record or report a fact or incident which is required of the member through Standing or Special Orders, this or any other Acts or Regulations; or

(x) knowingly makes a false or misleading or inaccurate oral statement relating to his duties; or

(y) knowingly omits to record or report a fact or incident which is required of the member through Standing or Special Orders, this Act or any other Act or Regulations; or

(z) knowingly fails to disclose the existence of any relevant evidence which is within his knowledge in relation to a criminal charge; or

(aa) without good and sufficient cause, destroys or mutilates an official book, document or record, or alters, erases or adds to an entry therein; or

(ab) without the consent of the Commissioner or a member authorized by the Commissioner, communicates to a person information which has come to his knowledge as a member of the Force, or shows or gives to a person a book or document prepared, used or kept in connection with the work of the Force, or publicly comments on administrative action by, or the administration of the Force, provided that this offence shall not apply to information given in good faith by a member in accordance with Standing or Special Orders; or

(ac) obtains or attempts to obtain the influence or interest of a person for the purpose of advantage or transfer or promotion in the Force; or

(ad) in his capacity as a member of the Force and without the consent of the Commissioner, directly or indirectly solicits or receives a fee, gratuity, present, benefit, subscription, reward or testimonial; or

(ae) through an intentional act or omission places himself under an obligation to a person which is likely to affect the proper discharge of his duties as a member of the Force; or

(af) improperly uses, or attempts to improperly use his appointment as a member of the Force for his advantage or the advantage of any other person; or

(ag) being a member of the Regular Constabulary Branch, carries on a trade, business or profession for remuneration, or accepts any remunerative employment outside the Force without the consent of the Commissioner; or

(ah) whether as principal or agent enters into a monetary transaction with another member by which interest or other return in money or kind is charged or paid or borrows money from a subordinate; or (ai) without good and sufficient cause fails to carry out a reasonable direction which has a bearing on the member's service to the Force, given by a legally qualified medical practitioner or, while absent from duty on account of sickness or injury commits an act or adopt any conduct calculated to retard his return to duty; or

(aj) fails to report promptly to his superior officer the loss of or damage to Force property issued to or used by the member or entrusted to his care; or

(ak) without lawful authority uses Government property for a purpose other than the execution of the member's duty; or

(al) is unfit to perform his duty by reason of being under the influence of alcohol or a drug; or

(am) finds a subordinate unfit to perform his duty on his shift by reason of being under the influence of alcohol or a drug and having authority to suspend such subordinate from duty for that shift or the remainder of that shift fails to do so; or

(an) aids or abets an offence against this Act or connives or knowingly aids, abets, counsels or procures the commission of an offence against this Act; or

(ao) supplies to another member, for use for a purpose not authorized by this Act certificates or testimonials relating to official capacity or performance of official duties; or

(ap) withholds a complaint or report against a member of the Force; or

(aq) misappropriates or improperly deals with property which comes into his possession or control by virtue of his office; or

(ar) fails to account for or fails to make prompt and true return of money or property received by the member in his official capacity; or

(as) being a member living in official accommodation enters or purports to enter into a polygamous marriage by custom or enters into an extra marital relationship in the nature of marriage; or

(at) sexually harasses another member; or

(au) commits a breach of a provision of this Act not otherwise referred to this section; or

(av) fails to comply with a direction for retraining imposed under Section 25; or

(aw) does or attempts to do anything in contravention of Section 136; or

(ax) being a member of the Regular Constabulary Branch registers or campaigns as a candidate for election to the National Parliament, or to a Provincial Assembly, or to a Local-level Government, or displays any political favouritism or support; or

(ay) commits an act or misconduct which may be a criminal offence, not being a purely indictable offence, under any Act, regulation, or by-law; or (az) acts in any manner, whether by word, conduct or omission which is prejudicial to good order and discipline in the Force, or which reflects discredit on the Force,

is guilty of a disciplinary offence and is liable to be dealt with and punished under this Division.

(2) For the purpose of this section, a member is sexually harassed where a person by the use of words (whether written or spoken) of a sexual nature or physical behaviour of a sexual nature –

(a) subjects the member to behaviour that is embarrassing, unwelcome or offensive to the member and which is either repeated or of such a significant nature that it has a detrimental effect on that member's employment, job performance, or job satisfaction; or

(b) makes a request of that member for sexual intercourse or sexual contact or other form of sexual activity and the request contains –

(i) an implied or overt promise of preferential treatment in that member's employment; or

(ii) an implied or overt threat of detrimental treatment in that member's employment; or

(iii) an implied or overt threat about the future employment status of that member.

(3) A member does not commit a disciplinary offence under Subsection (1)(ad) where –

(a) with the consent of the Commissioner he accepts –

(i) a public testimonial, presented on his retiral from the Force or on his removal from the locality in which he has been employed; or

(ii) a presentation from fellow members or from an organization within the meaning of industrial organizations in the Industrial Organizations Act 1962; or

(b) being a member of the Community Auxiliary Police, he receives a lawful honorarium or allowance'.

APPENDIX 3

SELF TEST

Would Your Decision Pass The Test?

YOU MUST ALWAYS CONSIDER:

Would your decision withstand Scrutiny?

Will your decision Ensure compliance?

Is your decision Lawful?

Is your decision Fair?

before you decide.

An unethical decision has adverse impacts.

APPENDIX 4

INVESTIGATION PLAN

INVESTIGATION PLAN
Offence/s Committed:
Background Information:
Investigation Goal(s):

Investigation Tasks And Time – Frames:

Resource Requirements:

Risk Management:

APPENDIX 5

VICTIM IMPACT STATEMENT

VICTIM IMPACT STATEMENT

Name:...

The victim must be informed:

- that the information is being gathered for submission to the judicial officer sentencing the offender if the accused is found guilty or pleads guilty;
- that the information must be true;
- that the information must be recorded and may be verified in the manner set out at the bottom of this form; and
- about who may properly see or make copies of the information ascertained, and about the orders, directions, and conditions , relation to disclosure and distribution of it that may be made.

Statement to take story form and to cover the following:

1. **Victim's Details** (if appropriate)

For example, age, occupation, sex, living arrangements, marital status, relation to the offender (if any), ethnic origin

2. **Physical Injuries**

For example, type and extent of injuries, long and short term effects, what treatment was required, was hospitalisation required.

Statement to take story form and to cover the following:

3. **Financial Costs**

For example, costs of treatment, replacement costs, repair costs, loss of wages or income, incidental costs and funeral costs.

4. **Emotional Harm**

For example, changes in behaviour, lifestyle and personal reaction and any treatment as a consequence.

5. **Any other harm or effects**

6. **Attach any supporting documentation**

7. **Victim or other person making the Victim Impact Statement:**

I have given the information in this Victim Impact Statement knowing that it is for submission to the judicial officer sentencing the offender and know that the information must be true. The information is true to the best of my knowledge and belief. I make it knowing that if it is tendered in evidence, I will be liable to prosecution if I have knowingly stated anything that is false or misleading in any particular.

Signature/Mark: .... (victim)

Name: .... (printed)

Date: ....

OR (if it is not practicable for the victim to sign):

I have advised the victim that the information in this Victim Impact Statement is for submission to the judicial officer sentencing the offender and that the information must be true. I have read it to the victim and am satisfied that the victim approves of it. I make it knowing that if it is tendered in evidence, I will be liable to prosecution if I have knowingly stated anything that is false or misleading in any particular.

Signature: ....

Name: .... (printed)

Designation: ....

Date: ....

APPENDIX 6

COMPENSATION FACTORS

COMPENSATION FACTORS

The following factors should be taken into account in respect of applications for compensation:

- Nature of the Injuries
  - Clearly outline the extent of the injuries;
  - Specify the duration of any pain or discomfort; and
  - Outline how the injury affected the complainant's life.
- Mental Anguish Caused

  Outline whether the complainant has suffered mental anguish as a direct result of the commission of the offence.
- On-Going Problems
  - Outline as per medical and/or dental advice;
  - Be specific as to the extent of such problems, duration of the problems and what treatment will be required in the future; and
  - Outline medical/dental expenses currently incurred and to be incurred in the future.
- Wages
  - Specify any loss of wages;
  - Explain why the complainant could not work;
  - Specify the amount of money lost; and
  - Specify the expected loss of wages in the future.
- Type Of Property
  - Detail the property in question;
  - Specify the condition of the property prior to the commission of the offence; and
  - Specify the value of the property prior to the commission of the offence.

- Damage/Destruction
    - Specify the extent of the damage/destruction; and
    - Explain how the property was damaged/destroyed as a result of the commission of the offence.
- Repair Costs
    - Explain what has to be done to ensure that the property is in the same condition as it was prior to the commission of the offence; and
    - Outline the cost of the repair.

APPENDIX 7

EXAMPLE OF A WITNESS STATEMENT

APPENDICES

STATEMENT

FIRST SHEET
Date: 3 October 2007

	Surname In Capitals	Christian Names
Name Of Witness:	MAPI	Julie
Occupation:	Unemployed	Age: 24
Address:	Kassia Village West New Britain Province	

On Friday 4th day of January 2010 I was at the Steamships Trade Store, Boroko when I saw my brother, Julian MAPI, enter the store.

At that time I was in line at a check-out.

I saw him walk over to where the men's trousers were located and select a brown pair of trousers.

The next time I saw him was when he walked to the check-out beside the check-out that I was in line for.

I said 'hallow brata' [in English 'Hello brother'] and he said 'hi'.

At that time he was carrying a pair of brown trousers in his right hand.

When it was his turn to pay for the trousers I saw him point a gun at the head of the lady at the check-out.

The gun was about 1 metre from her head.

All of the other customers then started to run away from the check-outs screaming and crying.

But I remained where I was standing because he was my brother.

I heard my brother say 'Putim han bilong yu antap, givim mi olgeta moni o bai mi kilim yu' [in English 'Hands up, give me all the money or you are dead'].

The check-out lady started to cry and yelled 'plis stap bai mi givim olgeta money' [in English 'Please stop I will give you all the money'].

Page 2 of Statement of Julie MAPI

I also started to cry and yelled to my brother 'Brata stap nau' [in English 'Brother stop now'].

The check-out lady opened the cash register and was grabbing all of the notes.

At that time a security guard was walking towards my brother with a large knife in his hand. He was yelling 'Yu stap nau' [in English 'You stop now'] over and over again.

When the security guard was about 2 metres from my brother, my brother then pointed his gun and shot him in the stomach.

The security guard then fell over and was yelling out in pain.

He was yelling 'Watpo yu sutim mi?' [in English 'Why did you shoot me?'].

I then ran to help the security guard.

As my brother was leaving the store he was tackled and arrested by a police officer.

Two men also helped the officer to stop my brother from running away.

I, Julie MAPI certify that this statement is true to the best of my knowledge and belief. I make it knowing that if it is tendered in evidence I will be liable to prosecution if I have knowingly stated anything that is false or misleading in any particular.

....

(Signature)

....

(Date)

APPENDIX 8

PROFORMA VOLUNTARY STATEMENT

VOLUNTARY STATEMENT

Date ....

Current Location ....

Name: .... **Age:** .... **Years**

Address: ....

Occupation: ....

Q1: If you wish to remain silent you may do so. If you wish to, you may give a written statement and it may be given in evidence. You can write it or I can. That is up to you. Do you wish to give a written statement?

A1: ....

Q2: Do you understand what I have said to you?

A2: ....

Q3: For the record I wish to tell you of your constitutional right to communicate in private with a member of your family, a personal friend or a lawyer of your choice. Do you understand?

A3: ....

Q4: Do you wish to contact any person before we commence?

A4: ....

I, ...,...

wish to make a statement. I want someone to write down what I say. I have been told that I need not say anything unless I wish to do so and that whatever I say may be given in evidence.

[All persons present, other than the suspect, are to sign the bottom of each page as an acknowledgement that it is true and correct. The suspect is only then to be requested to sign/mark the bottom of each page.]

Page 2 of a Voluntary Statement provided by [insert name of the suspect].

Q5: Do you agree that the time is now [specify the time]?

A5: …………………………………………………………………………………………………

Q6: Can you state your full and correct name and address?

A6: …………………………………………………………………………………………………

Q7: Are you currently over the age of 18 years?

A7: …………………………………………………………………………………………………

Q8: What is your date of birth?

A8: …………………………………………………………………………………………………

Q9: Are you currently affected by alcohol?

A9: …………………………………………………………………………………………………

Q10: Are you currently affected by drugs?

A10: …………………………………………………………………………………………………

[Exact Words of the Suspect]

[All persons present, other than the suspect, are to sign the bottom of each page as an acknowledgement that it is true and correct. The suspect is only then to be requested to sign/mark the bottom of each page.]

Page 3 of a Voluntary Statement provided by [insert name of the suspect].

Q11: Do you now wish to read this statement or do you wish an officer to read it to you?

A11: ……………………………………………………………………………………………………

Q12: Do you agree that [you have read this statement or this statement was read to you by (insert the name of the investigating officer)]?

A12: ……………………………………………………………………………………………………

Q13: Do you wish to correct anything, alter anything or add anything?

A13: ……………………………………………………………………………………………………

[Any correction should be done with a straight line through the relevant words and anything added should be included.]

The suspect should be required to initial any correction.]

Q14: Do you agree that there was no threat made to you to provide this statement?

A14: …….. ……………………………………………………………………………………………

Q15: Do you agree that you were not assaulted in order to make you provide this statement?

A15: ……………………………………………………………………………………………………

Q16: Do you agree that there was no promise made to you to provide this statement?

A16: ……………………………………………………………………………………………………

Q17: Do you wish to sign this statement?

A17: ……………………………………………………………………………………………………

[All persons present, other than the suspect, are to sign the bottom of each page as an acknowledgement that it is true and correct. The suspect is only then to be requested to sign/mark the bottom of each page.]

Page 4 of a Voluntary Statement provided by [insert name of the suspect].

I have read this statement or this statement was read to me and I have been told that I can correct, alter or add anything I wish. The contents of this statement are true and correct. I have made it of my own free will.

[If the suspect refuses to sign/mark
this fact should be noted here.]

Signature/Mark and Printed Name of Suspect

[Signature/s and Printed Name/s and Ranks of Other Officer/s and Signatures and Printed Name/s of Any Other Person/s Present]

APPENDIX 9

PROFORMA RECORD OF INTERVIEW

RECORD OF INTERVIEW

Date ……………………………………………………………………………………………

Current Location ……………………………………………………………………………

Name: ……… ………………………………………………………………………… **Age:** …………… **Years**

Address: ……………………………………………………………………………………

.

Occupation: …………………………………………………………………………………

Q1: This is a record of interview between [insert name and rank of interviewing officer] and [insert name of suspect] being conducted at [insert location]. Do you agree that [insert names of other persons present] [are/is] also present?

A1: ……………………………………………………………………………………………

Q2: Do you agree that the time is now [specify the time]?

A2: ……………………………………………………………………………………………

Q3: Can you state for the record your full and correct name and address?

A3: ……………………………………………………………………………………………

Q4: Are you currently over the age of 18 years?

A4: ……………………………………………………………………………………………

Q5: What is your date of birth?

A5: ……………………………………………………………………………………………

Q6: Are you currently affected by alcohol?

A6: ……………………………………………………………………………………………

[All persons present, other than the suspect, are to sign the bottom of each page as an acknowledgement that it is true and correct. The suspect is only then to be requested to sign/mark the bottom of each page.]

Page 2 of the Record of Interview between [insert name and rank of interviewing officer] and [insert name of the suspect].

Q7: Are you currently affected by drugs?

A7: ………

Q8: [Insert name of the suspect], I will now tell you what is alleged against you, do you understand?

A8: ………

Q9: [Insert name of the suspect], it is alleged that [briefly specify the allegation]. Do you understand?

A9: ………

Q10: Before I ask you any further questions I must warn you that you are not obliged to say anything unless you wish to do so but whatever you say will be taken down in writing and may be given in evidence. Do you understand?

A10: ………

Q11: For the record I wish to tell you of your constitutional right to communicate in private with a member of your family, a personal friend or a lawyer of your choice. Do you understand?

A11: ………

Q12: Do you wish to contact any person before we commence?

A12: ………

Q13: Do you understand English?

A13: ………

[All persons present, other than the suspect, are to sign the bottom of each page as an acknowledgement that it is true and correct. The suspect is only then to be requested to sign/mark the bottom of each page.]

Page 3 of the Record of Interview between [insert name and rank of interviewing officer] and [insert name of the suspect].

Q14: Do you wish to have this interview conducted in the English language?

A14: ………………………………………………………………………………………………………

[When questioning the suspect:

- give the suspect the opportunity to tell his or her own story;
- ask simple questions;
- ask short questions;
- do not ask more than one question at a time;
- ask questions in a logical sequence;
- clarify any issues raised by the suspect;
- focus on proving the elements of the charge/s; and
- focus on negativing any defence/s raised by the suspect.]

QX: Do you agree that there was no threat made to you to provide the answers you have given?

AX: ………………………………………………………………………………………………………

QX: Do you agree that you were not assaulted in order to make you provide the answers you have given?

AX: ………………………………………………………………………………………………………

QX: Do you agree that there was no promise made to you to provide the answers you have given?

AX: ………………………………………………………………………………………………………

[All persons present, other than the suspect, are to sign the bottom of each page as an acknowledgement that it is true and correct. The suspect is only then to be requested to sign/mark the bottom of each page.]

Page 4 of the Record of Interview between [insert name and rank of interviewing officer] and [insert name of the suspect].

QX: Do you now wish to read this statement or do you wish an officer to read it to you?

AX: ……………………………………………………………………………………………………

QX: Do you agree that [you have read this statement or this statement was read to you by (insert the name of the investigating officer)]?

AX: ……………………………………………………………………………………………………

QX: Do you wish to correct anything, alter anything or add anything?

AX: ……………………………………………………………………………………………………

[Any correction should be done with a straight line through the relevant words and anything added should be included.]

The suspect should be required to initial any correction.]

QX: Do you agree that the time is now [specify the time]?

AX: ……………………………………………………………………………………………………

I have read the record of interview or the record of interview was read to me and I have been told that I can correct, alter or add anything I wish. The contents of this record of interview are true and correct. I have made it of my own free will.

[If the suspect refuses to sign/mark

this fact should be noted here.]

Signature/Mark and Printed Name of Suspect

Signature, Printed Name and Rank of Investigating Officer

[Signature/s and Printed Name/s and Ranks of Other Officer/s and Signatures and Printed Name/s of Any Other Person/s Present]

APPENDIX 10

EXHIBIT LIST

EXHIBIT LIST

In The Matter Of

The State v ....

Exhibit No.	Exhibit	To Be Produced By Name Of Witness

APPENDIX 11

DRUG ANALYST AFFIDAVIT

The format of the affidavit is as follows:

IN THE DISTRICT COURT
HELD AT ...

IN THE MATTER OF POLICE
AGAINST [NAME OF ACCUSED PERSON]

I, [Full Name], **duly sworn make oath and say as follows:**

1. I am a drug analyst currently employed by [name of employer] at [location of work].

2. I am the holder of the following qualifications for the identification of [specify the dangerous drug such as cannabis and its derivatives]: [specify the qualifications]

3. At [location] on [date] I received a parcel from [person who handed in the parcel] of what appeared to me at that stage to be [specify the name of the dangerous drug] for the purpose of determining whether it was a dangerous drug as defined in the *Dangerous Drugs Act* (Ch. 228).

4. The recognised method used for the identification of such a dangerous drug is by [outline the usual method or methods used].

5. I analysed the dangerous drug by [outline as to how the dangerous drug was analysed].

6. As a consequence of that analysis I came to the conclusion that the substance was in fact the dangerous drug [specify the name of the dangerous drug, as referred to in the *Dangerous Drugs Act* (Ch. 228)].

7. The quantity of dangerous drug was [outline the weight of the dangerous drug].

....

[Full Name]

This page signed and sworn
at ... on ...
Before Me

....

Clerk of the District Court

APPENDIX 12

EXAMPLE OF A STATEMENT OF FACTS

APPENDICES

STATEMENT OF FACTS

At about 3.30pm on Friday 4th January 2010 the accused person Julian Mapi entered the Steamships Trade Store, Boroko with a loaded homemade gun hidden in his trousers.

He selected a pair of trousers from a shelf and entered the changing room.

On exiting the changing room he had the pair of trousers covering his right hand.

He then approached the check-out that was being operated by Mrs. Mary Kueng.

He then pointed the handmade gun at the head of Mrs. Kueng and said to her 'Em stilim, givim mi olgeta moni o bai mi killim yu dai' which translated to English is 'This is a robbery, give me all the money or you are dead'.

At that time a number of women and children who were at the check-out ran away in fear.

As Mr. Jamie Gutu, a security guard employed by the Steamships Trade Store, approached the accused person he was shot in the stomach and then fell to the floor.

At that time the victim was approximately 2 metres from the accused person.

Mrs. Kueng then handed the accused person all of the money in the cash register.

As the accused person was leaving the store he was tackled and arrested by Senior Constable Bosing who was off-duty.

Members of the public then assisted Senior Constable Bosing to restrain the accused person.

Upon being searched Senior Constable Bosing located K1202 in his shirt pocket.

Senior Constable Bosing took possession of that money and the homemade gun used by the accused person in the commission of the offence.

Senior Constable Bosing also observed that there were three other bullets in the firearm.

The accused person was then conveyed to the Boroko Police Station for questioning. Prior to questioning the accused person was cautioned in compliance with the Judges Rules. The accused person was also advised on his constitutional right to consult a friend or member of his family and a lawyer of his own choice. The accused person declined such consultation.

Upon being questioned the accused person admitted committing the offence. He stated that he only committed the offence because he was hungry.

As a consequence of this offence Mr. Gutu suffered a life threatening wound that required extensive surgery to his stomach. The full extent of his injury is still being ascertained. A medical report will be sought as soon as possible.

ANTECEDENTS

Name:	Julian Mapi
Age:	23 years
Marital Status:	Single
Address:	No Fixed Place Of Abode
Home Village:	Kassia Village, West New Britain Province.
Occupation:	Unemployed

APPENDIX 13

BAIL REFUSAL FORM

BAIL REFUSAL FORM

Section 9 of the Bail Act (Ch. 340) provides that bail may only be refused in exceptional circumstances. That section provides:

(1) Where a bail authority (meaning the officer-in-charge of the police station or a commissioned officer) is considering the question of granting or refusing bail, it shall not refuse bail unless satisfied on reasonable grounds as to one or more of the following considerations:

(a) that the accused person is unlikely to appear at his/her trial if granted bail:

Explain whether: (i) the accused person has a permanent place of residence; (ii) the accused person is married/single and the number of children to support; and (iii) the accused person has permanent employment (employed by whom and for how long):

....

....

....

In the case of a juvenile under parental control outline the circumstances:

....

....

....

(b) that the offence with which the accused person was charged was committed whilst the person was on bail:

Outline: (i) the offence/s for which the accused person is on bail; (ii) details of the bail conditions granted to the accused person; and (iii) which bail authority granted bail and when:

....

....

....

....

(c) that the alleged act or any of the alleged acts constituting the offence in respect of which the accused person consist or consists of (i) a serious assault; (ii) a threat of violence to another person; or (iii) having possession of a firearm, imitation firearm, other offensive weapon or explosive:

....

....

....

....

(d) that the accused person is likely to commit an indictable offence if he/she is not in custody:

If yes, outline briefly the criminal history of the accused person and explain briefly the reasons for your belief:

....

....

....

(e) it is necessary for the accused person's own protection for him/her to be in custody:

....

....

....

(f) that the accused person is likely to interfere with witnesses or the person who instituted the proceedings:

....

....

....

....

....

(g) that the alleged offence involved property of a substantial value that has not been recovered and the accused person if released would make efforts to conceal or otherwise deal with the property:

....

....

....

(h) that there are, in progress or pending, extradition proceedings against the accused person:

....

....

....

(i) that the alleged offence involves the possession, importation or exportation of a narcotic drug, other than for the personal medical use under prescription:

....

....

....

(j) that the alleged offence is one of breach of parole:

....

....

INFORMANT

FULL NAME AND SIGNATURE   RANK   STATION/SECTION   DATE

BAIL AUTHORITY

FULL NAME AND SIGNATURE   RANK   STATION/SECTION   DATE

APPENDIX 13

BAIL CERTIFICATE

Act Sec 7,8,10,11,12, 23 Reg. Sec. 2 Form 2

THE INDEPENDENT STATE OF PAPUA NEW GUINEA
BAIL ACT 1977

BAIL CERTIFICATE

To .... of ....

WHEREAS you have been charged with (state nature of offence) and you are required to be present at .... Court on .... 20........

This is to certify that you are entitled to bail on the following condition/s: --

1. Payment of K...... cash bail.*

2. A recuirement to reside at .... *

3. A requirement to be placed into the care of .... a [parent or responsible person] who agrees to accept you. [in the case of a juvenile]*

4. A requirement to report to the .... Police Station each .... between the hours of .... and ....*

5. A requirement to surrender your passport.*

6. A requirement to have no contact with .... who is/are to be called as witness/es by the prosecution.*

7. A requirement not to interfere with the on-going police investigation.*

Dated .... 20........

Issued by: ....

* Strike out whichever is inapplicable.

NOTE: You are required to keep this Certificate in your possession at all times.

APPENDIX 14

CERTIFICATE OF REFUSAL TO GRANT BAIL

Act Sec 16 Reg. Sec. 3 Form 3

THE INDEPENDENT STATE OF PAPUA NEW GUINEA
BAIL ACT 1977

CERTIFICATE OF REFUSAL TO GRANT BAIL

To .... of ....
WHEREAS you have been charged with (state nature of offence) and you are required to be present at .... Court on .... 20........, and the Bail Authority is satisfied on the following grounds that --

*	You will not appear at your trial if granted bail;
*	The alleged offence with which you are charged with was committed while you were on bail;
*	The alleged offence with which you have been charged with consists of -- (a) a serious assault; (b) a threat of violence to another person; and/or (c) having or possessing a firearm, imitation firearm or other offensive weapon or explosives;
*	You are likely to commit an indictable offence if you are not in custody;
*	It is necessary for your own protection for you to be in custody;
*	You are likely to interfere with witnesses to be called by the prosecution; or
*	The alleged offence involves property of substantial value which has not been recovered and it appears that if released you would make efforts to conceal or otherwise deal with the property;
*	There are in progress or pending extradition proceedings made under the Extradition Act against you;
*	The alleged offence involved the possession, importation or exportation of a narcotic drug other than for your personal medical under prescription; and/or
*	The alleged offence involves a breach of parole

you are refused bail.

Dated .... 20........

Issued by: ....
* Strike out whichever is inapplicable.

APPENDIX 15

WITNESS LIST

WITNESS LIST

In The Matter Of

The State v ....

Witness	Summary Of Evidence

APPENDIX 18

EXAMPLE OF AN INVESTIGATING OFFICER'S STATEMENT

APPENDICES

STATEMENT

FIRST SHEET
Date: 3 October 2007

	Surname In Capitals	Christian Names
Name Of Witness:	KUENG	Jason
Occupation:	Acting Sergeant	Age: N/A
Address:	Public Safety Unit Police Station Buka	

I am an Acting Sergeant of Police currently stationed at the Public Safety Unit, Buka Police Station.

On Wednesday 3rd day of October 2007 I was rostered 12mn to 8am with Constable John Scotty.

At approximately 1.50am we were directed to attend the Buka Town Market to investigate an alleged assault against Mr. Curtis Lehmann.

Upon arrival I spoke to Mr. Lehmann and obtained a statement from him.

I observed that Mr. Lehmann was suffering from bleeding cuts to the mouth and left leg.

Whilst I could smell liquor on the breath of Mr. Lehmann I noted that when I was speaking to Mr. Lehamnn his speech was not slurred and he had no trouble standing.

At the time of the alleged incident there were no other witnesses.

I was given a Rag and Chain at the Buka Town Market by Mr. Lehmann.

Senior Constable Scotty and I then went across the road from the Buka Town Market and located Mr. Errol Wilson, the accused person now before this Court.

At that time I noticed that the accused person was in possession of a Broom.

I requested the accused person to give me the Broom which he complied.

Upon request the accused person then accompanied us to the Buka Police Station.

At the Buka Police Station I together with Senior Constable Scotty conducted a Record of Interview with the accused person. At the commencement of the Record of Interview I advised the accused person of his right to silence in accordance with the Judges Rules. The accused person agreed to answer my questions. I also advised the accused person as to his right to consult a member of his family or personal friend and a lawyer of his choice. He chose not to consult any person. I then asked a series of questions in relation to the alleged assault on Mr. Lehmann.

At the conclusion of that Record of Interview I requested the accused person to read the Record of Interview and to sign each page if it was a true and correct record of our conversation. After reading the Record of Interview aloud the accused person stated that the Record of Interview was true and correct. The accused person then signed all pages of the Record of Interview.

Senior Constable Scotty and I also signed each page of the Record of Interview.

During the course of the Record of Interview Senior Constable Scotty was the Recording Officer.

During the course of the Record of Interview there was no force, threat or promise held out to the accused person to answer any of the questions or to sign the each page of the Record of Interview.

I now seek to produce that Record of Interview to the Court.

TENDERED AND MARKED AS EXHIBIT NO. ………………………………………………

During the course of the Record of Interview I showed the accused person a Rag that was given to me by Mr. Lehmann. The accused person admitted that he used the Rag that I showed him during the course of the alleged offence now before this Court.

I now seek to produce that Rag to the Court.

TENDERED AND MARKED AS EXHIBIT NO. ………………………………………………

During the course of the Record of Interview I showed the accused person a Broom that was taken possession of from him at the Buka Town Market. The accused person admitted that he used the Broom that I showed him during the course of the alleged offence now before this Court.

I now seek to produce that Broom to the Court.

TENDERED AND MARKED AS EXHIBIT NO. ………………………………………………

During the course of the Record of Interview I showed the accused person a Metal Chain that was given to me by Mr. Lehmann. The accused person admitted that he used the Metal Chain that I showed him during the course of the alleged offence now before this Court.

I now seek to produce that Metal Chain to the Court.

TENDERED AND MARKED AS EXHIBIT NO. ………………………………………………

At the conclusion of the Record of Interview I asked the accused person whether he wished to write a Voluntary Statement. The accused person stated that he wished to. I then advised the accused person of his right to silence in accordance with rule 4 of the Judges Rules. I again advised the accused person as to his right to consult a member of his family or personal friend and a lawyer of his choice. He chose not to consult any person.

At the conclusion of completing his Voluntary Statement I requested the accused person to read the Voluntary Statement and to sign each page if it was a true and correct record. After reading the Voluntary Statement aloud the accused person stated that the Voluntary Statement was true and correct. The accused person then signed both pages of the Voluntary Statement.

Senior Constable Scotty and I also signed each page of the Voluntary Statement.

During the course of the accused person providing his Voluntary Statement there was no force, threat or promise held out to the accused person.

I now seek to produce that Voluntary Statement to the Court.

TENDERED AND MARKED AS EXHIBIT NO. ………………………………………………

I then advised the accused person that he was under arrest.

He was later charged and upon being charged the accused person made no comment.

Later that afternoon I took two photographs of Mr. Lehmann.

I now seek to produce those two photographs to the Court.

Photograph 1 — This is a photograph of the face of Mr. Lehmann.

Photograph 2 — This is a photograph of the left leg of Mr. Lehmann.

TENDERED AND MARKED AS EXHIBIT NOS. ………………………………………………

APPENDICES

I, Acting Sergeant Jason Kueng certify that this statement is true to the best of my knowledge and belief. I make it knowing that if it is tendered in evidence I will be liable to prosecution if I have knowingly stated anything that is false or misleading in any particular.

....

(Signature)

....

(Date)

APPENDIX 18

ANTECEDENT REPORT

ANTECEDENT REPORT

THE STATE v ....

1. FULL NAME: ....

2. DATE AND PLACE OF BIRTH: ....

3. CURRENT ADDRESSS: ....

4. HOW LONG LIVED AT THAT ADDRESS: ....

5. PRIMARY SCHOOLING: ....
(School and Year)

   SECONDARY SCHOOLING: ....
(School And Year)

   TERTIARY SCHOOLING: ....
(School, Year And Qualification)

6. OTHER QUALIFICATIONS: ....

7. EMPLOYMENT HISTORY: ....

   ....

   ....

   ....

8. CURRENT INCOME PER FORTNIGHT: ....

9. MARITAL STATUS: ....

10. NUMBER OF CHILDREN: ....

11. PRIOR CONVICTIONS:

Date	Court	Offence	Sentence

APPENDIX 19

CHECK LIST

CHECK LIST

The State v. ....

Statute	Section No.	Offence
WRITE ANY OTHER OFFENCES ON REAR		

		Investigating Officer Yes/No	Prosecutor Agree Yes/No
1.	Correct Statute, Section and Wording of Charge? If not, write comments on rear.		
2.	Should additional charges be laid? If so, write comments on rear.		
3.	Each and every element able to be proven? If no, write comments on rear.		
4.	Does additional evidence need to be obtained? If yes, write comments on rear.		
5.	Is all the evidence admissible? If not, write comments on rear.		
7.	Have all the defences raised by the accused person been negatived? If no, write comments on rear.		
8.	Are all exhibits referred to in the statements? If no, write comments on rear.		
9.	Are all the police powers used in the investigation lawful? If no, write comments on rear.		
10.	Is the required documentation attached? If no, write comments on rear.		

INVESTIGATING OFFICER

....

FULL NAME, SIGNATURE, RANK & STATION/SECTION **DATE**

PROSECUTOR

....

FULL NAME, SIGNATURE & RANK **DATE**

INDEX

Page

A

B

C

INDEX

INDEX

D

INDEX

E

INDEX

Page

F

G

H

INDEX

I

INDEX

INDEX

INDEX

Page

N

P

INDEX

T

INDEX

INDEX

CPSIA information can be obtained at www.ICGtesting.com
Printed in the USA
LVOW09*0818240713

343816LV00003B/3/P

9 789980 945990